Politically

THE "GET SOME GUMPTION"

Handbook When

ENOUGH IS ENOUGH!

Helen Glowacki

Cover photo by Daniel Byers

Web Design by Daniel Patrick Landolfi

Novels by Helen Gumienny Glowacki

When God Broke Grandma's Heart
When God Took Grandma Home
When Grandma Chased the Spirits
The Granddaughter and the Monkey Swing
Grandma's Little Book of Poetry: The Story of God's Plan of Salvation
Abiding Faith, Hidden Treasure
And Then They Asked God

Non-Fiction Books by Helen Glowacki

To What Purpose?
Why God Why?
Why Trust Scripture?
What Should I Know About Life after Death And The Coming Tribulation?
Politically Incorrect: The Get Some Gumption Handbook
When Enough is Enough
What No One Wants You To Know About Addictions
Overcoming Depression: How To Be Happy

Coming Soon

What Does God Want Me To Do *RIGHT NOW*?
Do The Little Sins *Really* Count?

Authors Website: www.HelenGlowacki.com

Face book: http://www.facebook.com/pages/The-Grandmother-Series/155300907853909?ref=ts

Politically

THE "GET SOME GUMPTION"

Handbook When

ENOUGH IS ENOUGH!

Helen Glowacki

Cover Photo by Daniel Byers

Website by Daniel Patrick Landolfi

Copyright © July 2011 by Helen Glowacki

Library of Congress Control Number:
Softcover: ISBN 978-1-4507-9074-1

All rights reserved. No part of this book may be reproduced or transmitted in any form or by any means, electronic or mechanical, including photocopying, recording or by any information storage and retrieval system, without permission in writing from the copyright owner except in the case of brief quotations embodied in critical articles or reviews.

This book was printed in the United States of America

The King James Version (KJV) of the Bible, which is public domain in the United States of America, is used for all scriptural references throughout this book. The information contained herein is based upon the opinion, research and religious belief of the author. Matters pertaining to one's spiritual life, or application of the information contained herein should be discussed with a theological professional.

Cover photo by Daniel Byers, St. Petersburg, Florida

To order additional copies of this book visit:
www.HelenGlowacki.com
For more information or bulk order prices email the author at: helen@helenglowacki.com

Mission Statement:

TO SERVE GOD

WITH ALL

OUR STRENGTH

AND ALL OUR HEART

Helen Gumienny Glowacki, Daniel Patrick Landolfi

DEDICATION

To those who gave their life and effort to defend our country, our freedom, and our Christian principles, and to those who now fight to keep our country safe and keep it a nation under God.

NOTE TO THE READER

The King James Version (KJV) of the Bible, which is public domain in the United States, is used throughout this book. However, for further study, the author recommends the New King James Version (NKJV) of the Bible for easier reading and less usage of the old world language while remaining true to the original text.

All rights reserved. No part of this publication may be used or reproduced, stored in a retrieval system, or transmitted in any form or by any means, electronic, mechanical, photocopying, recording, or otherwise, without the prior written permission of the author, except in the case of brief quotations embodied in critical articles and reviews.

The non-fiction works by Helen Glowacki contain information based upon the research and the personal experiences of the author and her interpretation of scripture. All matters pertaining to one's spiritual life should be discussed with a theological professional. The publisher and author are not responsible for any adverse effects or consequences resulting from any of the material discussed in this book.

The novels by Helen Glowacki are works of fiction, but the applied scripture are actual verses taken from the King James Version (KJV) of the Bible and applied to the situations of the characters based upon the personal experiences and interpretation of the author. The publisher and author are not responsible for any adverse effects or consequences resulting from imitating the character's application of scripture and recommend discussing intent with a theological professional. References to real people, events, organizations, or locales are intended only to provide a sense of authenticity, and are used fictitiously. All other characters and all incidents and dialogue are drawn from the author's imagination and are not to be construed as real except for many of the experiences of faith which the characters live through and which were related to the author by various people and used with permission. Any resemblance to actual persons, living or dead is entirely coincidental.

This book contains scriptural quotes in its text and scriptural references at the end of each chapter. Instead of assembling an index according to the Chicago Manual of Style, the scriptures are provided in a format which the author deemed more useful to the reader. Key points highlighting the chapter content are listed at the end of each chapter and below them are listed the verses which address the issue under discussion. This index style will better support a teaching program which may utilize this book as a guide for Bible study and determining a Christian's position on a given issue.

ACKNOWLEDGEMENTS

To my husband Wally who is an incredible support, a champion for my work, the wind beneath my wings and the genius who patiently cajoles my computer into behaving; to my children and grandchildren for their love and encouragement. Special thanks to Daniel Patrick Landolfi who tirelessly helps with the website, and many other chores associated with my work. Special thanks to Colette Van Loggerenberg of Pietermaritzburg, South Africa, for providing or editing the photography used in the Why God Why series, for promoting my books in South Africa and distributing many to cancer centers, drug rehabilitation centers, prisons and other areas where there may be souls who hunger to learn of God. Special thanks to Kevin Speranza for locating and developing additional venues for this work. Thanks to Matthew Burniston for his photography and for promoting and distributing my work in the UK, and to Michelle Mascatello, Andre Myrick and Daniel Byers and many others who have offered their photos. Special love to Richard Levinson whose kindness can never be repaid; to the ministers and deacons of The New Apostolic Church; to new friends and old friends who pray for me, and grant me the greatest friendships I could ever ask for; and to the readers and Facebook friends who ask me to keep writing and comment so favorably on my work. Special thanks to those who diligently uplift me in my spiritual life, and keep me in their hearts and in their prayers; and most importantly, to my Heavenly Father who guides my life, gives so much, loves so much, and made all this possible! MY HEARTFELT AND HUMBLE THANKS

MESSAGE FROM THE AUTHOR

Confusion reigns in today's world not by chance, but by design. We are led to believe that our confusion is the result of our busy and harried lives, but in reality it has been carefully planned and executed by the architect of Christian complacency. He knows that confusion leads to doubt, doubt leads to complacency, and complacency leads to a lack of involvement. There is however a new ploy which Satan uses quite effectively to create this complacency. It is called "political correctness" and has nudged us into the loss of our Christian convictions about many important issues. Thus, we no longer take a stance against sin and we no longer know what we can do or say about what was once considered displeasing to God. Instead, we choose the easy route of ignoring how political correctness is destroying the moral fiber of our country and supports the corruption of everything our forefathers fought and died for. Political correctness is so powerful that it also leaves us wondering if we dare to disagree. We cannot continue in our complacency and simply allow our Christian values and liberties to be attacked and possibly lost. We must define what we believe, clearly understand what God says about our values, and find the courage to act. It's time for us to do as Isaiah 1:18 tells us: *"Come now, and let us reason together......"*

Prior to writing this book, I published seven novels in which I incorporated the principles God provides for guiding us through the trials and tribulations in our lives. I also published four non-fiction mini-books which I send all over the world. I have written this book to provide a concise and topic-specific guide to gaining immediate insight into what stance Christians must take in today's world to avoid the subtle trap which is robbing us of our values and attacking the God given Constitution of our country. While an author writes to develop a reading experience which informs, comforts, or entertains, this book is directed specifically toward informing.... quickly and concisely. It is designed to explain what Christians must consider as we face our many dilemmas and as we see our Christian way of life attacked. If we don't respond scripturally, with conviction and a united stance, the moral fiber and Christian principles of our country could be lost. We no longer take the time to read the Bible and discuss how God's words apply to today's situations, nor do we seek to learn how we should react to these situations. It is important that we learn what God tells us and protect what we have been given.

This book specifically addresses the Christian principles we must apply toward contemporary issues. It differs from my novels where I use characters plagued by heartbreaking circumstances to explain why God allows pain and confusion to exist before He steps in. In this book each chapter addresses a timely issue and provides concise direction for how Christians should view and address that issue. Those familiar with scripture are aware that scripture provides the answers to our questions on any issue, but we all understand that today's world saps our strength, and our time, leaving us bereft of the ability to seek these answers. My challenge herein is to create a thorough, but concise understanding of the complex issues Christians face and what God wants us to know about them. Exploring these daily concerns is a daunting challenge for every Christian who wears many hats and feels crushed by their weight. With no time and energy left to pursue God's words, guilt can set in and add depression and lethargy to the mix of confusion and anxiety which stalks us every day. Thus, this book addresses the questions we face by researching scripture through which we can obtain a guide for answering those questions. While writing requires only a simple succession of words, to be effective those words must touch the mind with common sense and move the heart with the desire to act. Those words must also touch the soul with the importance of taking a stand and recognizing that we are engaged in a spiritual warfare so malevolent and desperate that we are in jeopardy of losing those things we have always cherished. God wants to help us. He wants to bring us through our difficult situations. But if we don't know what He wants to tell us, we are lost. God's love for us is so great that He provides us with every possible tool to learn His words. If we do not read scripture, He has given us ministers who do read scripture, books which provide this information and role models who are an example of what God wants us to be and do. God provides all these venues to bring His word to us. However, whether we listen or not, whether we accept His direction or not, is solely up to us. I hope that this book will answer the questions stirred by our current world crisis and show us how to bring forth the courage required to stand firm in our faith and be willing to fight for our principles. Our courage to do so will come from the conviction of our position.

Many forget that we have a powerful enemy who fights God and that we are the pawns used in that effort. This enemy encourages the complacency we have long been exhibiting, to prevent God from completing His plan of salvation. He needs to destroy our faith, and by reducing our values and our freedoms, he also steals our hope and increases our complacency. We cannot thwart the goal of this enemy if we do not tap into the power of love, the power of prayer, and the power of the perfect plan God placed into the physics of our world to help us. To do this we need to know what to believe and what to do to defend those beliefs. Those who hunger to learn more about what scripture tells us are not alone; others are also searching for the godly answer to the complex situations we face today. Our Heavenly Father knows that we can become exhausted from the constant battles we face. He knows that there seems no end to our job list and no time to study His word. He also knows that as we learn, and gain an understanding of what He wants us to do we will gladly take up the banner and fight to protect the gifts He has so freely given us.

What I hope to impart through this book, and through my novels, is an understanding of the enemy we face on a daily basis, why he does what he does, how we can thwart his efforts and most of all, exactly how we are to do battle. When we engage in a battle which we understand it helps remove our fear and creates a more formidable Christian warrior. We will also fight wiser. But when we do not understand this spiritual warfare, when we wonder why our world has been reduced to what we are witnessing today, when we are not sure how to address the difficult questions, we lose our conviction and become complacent; we lose our hope and our strength. But as we learn of God, His enemy, and His plan of salvation, we also learn that He is always with us to uplift us, protect us, and provide us with the energy and determination we need to see this battle through to the end. We can't effectively fight an enemy when we don't know our own position which should be the position God wants us to take. Sadly, few do know this, and if we do not understand, we cannot teach others. God wants us to win this battle and will help us. It is through God's words that we learn how to fight and what to believe, and gain the courage to make a stand. God gifted us with a country built on Christian principles and He has gifted us with the freedom to practice those principles. It is only through our united front that we can become a formidable force against what is happening in our country. Let's develop a new appreciation of God's gifts and join the populous eager to learn and determined to protect these gifts. Let's demand more from our school systems, text books, politicians and government. Let's fight for the honesty, integrity, morality, faith, and loyalty our faith teaches us. Sadly, however, many stand back, afraid to become involved, afraid of the few…only 14%… who want to turn aside our Biblical principles in the name of social justice. We should be shocked by the fact that so few have had the power to take these principles from our schools, our government, our churches, our press, and even indoctrinate our children and do so in order to oppose and negate our faith. But their power comes from Satan and it goes forth easily only because we have been complacent. We need to fight back.

Our struggles have increased because we are moving closer to the ultimate goal of our faith, the First Resurrection, and Satan must work harder than ever. He knows that his end will come when the number God longs for is fulfilled, and must work to prevent God from fulfilling that number. We need to do our part as children of God and stand up and be counted. But to do this we need to know what we stand for. We can accomplish this noble goal only if we know what God says. Further we are being tested for our constancy, our example, our loyalty to God and this requires us to live our faith every day, not just on Sundays….and live our faith as Christ asked us to live it. But it also requires our courage to *fight* for our faith and our values, and can only be effective when we think about what these values are and where we stand on them. Malachi 2:8 warns, *"But ye are departed out of the way; ye have caused many to stumble at the law; ye have corrupted the covenant of Levi, saith the Lord of Hosts."* If we don't protect our values, we will cause our children to stumble. God not only shows us what dangers we should watch for, but He also shows us how to live together, how to set the right example, how to instruct our children, and clearly and unequivocally promises wonderful rewards for doing so. He promises us His protection. He gives the ultimate guarantees about our life and our home. This doesn't say we won't have problems, but it does say we will be brought through those problems, we will be refined in the process, and that we need not fear the outcome when we fight for right. As Biblical values are lost, so are mankind's ability to recognize the same lies offered today which Satan used to trap Eve. By fighting back we will be taking a stand against political corruption and terrorists who plot the death of our faith, our way of life and our country. However, if we are complacent in the face of the destruction of our individual right to pray, the destruction of an unbiased education and a free and honest press, and the destruction of a corruption free government, we give Satan a huge platform from which to work. God's word is our most potent protection and the most potent protection our country can have against its current onslaught. Instituting God's words into our minds and hearts and thus our lives can help us immensely not only because we now live in a world of uncertainty, but also because we long to attain the goal of our faith….an eternity with God.

Most of us are tired of the "political correctness" which seeks to prevent us from standing up and saying "enough is enough". Even though our lives require us to wear many hats to make ends meet and this tires us, and has made us complacent, surely we can stand against that 14% who have changed the textbooks our children read, removed prayer from our schools, disallowed Nativity displays for Christmas, challenged our Constitution, and still want more. Wouldn't God want us to stand up and be counted....fight for the values upon which our faith and country was founded and which He then blessed?

I hope that this book will show you the worthy stance of a Christian on many contemporary issues and inspire you to cherish our faith and our values, and cling to them even if they are lost to the world. If you, the reader, will share what you know and what you learn about God's plan with others so they too can understand, you will touch the heart of God and help protect our faith and our country. May God bless you and keep you always and may He grant you the wisdom to understand His ways, His words, and the future He so freely offers us all. And may He open your understanding to the wonder of His word and to His all-encompassing love for you.

Helen Glowacki

"Preach the word; be instant in season; reprove, rebuke, exhort with all longsuffering and doctrine. For the time will come when they will not endure sound doctrine; but after their own lusts shall they heap to themselves teachers, having itching ears. And they shall turn away their ears from the truth, and shall be turned unto fables. But watch thou in all things, endure afflictions, do the work of an evangelist, make full proof of thy ministry."   *2 Timothy 4:2-4*

TABLE OF CONTENTS

Dedication	Page 06
Note to the Reader	Page 07
Acknowledgements	Page 09
Message from the Author	Page 10
Table of Contents	Page 17
Chapter 1: Godly Wisdom	Page 21
Chapter 2: The Stealthy Attack of Evil	Page 27
Chapter 3: What is a Relationship with God?	Page 35
Chapter 4: The Mystery of Scripture	Page 41
Chapter 5: Creation and Evolution.	Page 49
Chapter 6: Why Fellowship is Important	Page 57
Chapter 7: Christians and Politics	Page 63
Chapter 8: Do I Have To Vote?	Page 73
Chapter 9: Counsel and Compassion	Page 79
Chapter 10: Sacraments and Passports	Page 85
Chapter 11: Why God Allows Heartache	Page 91
Chapter 12: The Plan of Salvation	Page 99
Chapter 13: Life after Death	Page 104
Chapter 14: Satan's and his Helpers	Page 114

Chapter 15: The Overcomer	Page 123
Chapter 16: Large Sins and Little Sins	Page 129
Chapter 17: The Right to be Angry	Page 135
Chapter 18: Forgetting and Forgiving	Page 145
Chapter 19: Forgiving Yourself	Page 151
Chapter 20: From Anger to Blessing	Page 159
Chapter 21: Addictions and Spirits	Page 167
Chapter 22: Why Tough Love is Real Love	Page 177
Chapter 23: When to Hold and When to Fold	Page 185
Chapter 24: Debating the Unbeliever	Page 193
Chapter 25: Rules for Christian Parents	Page 199
Chapter 26: Kids and College	Page 205
Chapter 27: Husbands, Wives & Role Models	Page 211
Chapter 28: When we are Unequally Yoked	Page 219
Chapter 29: Prayers to Touch God's Heart	Page 225
Chapter 30: The Elusiveness of Self Esteem	Page 233
Chapter 31: Devastating Life Changes	Page 239
Chapter 32: No Job, No Money, No God	Page 245
Chapter 33: Pretty and Petty Pride	Page 255
Chapter 34: Should Christians Make Waves?	Page 261
Chapter 35: The Apocrypha	Page 267

Chapter 36: Differing Doctrines	Page 273
Chapter 37: Collective Redemption	Page 285
Chapter 38: Hatred by Any Other Name	Page 293
Chapter 39: The Danger of Halloween	Page 301
Chapter 40: The Truth about Feng Shui	Page 307
Chapter 41: Astrology, Tarot & Divination	Page 315
Chapter 42: The Gift of Divine Proportion	Page 321
Chapter 43: Immersion Baptism	Page 329
Chapter 44: Timely, Touching Testimony	Page 337
Chapter 45: Tools of the Trade	Page 343
Chapter 46: Is Meekness Weakness?	Page 349
Chapter 47: Transformation: A New You	Page 357
Chapter 48: Celestial Body/Second Death	Page 363
Chapter 49: The End Times	Page 371
Chapter 50: Peace: The Art of Being Happy	Page 379
Bibliography	Page 388
About The Author	Page 389
Synopsis of Books by this Author	Page 390
Book Reviews	Page 397
Description of novel characters	Page 406

Chapter One

THE IMPORTANCE OF GODLY WISDOM

We live in such a harried world that it is a struggle to find the time or energy to devote to God and family. When we find a respite in our busy schedule, we seek comfort or some form of entertainment to help us relax from a stressful and exhausting schedule. We seldom realize that the troubles we find in today's world are not by God's design, but by Satan's efforts whose sole purpose is to keep us from learning and sharing God's words and thereby learning what is required to become a part of the bride of Christ. Because we are so busy, we no longer seek the treasures of scripture even though scripture will answer the age old question of why those who strive to do what is right seem to struggle while those who are evil appear to prosper. Scripture also tells us about the spiritual warfare in which we are engaged and which we rarely now consider. Yet, the evil we face is malevolent and desperate and places us all in jeopardy, especially our children. They, like us, sometimes ask God why we are so harried, why we suffer heartache and why He does not provide His help in what *we* think is a timely fashion. When we don't know why we suffer or why some problems don't resolve, we can despair. That despair blocks our Godly pursuits and keeps us from understanding that we are pawns used by Satan to prevent God from completing His plan of salvation. Neither do we understand that we can thwart evil when we tap into God's words and the power of the perfect plan God placed into the physics of our world. Godly wisdom helps us fight harder and wiser, but without that wisdom we do not understand evil, and our heartache causes bitterness and the loss of hope which strengthens the hold of evil. We no longer bring to mind that we are in a desperate battle…..a fierce and unrelenting battle where our enemy must keep us from God to prolong his freedom. We forget that he is in a life or death battle in which he not only targets us, but targets our children and grandchildren in that effort. Titus 1:9 warns us to hold fast to the faithful word of God and Ephesians 5:11 to have no fellowship with darkness.

We all have struggles and questions about life. We are not alone, others also have heartache, feel despair and ask "why". Many are exhausted from their battles, see no end to their problem and no reason for it, and while some turn to God to learn why they are under attack, by whom, and how they can win their battle, others give up. But God tells us in Ephesians 6:10 to find our strength through him. Sadly, we cannot fight an enemy we don't know exists. We can't effectively fight when we don't know how to identify the enemy, and don't know how or why he attacks. Sadly, few understand this, and if *we* do not understand, we cannot teach our children. Thus, fewer and fewer children learn of their powerful and selective enemy and grow into adults with no understanding of evil…and cannot therefore teach their own children. Truly loving God requires that we learn and follow His words. It is through God's words that we know Him and understand why we face a battle. We are in a spiritual war between good and evil where the gripping struggle of our daily lives is meant to prevent us from learning how to address our challenges and what we are to do. It is imperative that we learn how to fight the contemporary conditions we face. Throughout scripture we find warnings about Satan and the power he wields. 2 Corinthians 2:11 tells us not to let Satan get an advantage over us. Amazingly, scripture clearly warns us of the enemy who brings such harm. Scripture tells us that Satan can blind men to God's words, and cause them to act as they do. He does this by filling our lives with so much stress and robbing us of the time we might apply to studying scripture. Knowing this, God has provided other avenues of learning for us; even avenues which are entertaining and relaxing. He has inspired Christian books and movies. He has given us ministers and their sermons, and newsletters and magazines. We can engage in various church activities such as Bible studies, and fellowship with Christian role models. While we may agree that we all must answer for our actions, we rarely take responsibility for our inaction, or for the stumbling our action or inaction may cause others. When we do not pursue God and do not teach our children about God we become a stumbling block to our children, and when we do not rebuke the sin of those who reach out to us, we contribute to that sin. Mark 9:42 warns: *"And whosoever shall offend one of these little ones that believe in me, it is better for him that a millstone were hanged about his neck, and he were cast into the sea."* And Luke 17:1 warns: *"Offenses will come, but woe unto him, through whom they come."*

The subtlety of our enemy and the spirits which serve him is a great danger. John 8:44 tells us that Satan is a liar, and Genesis 3:1 warns us about how subtly he works. Satan and his minions lead us astray through envy and fear, complacency and exhaustion, perversions and addictions, hatred and misconceptions, money and power. Our enemy is not only clever, but also seductive, tempting and as dangerous as He was when he brought sin to everyone who ever lived or died through Adam and Eve. It is easy to forget that this powerful enemy still lurks today, more potent than ever, still the sly and enticing stalker who revels in the chaos of our daily lives. Satan rarely takes the obvious path; he uses people to harm people and thus there is much evil in this world. Many professing faith in God, act not by God's words, but by the subtle influence of evil. Malachi 3:10 warns us to prove whatever we see and hear so we can know it comes from God. We must embrace our climb from the fall of man which we have all experienced and triumph over the evil which draws so many to its misconceptions. God's word is our most potent protection and He knows that without it we will be lost. In Hosea 4:6 God laments our lack of this knowledge which He warns will cause our fall. But throughout scripture we learn that God will bless our efforts to learn of Him… and part of that blessing is how little these efforts will take from our busy schedules. Whatever time we give to God, He gives back to us by helping us in our daily lives. As we learn, and as we share the warnings and principles of scripture with others, we bring a blessing to ourselves and to our families because we then have touched the heart of God.

Bullet Points

Evil is alive and well in today's society.

Evil creates our busy schedules to keep us from God.

Evil wants us to become complacent and excuse sin.

Scripture tells us why evil exists and how to be protected. Our children are the primary targets of evil.

God helps us meet our obligations when we study His word.

Supporting Scripture

1 Corinthians 14:33,	Colossians 3:15,
Daniel 12:4,	Mark 9:42,
Revelation 2:2-3,	Revelations 2:25,
Matthew 11:29,	1 Timothy 6:11,
Mark 4:15,	Acts 18:9.

Chapter Two

THE STEALTHY ATTACK OF EVIL

Scripture tells us that there will be little faith on earth when Christ returns to gather the number of souls God wants for the First Resurrection. 1 Timothy 4:1 warns, *".....in the latter times some shall depart from the faith, giving heed to seducing spirits, and the doctrines of devils."* Scripture also tells us that our spiritual destruction will occur because we have not learned and applied God's words. Hosea 4:6 tells us: *"My people are destroyed for a lack of knowledge..."*

Television shows, reading materials, and movies which entertain by glamorizing evil, witches, vampires, werewolves, supernatural events and powers, all work toward negating the reality of evil. When evil becomes entertaining rather than personally threatening to our soul salvation, it lowers our guard and opens us up to danger. This is not by fluke, but by plan. These benevolent or entertaining portrayals of evil are used to lull us into dismissing the warnings in scripture which tell us that Satan and his fallen angels walk this earth wielding the power to harm the faith of God's children. As a result, we no longer understand or teach the seriousness and subtlety of the spirits which attack Christians. Acts 20:29-31 warns: *"For I know this, that after my departing shall grievous wolves enter in among you, not sparing the flock. Also of your own selves shall men arise, speaking perverse things, to draw away the disciples after them. Therefore watch..."*

Satan is God's enemy and he is our enemy. He must thwart God's plan of salvation in order to continue his existence. Because he knows scripture well and knows God's plan, he knows when and how his present life will end. He believes that if he can prevent God from obtaining the number of faithful souls God wants by breaking our faith, he will delay the return of Christ and thus delay his fate. Sadly, many do not understand why this powerful enemy fights, what his goal is, or how to protect themselves. Therefore they have not protected themselves, and cannot teach these principles to their children. It is why we live in a world where actions which scripture tells us are harmful to our soul are so widely accepted. Only when Christians understand evil and the spirits of evil as a daily and insidious threat to their soul, will they survive its onslaught and be prepared for Christ's return.

Satan's Powers

The Bible clearly describes Satan's powers throughout its pages and includes the following:

Satan can move men to do his bidding (1 Chronicles 21:1), can walk back and forth on the earth (Job 1:7), can cause illness (Job 2:7), can take God's word from men's hearts (Mark 4:15), can enter man (Luke 22:3 and John 13:27), can blind the minds of them which believe not (2 Corinthians 4:4), can transform himself (2 Corinthians 11:14), can send messengers to hurt man (2 Corinthians 12:7), can hinder people (1 Thessalonians 2:18), can produce signs and has powers (2 Thessalonians 2:9) and uses them to convince us to accept his perversions.

"……the working of Satan with all power and signs and lying wonders." The simple tweaking of God's words….the slightest perversion…..causes confusion and leads to doubt and indecision. This creates the lukewarm attitude and inaction which prevents us from reaching the goal of our faith.

Why Satan and his minions do what they do:

God longs to fill His kingdom with souls who love Him and His Son, and one another. He wants these souls to value love, integrity, and loyalty, and to practice these attributes voluntarily. Thus He developed a plan and placed it into the physics of our world to encourage each soul to hunger for these values. God created Adam and Eve as the first souls He hoped would grow in love and loyalty. But in the heavens the angel Lucifer, later known as Satan, rebelled because of his jealousy toward Christ, and toward mankind whom he knew God would elevate above the angels. Satan and those who rebelled with him were thrown to earth knowing they would enter Hell for their rebellion when God's plan was completed. To forestall his end, Satan (Lucifer) destroyed God's relationship with Adam and Eve by enticing them to sin. But God provided a way for Adam and Eve, and the generations to follow, to escape the captivity Satan proposed for them. Christ offered Himself as the perfect sacrifice by which man's sins could be forgiven. At every turn, Satan interfered with God's plan, trying to break those who followed God, even trying to break Christ so he could forestall his destruction and prolong his freedom. Yet many who are tested by Satan are strengthened through these attacks, and from these souls, God is building what the Bible calls The Bride of Christ.

Christ will return at the First Resurrection to take His bride to the wedding feast in Heaven. After the great tribulation which will culminate on earth while they are gone, they will return to earth to bring testimony during the thousand years of peace when all mankind will accept and return God's love because Satan will be bound. But after one thousand years, Satan will be loosed again so those who newly accepted what God offers can be tested. Satan will wreak havoc on those not firm in their faith knowing that when the Day of Judgment arrives he will be bound forever. Those souls who succumbed to Satan, which the Bible calls the "goats", will be cast into hell with Satan, while those who stood firm, called the "lambs", will inhabit God's new kingdom where there will be no sorrow, no tears and no evil. Thus, all of us are caught in this battle and as Satan fights to remain free and powerful, we must fight to remain faithful. Knowledge is power and knowledge of God's words the most powerful.

The Protections God offers:

Throughout scripture, God advises we wear the armor He provides. When we use everything God gives us and do what He asks of us, God refers to us as an "overcomer" and says in Revelation 3:21: "*...to him* *that overcometh, will I grant to sit with me in my throne....*" An overcomer is described as putting on a clean robe, indicating that sin has been washed away through the sacrifice of Christ. Revelation 7:13-14 says: "*......What are these which are arrayed in white robes?............These are they which came out of great tribulation, and have washed their robes, and made them white in the blood of the Lamb".*

The blood of the Lamb refers to the blood Christ shed in His sacrifice for us so our sins can be forgiven. Scripture assures us that *nothing* is too difficult for God and that all heartache can become a blessing. Jeremiah 32:17 says, "*...thou hast made the heaven and the earth by Thy great power and stretched out thy arm, and there is nothing too hard for Thee.*

We know from Revelation 7:17 that to be an overcomer isn't easy: "*......and God shall wipe away all tears from their eyes*". We may suffer for a while, but if we stand firm and withstand evil we will be an overcomer. Ephesians 6:13 tells us: "*Wherefore take unto you the whole armour of God, that ye may be able to withstand in the evil day, and having done all, to stand."* God reiterates in Romans 13:12: "*The night is far spent, the day is at hand: let us therefore cast off the works of darkness, and let us put on the armour of light"* The armor of light is God's words and the teaching and sacrifice of Christ. Revelation 4:20 says: "*Behold, I stand at the door, and knock; if any man hear my voice, and open the door, I will come in to him, and will sup with him, and he with me."* In Matthew 11:29, God says: "*Take my yoke upon you and learn of me...."* And 2 Timothy 2:7 says: "*Consider what I say; and the Lord give thee understanding in all things."* We are warned in Hebrews 3:7, 8: "*Wherefore, as the Holy Ghost saith,*

Today if ye will hear his voice, Harden not your hearts, as in the provocation, in the day of temptation in the wilderness." In Mark 13:33 God also warns us to watch: *"Take ye heed, watch and pray: for ye know not when the time is."* He also advocates that we flee evil and says in 1 Timothy 6:11: *"But Thou, O man of God, flee these things; and follow after righteousness, godliness, faith, love, patience, meekness."*

To flee evil we must recognize its subtleties and teach our children of them. We must help our brothers and sisters in faith, and all others to understand the importance of God's words about evil. We must help others recognize how serious this battle is, and to pray for their understanding, acceptance and protection. God helps us and He directs His angels to help us, but He also uses people, from ministers to strangers, to help us. As we learn how God looks after us, we must be willing to look after others, and teach others that *every* day we enter into a fierce battle against a formidable enemy who wants to thwart God's plan. God will help us, but when we know His words, we are better equipped to use His help and offer it to those we love.

Bullet Points

Satan rebelled against God because he was jealous of Christ and of mankind.

Satan's goal is to destroy the Bride of Christ and thus delay Christ's return.

There is danger in our lack of scriptural wisdom.

"Wolves" will enter among us to destroy our faith.

Many people, called the "goats" will be cast into hell with Satan.

God offers us a special "armour" with which to fight evil.

Our sorrows will end when Christ returns if we have made ourselves ready.

<u>Supporting Scripture</u>

Hosea 4:6,	Acts 20:29-31,
Jeremiah 32:17,	Revelation 7:13-14,
Revelation 7:17,	Ephesians 6:13,
Matthew 11:29,	Hebrew 3:7-8,
2 Timothy 2:7,	Revelation 4:20,
Mark 13:33,	1 Timothy 6:11,
Mark 4:15,	2 Corinthians 4:4.

Chapter Three

WHAT IS A RELATIONSHIP WITH GOD?

It's easy to say that by virtue of being a Christian we have a relationship with God. Some feel that demonstrating our faith by attending church, believing that Christ died for us, and being "good people" automatically provides us with a true relationship with God. While these are commendable, they do not guarantee the kind of relationship God longs to have with us nor is it enough for the Bride of His Son. It's a start, but it is not what truly touches the heart of God. An example of a truly intimate relationship can be found when we examine the relationship which exists between a husband and wife. If a husband and wife spend time together every evening, believe in their marriage, and are "good" people, yet do not share a true and intimate relationship through these deeds, what then is a good relationship? Revelation 3:15–16 warns: *"I know thy works, that thou art neither cold nor hot: I would thou wert cold or hot. So then because thou art lukewarm, and neither cold nor hot, I will spue thee out of my mouth."* To understand these words let's examine the relationship between a young married couple who are very much in love and let's discuss how they might interact with one another.

When we first fall in love, we care so much for the one we love that we devise many ways to demonstrate our love. We may place a note into the briefcase of the one we love as a surprise to be discovered sometime during their hectic day. We might purchase a special treat for them or telephone just to say hello or to provide an endearing word. At home we might touch or hug when we pass our loved one in a hallway or as we move from room to room. We may complete a chore for them that they have wanted to complete but had not yet found the time to do so. We would also communicate intimately with the one we love, share our concerns and ask what their concerns are. We would communicate about the good and the bad parts of each day, ask advice about how to handle a particular problem and often remind them of how much we love them. We would discuss the purchases we wish to make and the state of our joint finances. We would act like one entity, entwined in heart and mind and spirit. We would be like-minded. We would appreciate one another and express that appreciation. This is what would keep us close. Every expression of love and endearment would make our hearts soar. Our children would learn from hearing us speak to one another, and from how we respond to people who hurt us, and how we appreciate those who support us. Our children would learn from the prayers we say aloud with one another, and our own hearts would be touched by the prayers we hear from the one we love. We would be a happy family because we are openly expressive with one another. We would not be lukewarm with one another. We would articulate our love for one another and share our triumphs and our burdens with one another.

Would we be happy in a relationship where we are treated with indifference, where the person we love is uncommunicative, acts neither hot nor cold, neither caring nor uncaring. Would we feel loved, important to that person, feel that they cared? Would our love for them become cool and lukewarm? Which type of relationship do we have with God? Do we converse with God as we do with those we love and do we do this many times each day? Do we speak to God of our difficulties and our triumphs as we would with our loved one? Do we trust God and ask His advice as we would with the one with whom we share our temporal life? Do we seek to do little things every day to show God how much we love him as we do with the person we fell in love with? Do we make an effort to learn what pleases God as we did the one with whom we fell in love? If we do not do the things which all good relationships require we haven't yet developed the relationship with God which allows Him full entry into our hearts and minds, into our spirit and our future. And if we haven't yet developed that relationship, we really don't know Him. If we have not developed that degree of intimacy with God, we will be classified as lukewarm toward God, and He will rightly say that He knows us not. God wants to develop a bride for His Son, and inhabitants for His new heaven and new earth who will desire to give and show love. How then can He accept those who are not willing to work for the kind of a relationship with Him, which exists between a man and a woman who are deeply in love? How can we love someone to whom we give no time or effort? Only we can answer this question about the relationship we have fostered with God. Only we can answer this for ourselves. Each of us must learn what love really is and begin by helping and encouraging one another to understand what a relationship with God entails. Matthew 25:12 warns us that to some God will say, *"I know you not"*. But when we bring an act of love to God by learning how to love and how to express our love, we will please Him. If we do try our best to show our love and act with love we will be equipped to become the bride God wants for His Son and have a loving relationship with God. Love is expressed when we whisper the words "Thank You" to our Heavenly Father many times each day. It is expressed when we find ourselves angry yet bite our tongue and then tell our Heavenly Father that we are trying to live as He asks us to live and request His help. Love is the trust with which we describe our worries to Him and ask Him to guide us, trusting that He will. Love is the intimacy through which we ask Him to bless us and teach us and protect us every day. Love is having the courage to stand firm and fight to retain the values and treasures He has given us. This, along with our repentance, our tithing and effort, our willingness to learn His words and to help others, will result in a true relationship of love and trust. And when our hearts are moved, and our eyes fill with thankful tears for the love God gives us, and our goal is to strive to be an overcomer, we know that we have finally allowed God to touch our hearts and that we have touched His. That is a relationship with God.

Bullet Points

The relationship between two people in love is the kind of relationship we should want with God.

If we do not have a relationship with God we cannot know Him.
Scripture warns that if we do not know God, He will "spue" us from His mouth.

Love that begets trust and integrity is required for all good relationships.

Regular and intimate communication helps maintain a good relationship.

How well Christians express their relationship with God impacts their children.

Supporting Scripture

Revelation 3:15-16,	Matthew 25:11-12,
1Timothy 2:4-6,	Romans 8:28,
Matthew 22:37,	Joshua 24:15,
Proverbs 29:23,	11 Timothy 4:2,
Ephesians 6:4,	Matthew 25:21,
11 Corinthians 2:11,	Ephesians 6:11-12.

Chapter Four

THE MYSTERY OF SCRIPTURE

Most of us feel incredible awe for the wondrous love God has for us through which He sent His Son in order for us to be ransomed from sin. These are the greatest gifts we could ever ask for; they are priceless....they are treasures. Yet God has provided us with yet another gift which greatly assists those who seek Him with an open heart. It allows us to fully understand what these other gifts mean to us by teaching us how we can reach the goal of our faith. It is the gift of scripture.

Many people, believers and unbelievers alike feel that scripture is difficult to understand. Others find scripture fascinating and timely, and appear to fully understand what they read. While many question this phenomenon, scripture clearly tells us that the Bible is a mystery whose words are not unveiled to everyone. Yet, scripture shows us the beauty and goodness which lives in the heart of God and demonstrates His emotion, His love, His goals, His plan, His desire, His righteousness, and His power. Scripture teaches us about His enemy, why that enemy seeks the destruction of our faith, and how we can protect our faith. It teaches us how to love and how we are to treat one another. It helps us become worthy to spend eternity with Him and His Son.

None of us want our children to marry someone abusive or someone who thrives on contention. Similarly, our Heavenly Father seeks those who employ their free will to become a people who choose to love, who choose to be kind and loyal, who choose honor and integrity in all facets of their lives, and will spurn all things evil. God wants love and righteousness to reign in the new heaven and earth and graciously provides us with everything we need to accomplish this goal. Scripture is our best teaching tool, and when we seek to understand what God wants to tell us, and do so with an open heart, all is revealed to us as our understanding grows and our soul is ready to learn.

It is one of the fascinating components of scripture that its wisdom is easily read and understood by many, yet hidden from others, and that amazingly more is revealed as we grow in faith. The Holy Spirit opens the secrets of scripture to those who seek them with a pure, honest and humble heart. The Holy Spirit provides this wisdom at just the right time and to those who have been "made ready" to understand its deepest elements. This is called the "mystery" of the Bible and is another component which demonstrates how much God loves us, protects us, and guides our steps toward a perfect understanding.

King David loved God so deeply that despite his many faults and failings he could always touch God's heart. He trusted God and said in Psalms 18:28, *"For thou wilt light our candle: The Lord my God will enlighten my darkness."* This was a plea from David to God for a greater understanding. His use of the word "will" indicates the trust he had that God would provide him with that enlightenment.

Matthew 13:11 teaches us that understanding the things of God is a mystery not understood by everyone. *"Because it is given unto you to know the mysteries of the kingdom of heaven, but to them it is not given."* Further along in that chapter we learn that not all who see or hear will accept and follow. We also learn that God can open our understanding if we ask with a pure heart for Him to do this. Luke 24:31 tells us, *"And their eyes were opened, and they knew him....."* Sadly, some arrogantly believe that they already know all there is to know, or need only to believe, and this attitude can shortchange one's spiritual growth…and be deadly.

We must pray that we are continuously enlightened; open to where God wants to lead us, and protected from false teachings and complacency. As the Holy Spirit fills us, we will be liberated from the spirits of this world which want us bound, kept from the fullness of God's truths and lazy in what we offer God.

Scripture does not change, but hopefully we do. By giving our hearts and lives to God, by striving to do His will, by loving one another, and by praying for enlightenment, God will open the mysteries and truths of scripture to us. Our striving should be to grow in Spirit so we can learn and make of ourselves all that our

Heavenly Father wants us to be, all that He wants for the bride of His Son!

If we try to teach a new born infant to make a bed, they cannot. If we try to teach an infant to solve a complex physics problem, they cannot. But when they grow, and are taught the proper basic instruction which prepares them for more complex tasks, they can learn, and in time, can accomplish much more than they could earlier in life. Similarly as God's children, we must bring a willing heart to our life of faith and *apply* ourselves to become all God wants in a bride for His Son. As our understanding is opened, our trust increases and we can obtain the fullness of God's blessing.

1 Corinthians 2: 10, tells us, *"But God hath revealed them to us by his Spirit; for the Spirit searcheth all things, yea, the deep things of God."* Ephesians 3:4,5 tells us, *"Whereby, when ye read, ye may understand my knowledge in the mystery of Christ, which in other ages was not made known unto the sons of men, as it is now revealed unto his holy apostles and prophets by the Spirit;* and Luke 12:12 says, *"For the Holy Ghost shall teach you . . ".*

Satan uses mankind to perpetrate his evil and separate us from God. He also uses mankind to pervert the Gospel of Christ as written in scripture just enough to cause some to lose their way and create disputes. Satan can blind the eyes of men from correctly interpreting scripture. This is why we are urged to ask God for help, ask that the Holy Spirit guide us when we read scripture.

The very last words of the Bible warn us not to misapply, misinterpret or change what scripture tells us.

Revelation 22:18,19 warns, *"For I testify unto every man that heareth the words of the prophecy of this book, if any man shall add unto these things, God shall add unto him the plagues that are written in this book. And if any man shall take away from the words of the book of this prophecy, God shall take away his part out of the book of life, and out of the holy city, and from the things which are written in this book."*

God has provided us with scripture. The faithful who ask Him to help them understand are provided with the ability to unveil its mysteries. Luke 24:45 tells us, *"Then opened he their understanding, that they might understand the scriptures."* And Matthew 13:11 tells us, *".. . .Because it is given unto you to know the mysteries of the kingdom of heaven, but to them it is not given".*

The Apostle Paul, who was also given the ability to understand the mysteries of God, wrote in Ephesians 3:3,4,8,9, *"How that by revelation he made known unto me the mystery; (.....Whereby, when ye read, ye may understand my knowledge in the mystery of Christ) Which in other ages was not made known unto the sons of men, as it is now revealed unto his holy apostles and prophets by the Spirit………Unto me, who am less than the least of all saints, is this grace given, that I should preach among the Gentiles the unsearchable riches of Christ; And to make all men see what is the fellowship of the mystery, which from the beginning of the world hath been hid in God, who created all things by Christ Jesus."*

We are taught by scripture not to believe everything we hear or read. 1 John 4:1-2 warns, *"BELOVED, believe not every spirit, but try the spirits whether they are of*

God: because many false prophets are gone out into the world. Hereby know ye the Spirit of God . . ." Scripture teaches us to prove what we hear and read by comparing it to what God tells us, and to be careful when asked to trust only in the wisdom of men. 1 Corinthians 2:13 tells us: *"Which things also we speak, not in the words which man's wisdom teacheth, but which the Holy Ghost teacheth; comparing spiritual things with spiritual."*

When we understand that scripture is a mystery which God hides from those who desire to negate the word of God, and we understand that God delights in unveiling its mystery to His children, we see yet another miracle which God provides for us. We also learn to appreciate the power and majesty in God's all encompassing and perfect plan of salvation which He instituted just for us.

We live in a dangerous time. We have been warned of false prophets and of the satanic power they will bring to their words and to creating our complacency. We have been instructed to test those words and actions against the true Gospel of Christ, to pray unceasingly and to be rooted in the traditions of our faith and not justify sin by claiming it to be the times in which we live. 1 Timothy 4:13 tells us, *"Till I come, give attendance to reading, to exhortation, to doctrine."* And in 1Timothy 4:16, *"Take heed unto thyself, and unto the doctrine; continue in them: for in doing this thou shalt both save thyself, and them that hear thee."*

Bullet Points

Not everyone understands scripture.

Scripture itself tells us that scripture is a mystery which God will unveil to some, but not to all.

God provides us with ministers and other Christians to help us understand scripture.

Scripture tells us to prove what we are told so we are not misled by false doctrines.

When we seek to learn with a pure and open heart, God will open the mystery of scripture to us.

Supporting Scripture

1 Corinthians 2:10,	Ephesians 3:4-5,
Luke 12:12,	Revelation 22:18-19,
Matthew 13:11,	Luke 24:45,
Ephesians 3:3-4,	1 John 4:1-2,
1 Corinthians 2:13,	Ephesians 3:8-9,
1 Timothy 4:13,	1 Timothy 4:16.

Chapter Five

SCRIPTURE MARRIES EVOLUTION AND CREATION

Millions of people are joining a movement which requires that Biblical principles be brought back into our schools, our country, and those who govern. The return to Biblical principles has also drawn historians to the rediscovery that the intent of the founding fathers was to keep church in government, but government out of the church. They have also discovered that textbooks have been changed to negate the Judeo/Christian beliefs upon which this country was founded, and that our founding fathers *expected* textbooks to teach the principles explaining that God is our benefactor and protector, and that our Constitution was inspired by God. Parents have been surprised by these revelations and, looking more carefully at the quality of the education their children are receiving, have found it lacking and biased. Thus they are now confidently formulating bold questions and demanding change. One such issue is why evolution is taught to our children while creation is not when according to scripture, evolution and creation can co-exist.

Before studying the scripture which provides this information, one needs to address the question of what we believe creates our concept of time; our twenty-four-hour day. Simply put, it is the relationship between the earth and the sun. It is the speed and manner in which the earth revolves around its axis which creates the day and the night, and which for us occurs every twenty-four hours. The twenty-four hours it takes the earth to make one turn on its axis determines the length of time that one day and one night can claim. When the part of the planet we personally occupy is facing the sun, it is daylight, and when the earth rotates so we are not facing the sun, it is nighttime. The angle of the earth to the sun, how far it is from the sun, whether it faces toward or away from the sun, and how fast it spins on its axis, determines our days and nights, our seasons, and our time. The earth moves in a sort of egg-shaped or elliptic orbit around the sun, yet its axis always remains tilted in the same direction relative to the plane of the orbit. This tilt causes the sun's rays to strike each part of the earth at various angles throughout the orbit. The angle that the sun's rays hit the earth and the distance of the earth from the sun causes the seasons. One full orbit around the sun brings the earth back to the starting point and the amount of time required for this leads to our concept of the year. This, together with the rotation of the earth on its axis which causes our night and day, gives us our concept of time. Without the earth's rotations around its axis and around the sun as they are now, we might have a twenty-eight-hour day, or always be cold or always be warm. Thus, the angle of the earth to the sun, how far it is from the sun, whether it faces toward or away from the sun, and how fast it spins on its axis, determines our days and nights, our seasons, and our time.

The Book of Genesis tells the story of how the world was created and although commonly accepted that it took seven days to create, it actually took six days to create because on the seventh day, God rested. If we look carefully at the word "days", the Bible gives us an incredible clue about how carbon dating, along with some parts of evolution, is compatible with creation and how the two apparently contradictory theories, creation and evolution, could be quite compatible. Much of the conflict arises because "days", as we know them, are made up of a period of twenty-four hours each and exist only because of the relationship between the earth and the sun. When we read the first verse in Genesis and then follow this accounting from the first verse to the nineteenth verse, we find that the sun and moon and the 'seasons, days, and years' were not created until the fourth day. Therefore, we can conclude that it wasn't until this fourth day that we could have entered into time as *we* know it. We read about the creation of the sun and moon in Genesis 1:14, 16 and 19 which tell us: *"And God said, Let there be lights in the firmament of the heaven to divide the day from the night, and let them be for signs, and for seasons, and for days, and years." "And God made two great lights; the greater light to rule the day, and the lesser light to rule the night; he made stars also." "And the evening and the morning were the **fourth** day."*

Thus the first four "days", or two thirds of the time it took God to produce our world, are not days as we know them because time, as we now know it, was not yet introduced into the Creation. Thus, the verses from 1 through 13 in Genesis chapter 1 describing the Creation don't correspond to time as we currently experience it. Therefore many of the years relative to carbon dating may fall into this period before the completion of the work of the fourth day. Verses 1 through 13 speak of the form, the darkness, the waters, light and darkness, the firmament, and finally the division between dry land and the seas. Genesis 1:9 and 10 says, *"And God said, Let the waters under the heaven be gathered together unto one place, and let the dry land appear: and it was so. And God called the dry land Earth; and the gathering together of the waters called the Seas: and God saw that it was good."* This occurred on the *third* "day", one "day" *before* the sun and moon, days and nights, and seasons were established, and before time as we know it was established. Thus, many thousands of years could have gone into the making of everything up to the end of the fourth "day" when God completed the sun and moon for the earth, which then created the seasons, days, and years as we experience them. What the Bible says indicates that creation and evolution are more compatible than we recognize because carbon dating and many parts of evolution derived from it seem fully compatible with scripture. In fact, carbon dating supports the relationship scripture describes of evolution and creation rather than disproves it. Further, scripture describes God's work on the fifth day adding in Genesis 1:24: *"Let the earth bring forth the living creature **after his own kind.**"* What this could indicate is that because of the limits placed on time as described in the previous verses, **no longer would these creatures change through the process of evolution into new species;** they would instead bring forth only other creatures just like themselves. As we wonder why this debate still exists we can again look to the Bible for the answer. By reading about the encounter between Eve and the serpent in the Garden of Eden, and subsequent encounters between man and evil, we recognize that according to the Bible, mankind has an enemy who wishes to separate man from God. Thus, this debate is important to Satan as he would be interested in preventing man from accepting scripture as truth. He encourages unbelievers to denounce that creation and most parts of the theory of evolution can co-exist, for if he did not, more men might believe in God simply because they recognize the amazing accuracy of the Bible and the incredible feat of the creation.

Our concept of time is also addressed in Mark 13:19 where we read: *"………. And except that the Lord **had shortened those days**, no flesh should be saved: but for the elect's sake, whom he hath chosen, **he hath shortened the days.**"* If we consider the words 'hath shortened' to indicate that God had *already* shortened the days and that He did this when He created our sun and moon on that fourth day, this would give even more credence to the argument that days, before the sun and moon existed, were much longer. Revelation 10:6 says, *"And I sware by him that liveth for ever and ever, who created heaven, and the things that therein are, and the earth, and the things that therein are, and the sea, and the things which are therein, that there should be time no longer."* The words 'there should be time no longer' indicate that we will live without the confinement of time as we know it when God creates the new heaven and the new earth. This indicates that God controls time and that time might have been created just for us and for a specific span of time. Joshua 10:13–14 tells us, *"And the sun stood still, and the moon stayed………"* "……

So the sun stood still in the midst of heaven, and hasted not to go down about a whole day. And there was no day like that before it or after it." Here is another indication that God controls time.

Scientists claim that our universe is made up of dark matter which contains a kind of web which connects multitudes of superclusters, which themselves are made up of about one hundred billion galaxies. We live in the Mergo cluster in the relatively small Milky Way galaxy, which contains one hundred billion stars, one of which is our sun. Interestingly, in the beginning of Genesis, *before* God created our sun and moon and thus provided time as we know it, the words firmament, void, waters, darkness, and light are used. Webster's dictionary says that firmament means the vault or arch of the sky and also means a 'support.' The word void could be the dark matter itself, and the word firmament could refer to the webs within the dark matter which hold together the superclusters of galaxies. Darkness, according to the dictionary means devoid of light, not reflecting, receiving, transmitting, or radiating light, and could be what existed before the stars were created. One of the definitions of the word light says it is an electromagnetic radiation in the wavelength range including infrared, visible, ultraviolet, and X-rays traveling in a vacuum with a speed of about 186,281 miles per second. If Biblically this refers to stars it would support the big bang theory which Christians believe was *a controlled event with an engineered result,* not a haphazard event with an unpredictable result.

Bullet Points

The Bible shows us that evolution and creation coexist.

Time as we know it began with the creation of the sun and moon.

The sun was not created until the end of the fourth day.

The earth's rate of spin and the proximity to the sun create our twenty four hour day.

In the new world, time will exist no more.

God controls time and can change it

Supporting Scripture

Genesis 1:14,	Psalm 90:4,
2 Peter 3:8,	Genesis 1:9-10,
Genesis 1:19,	Genesis 1:1-13,
Mark 13:19,	Joshua 10:13-14,
Genesis 1:16,	Revelation 10:6,
Hosea 4:6.	

Chapter Six

WHY IS FELLOWSHIP IMPORTANT?

One of the most wonderful gifts God has provided for His children is the comfort of others who share their faith. In Galatians 6:2, the Apostle Paul told his congregations to *"Bear ye one another's burdens, and so fulfil the law of Christ"*. And in Galatians 6:6, he said, *"Let him that is taught in the word communicate unto him that teacheth in all good things."*

Further, in Ephesians 2: 19-22 tells us, *"Now therefore ye are no more strangers and foreigners, but fellowcitizens with the saints, and of the household of God. And are built upon the foundation of the apostles and prophets, Jesus Christ himself being the chief corner stone; in whom all the building fitly framed together growth unto an holy temple in the Lord; In whom ye also are builded together for an habitation of God through the Spirit."*

These words coupled with words such as fellowship, friend, fellowservant, fellowsoldier, fellowworker, fellowdisciple, and fellowlabourer indicate the bond which God's children should have, and the love toward one another which should emanate to and from them. Fellowship is defined by Webster's dictionary as "companionship", and "the company of equals". This describes a kind of kinship or friendship which God encourages among believers.

As an example, if we were to relocate from the Northern states of our country to the Southern states for an extended period of time we may begin to adopt the southern drawl which is prevalent in that region because what we surround ourselves with will leave its mark on us. Because we are so easily influenced by our surroundings, God warns us not to have fellowship with evil but with good… and says in 1 John 1:6-7, *"If we say that we have fellowship with him, and walk in darkness. We lie, and do not the truth: But if we walk in the light, as he is in the light, we have fellowship with one another, and the blood of Jesus Christ his Son cleanseth us from all sin."*

As the Apostles traveled from city to city to bring the gospel to others, God told them to search for someone they knew, someone in their congregation of believers who resided in the city to which they traveled. If they found no one and were to preach to those they wished to convert, God told them that He would choose someone in that city who would help them and believe in their cause. The Apostles enjoyed being with believers, but also being with new converts, and those willing to listen, because in such a group they felt safe, comfortable and comforted. God wants no less for us. He knows that when we are tired, or overburdened, or if we feel defeated, those who are close to God and who share our faith will help us and uplift us. Those who love God can pray together, and break bread together as the Apostles did. It is this spiritual comfort which encourages Christians to have fellowship with one another. But it is also because we can find godly advice in this circle as well as any needed admonition.

Sometimes we don't recognize when our path is a dangerous one. But in fellowship with other believers, those who do recognize this danger can remind us what Ephesians 5:11 says: *"And have no fellowship with the unfruitful works of darkness, but rather reprove them."* And in 1 Corinthians 10:20, *"But I say that the things which the Gentiles sacrifice, they sacrifice to devils, and not to God; and I would not that ye should have fellowship with devils."* It is also comforting to know that when we do make a mistake we are forgiven, encouraged and still loved and welcome in the circle of believers. 1 John 1: 3 tells us, *"That which we have seen and heard declare we unto you, that ye also may have fellowship with us: and truly our fellowship is with the Father, and with his Son Jesus Christ."* And in Galatians 1:9, *"God is faithful, by whom ye were called unto the fellowship of his Son Jesus Christ our Lord."*

Fellowship with other believers should be an important factor in the life of a Christian. We are not pulled in two directions when we share good food, camaraderie, or some form of entertainment with believers because we are like-minded and cognizant of how God wants us to behave. Our fun will be righteous healthy fun and our conversations kind, and often about our faith or how we can help those in need. What we seek to understand of scripture can also be revealed to us as we share conversation with believers. When one is weak in faith others can provide strength, when one lacks understanding others can teach, when one is weary, another will uplift. When our children are exposed to the conversations of believers they too are blessed with the growth of their faith and love. The hand of friendship we receive, and the trust we can obtain through those friendships is precious. The conversations and the role models we are given bring us consolation, comfort, instruction, and love. Philippians 2:1 tells us, *"If there be therefore any consolation in Christ, if any comfort of love, if any fellowship of the Spirit......"* And in Philippians 3:10 we are told, *"That I may know him, and the power of his resurrection, and the fellowship of his sufferings, being made conformable unto his death."*

If we have never been offered the hand of friendship from those in our congregation then we should extend our own hand. Galatians 2:9 gives us this example: *"....they gave to me and Barnabas the right hand of fellowship; that we should go unto the heathen....."* As Christians we will find a blessing in imitating the actions of the Apostles which scripture relates in Acts 2:42, *"And they continued stedfast in the apostle's doctrine and fellowship, and in breaking of bread, and in prayers."* And in Colossians 4:11, *"..........These only are my fellowworkers unto the kingdom of God, which have been a comfort unto me."*

Bullet Points

If we know God's words we will know the value of seeking fellowship with one another.

Scripture tells us to continue in the Apostle's doctrine and in fellowship.

Our fellowworkers in Christ bring us comfort and help us bear our burdens.

Christians are to offer one another the right hand of friendship.

Bringing God's words to the unbeliever is a part of the Christians duty.

Scripture tells us to have no fellowship with evil.

<u>Supporting Scripture</u>

Galatians 6:2,   Ephesians 2:19-22,

1 John 1:6-7,   1 Galatians 1:9,

Philippians 2:1,   Galatians 2:9,

Galatians 6:6,   Philippians 3:10,

Acts 2:42,   Colossians 4:11,

1 John 1:3,   Ephesians 5:11,

1 Corinthians 10:20.

Chapter Seven

CHRISTIANS AND POLITICS

Contrary to public opinion, there has never been an official document written by the founding fathers which intended a separation of church and state. This was a concept put forth by an ACLU attorney named Leo Pfeffer in 1947. The Supreme Court in the case of Everson versus Board of Education of Ewing Township used his words, "the separation of church and state" to impose a decision by a five to four vote which coupled that phrase with the First Amendment. In truth, the First Amendment was not intended to remove Christian principles, nor the proclamation of our nation's dependence on God, from government. The First Amendment simply states, *"Congress shall make no law respecting an establishment of religion or prohibiting the free exercise thereof."* The founding fathers wrote those words to assure that each state would have the freedom to worship as the people desired and that government could not prohibit worship nor impose its own religion. Thus, a grave error evolved regarding the separation of church and state which historians and constitutionalists are now re-examining.

David Barton, founder of Wallbuilders, Inc., states that the ACLU and other anti-Christian Organizations and individuals, as well as evolutionists use the phrase "separation of church and state" to harass Christians, and use this court ruling to keep a theistic explanation of origins out of the public schools. He also contends that they have used this ruling to completely revise history books and thus change what our children are taught about our nation. He further explains that the basis for their argument came from an out-of-context quote from a letter written by Thomas Jefferson from which they claimed that Jefferson was a deist, meaning that he believed in God but not in God's personal and continuing interest in man, rather than being the committed Christian his writings show him to be. Sadly, the truth about our history and the Christian foundation upon which our country was founded is very different than what revised history books have been portraying to students over the past sixty years. The founding fathers' intent for the First Amendment is documented in discussions recorded in Congressional Records from June 7th through September 25th of 1789. Their goal was to prevent America from falling under the same rule which forced them to flee Great Britain where one religion was imposed by the government on all the people. The founding fathers intended that our nation would not dictate any single denomination for the nation, yet wanted Biblical principles and the acknowledgement of our dependence on God to continue to dictate behavior. It is interesting to note that twenty seven of our fifty six founding fathers earned degrees from a Christian seminary and specifically developed the Constitution and the Declaration of Independence to assure that the church was protected from the government and not that the government was protected from the church. The majority of founding fathers were committed Christians whose speeches contained direct quotes from the Bible and whose intent was to obtain and retain God's blessing on our nation. Research demonstrates that they desired our nation to be built and maintained upon a foundation of Biblical principles which they understood was paramount to the continued success and protection of our country. This is why our Constitution, Declaration of Independence, and Bill of Rights, along with our government buildings, currency and original text books, clearly acknowledge the Divine Providence of our country. Even earlier, on October 11, 1782 a congressional proclamation declared that Thanksgiving Day was a day when our nation was to give thanks to God for the variety of blessings He bestowed on our country and in our lives. The Bill of Rights and all laws were passed on the basis of Biblical principles and the assumption that they were and always would be subordinate to the more authoritative Bible. The assumption and expression of Divine Providence was thought to be common knowledge. Even the Establishment clause dating back to 1791 when the United States Constitution was officially ratified, lacks any mention of a separation of church and state. Its intent was also based on the assumption that Judeo/Christian Biblical principles are the basis upon which our country was founded. This document sought only to protect religion and allow the people of the nation to worship freely with no government interference. Revolutionary Patrick Henry said that this great nation was founded by Christians; not on religions, but on the gospel of Jesus Christ. As Chief Justice of the State of Maryland and a signer of the Declaration of Independence, Samuel Chase declared in a court ruling in 1799, *"By our form of government, the Christian religion is the established religion, and all sects and denominations of Christians are placed on the same and equal footing."* Later, in 1950 President Harry Truman told an Attorney Generals Conference that the fundamental basis of this nation's laws was given to Moses on the Mount and that the fundamental basis of our Bill of Rights comes from the teaching we can obtain from Exodus, the Apostle Matthew, from Isaiah, and from the Apostle Paul. He also said that without a proper moral background we would end up with a totalitarian government. Despite the erroneous Supreme Court ruling in 1947 and its detrimental consequence of no church in government as opposed to no government in churches, over the past few years an incredible revival of faith and patriotism has been sweeping this country. Ministers, Rabbis, Priests and even Imams have come together to fight for the reinstatement and proclamation of returning God to our schools and government. Rightfully so, these brave men are standing together to teach their congregants to fight for the fundamental faith upon which this country was founded. They have reinstituted the "Black Robe Brigade" of the founding fathers' era. The name evolved from the black robes which all ministers wore in those days when behind the pulpit. According to David Barton this group is made up of thousands of well known and well respected religious leaders representing huge congregations across the country. The original Black Robe Brigade was initiated by a Lutheran Minister named John Muhlenberg who became a Virginia Colonel in Washington's army in the fight for religious freedom. Washington asked Muhlenberg to help him raise a regiment of volunteers, and as Muhlenberg gladly complied, he gained the support of a large number of ministers. They began to preach that Christianity was the foundation of our country and urged their parishioners to fight for the Biblical concept that all men are created in the image of God, entitled to equal treatment and inalienable rights, and that the government must never interfere with the advancement of Christian liberty. The goal of the *new* Black Robe Brigade is to teach Christians once again that they must put forth their powerful and united voice to retain their religious freedom and their religious expression. They hope to teach Christians that they must fight to undo the damage that the Progressive Movement has wrought by stifling Christian expression, and by removing any expression of God and the Biblical principles upon which this nation was founded from our government, our schools and our children's textbooks. These courageous ministers are leading our nation back to a place where God can once again bless us and bless this nation. But it is up to Christians and other people of God to support their efforts and also demand this effort from their politicians, their school boards, those who write text books, and those who teach our children. It is interesting to note that according to David Barton, 33 tapes of sermons which address these admonitions to congregants were sent to the IRS in 2008, and 84 were sent in 2009, challenging the IRS to prevent these sermons by withholding tax credits to these churches. They expect to have thousands of ministers participating this year and have a bevy of attorneys ready to meet this challenge. However, to date, the IRS, apparently acknowledging that they would lose such a challenge in court, have looked the other way proving these brave men right. These sermons and future sermons which encourage congregants to take back their country and their Biblical values have come to be known as "Pulpit Freedom Sundays". Christians need to stand behind these courageous men of God and take an interest in the values of those they elect to any governing office. Scripture provides both direction and warning about governing and describes the attributes of those who should govern as those who walk in truth and fear God. Further, it warns that those who do not follow these admonitions will pay a heavy price personally for the damage that will befall their nation. Here are but eight of the many verses in scripture which address governing, the nations which are governed, and the people who are governed. Exodus 18:21 teaches, *"Moreover thou shalt provide out of all the people able men, such as fear God, men of truth, hating covetousness; and place such over them to be rulers of thousands, and rulers of hundreds, rulers of fifties, and rulers of ten."* This clearly tells us to support and vote for men of truth who fear God. 11 Chronicles 19:5-7 tells us, *"And he set judges in the land throughout all the fenced cities of Judah, city by city. And said to the judges, Take heed what ye do; for ye judge not for man, but for the Lord, who is with you in judgment. Wherefore now let the fear of the Lord be upon you; take heed and do it: for there is no iniquity with the Lord our God, nor respect of persons, nor taking of gifts."* Here a warning is clearly issued to those who govern. They are told to fear God and govern according to His will. 11 Chronicles 19:10 adds, *"....between law and commandments, statutes and judgments, ye shall even warn them that they trespass not against the Lord, and so wrath will come upon you, and upon your brethren; this do, and ye shall not trespass."* Here scripture tells us that where governing occurs, no trespass upon God must occur and that *"ye"* shall warn them or we will all suffer God's wrath. Psalms 9:16-17 warns, *"The Lord is known by the judgment which he executeth; the wicked is ensnared in the work of his own hands....The wicked shall be turned into hell, and all the nations that forget God."* Here we are warned that we will be ensnared by our allowance of evil lawmakers, and that our nation will suffer when we are ensnared by what wicked lawmakers have wrought. Further, that if we forget God, as a nation we may face hell. 11 Chronicles 7:14 comforts us with the words, *"If my people, which are called by my name, shall humble themselves, and pray, and seek my face, and turn from their wicked ways; then will I hear from heaven, and will forgive their sin, and will heal their land."* Clearly God is offering us a second chance to stop the wickedness and turn back to Him. If we add works to our faith to accomplish this, He will heal our nation. Malachi 2:8 acknowledges, *"But ye are departed out of the way; ye have caused many to stumble at the law; ye have corrupted the covenant of Levi, sayeth the Lord of hosts."* Christians have clearly departed from God by allowing, even encouraging the corruption of government to continue and by their inaction have *allowed* it to occur. God notices those who have been corrupt and who cause our nation and their people to stumble. Matthew 18:6 warns, *"But whoso shall offend one of these little ones which believe in me, it were better for him that a millstone were hanged around his neck, and that he drowned in the depth of the sea."* This scripture clearly warns those who were and are responsible for removing God, and the Biblical principles upon which this nation was founded from the schools and textbooks of our children. Malachi 2:17 warns, *"Ye have wearied the Lord with your words.....When you say, Every one that doeth evil is good in the sight of the Lord, and he delighteth in them; or Where is the God of judgment?"* Here God acknowledges that we are complaining about our situation. However, He also tells us that our complaining wearies Him and will be of no avail because *we ourselves* are the cause of allowing our Biblical principles to be lost. These are just a few verses from scripture which address the governing of the people. In every verse, God warns that His principles and His might must always be respected. We as Christians need to find the backbone to fight against corruption and fight against the removal of God from our government and our schools. We should encourage politicians, ministers and teachers to support the adherence to the Biblical principles basic to Christianity and to Judaism from which it flowed. God wants them to encourage those they teach and help their congregants understand that scripture tells us to appreciate our freedoms, appreciate that we can vote for them, and choose carefully to whom we give our vote. Each of us must value what God gave us enough to fight to retain them. If we don't, we will lose those gifts, and lose the blessing of God for ourselves and our country.

<u>Bullet Points</u>

27 of the 56 founding fathers earned Christian seminary degrees.

It is a falsehood that the First Amendment requires a separation of church and state.

The founding fathers wanted to prevent government from dictating a specific religion but agreed that to flourish this nation must retain its Judeo/Christian Biblical principles.

The separation of state and church fallacy developed from a phrase coined by an ACLU attorney by taking out of context words from a letter by Thomas Jefferson.

In 1947 a Supreme Court case was won by a vote of five to four to support an anti-Christian movement to remove God from all government run or assisted entities.

Thousands of ministers are now working together to re-instate the original Black Robe Brigade of ministers who supported the founding fathers and work together for the right to re-instate and proclaim our nations Judeo/Christian principles.

Supporting Scripture

Exodus 18:21,	11 Chronicles 19:5-7,
11 Chronicles 19:10,	Psalms 9:16-17,
11 Chronicles 7:14,	Malachi 2:8,
Matthew 18:6,	Malachi 2:17.

Chapter Eight

DO I HAVE TO VOTE?

Yes, Yes, Yes! Colossians 2:8 says, *"Beware lest any man spoil you through philosophy and vain deceit, after the rudiments of the world, and not after Christ."* Ephesians 4:26 tells us *"Neither give place to the devil."* And in 5:11, *"Have no fellowship with them."* And Acts 18:9 says, *"Be not afraid but speak and hold not thy peace."* Luke 20:25 teaches: *"Render unto Caesar the things which are Caesar's and unto God the things that are God's."* which is better understood when we also read in Romans 13:1: *"Let every person be in subjection to the governing authorities. For there is no authority except from God and those which exist are established by God."* What we learn from these verses is that the privilege to vote is an authority given us by God and that we are to obey that authority, beware some philosophies, and not be afraid to speak against them. Further, in the previous chapter we discussed the words of Exodus 18:21 and 11 Chronicles 5-7 which tell us to choose leaders who fear God and speak the truth. This admonition, coupled with the verses listed above, helps us understand that God wants us involved in these political selections and that He has gifted us with the freedom to do so.

In recent years, there has been an incredible rally of political interest and thus the awareness that we have lost many of our Christian principles. Many are refusing to accept the continued loss of these values and the lower moral standards this spawns. This has created a populous eager to change direction and determined to demand that school systems, text books, teachers, politicians, church boards, ministers, and elected officials act with Christian integrity and become role models who willingly uphold godly values.

As this country began to awaken to the insidious attack on Christian values, many regretted their lack of engagement in the political process and in the responsibility to watch and guard what is precious. They recognized what they lost and want to prevent the further loss of those things God so graciously gave us and work towards their re-instatement. Sadly, we have become lax about learning the word of God, negligent in supporting our beliefs, lazy in teachings the ways and wiles of Satan, and irresponsible in allowing ungodly political ideologies to govern. Our good intentions have been thwarted because we no longer know what God says and because we have become irresponsible, unappreciative, and complacent, and have perhaps lost our courage and conviction. We have learned that when Biblical values are lost, so is mankind's ability to identify and prevent the lies and rhetoric which will destroy what we hold dear.

Each of us needs to be committed to adding our support to this fight and to speak openly against deception and evil not only in our homes, and churches, but also in our government. Yet seldom do we address the issue of our personal responsibility regarding government. We have foolishly left it to others. Christians and Christian leaders must take responsibility for a corrupt government and advocate that the privilege to vote is a gift and if we ignore that gift, we negate that which scripture tells us. Church leaders understand that Satan wants man to harm man by destroying faith and righteousness and that he is accomplishing this goal through a variety of arenas, one of which is our political system. It is this system through which the parameters of behavior are defined through our laws, and trickle down into the parameters of how we live and what behaviors we tolerate. When we do not vote we abdicate the gift of freedom and leave this arena to those who may not espouse Christian values. This may in time also deny us the right to vote in the future, for many countries either do not provide the right to vote, or do not offer a vote which carries any meaning.

Christians must stand up for and honor God's gifts and precepts, and cling to them even if they are lost to the world. Those precepts must live in our heart and be placed into our children's hearts to develop the unity of purpose so necessary to the survival of the values put forth by Christianity. The incredible Christian energy which has surfaced recently is God's way of giving us a second chance. We can still win this battle between a corrupt and godless government, and a truthful and godly government if we begin to carefully vet our candidates and we all voted. There are hundreds of organizations comprised of moms, dads, neighbors, college students, retirees, even children who want to learn about politics, are willing to teach one another, and will support one another in the goal to bring our country back to a nation under God, along with the fiscal responsibility and Christian values our forefathers espoused. This is a matter of principles, not party lines or political correctness....it is a matter of helping one another demand personal values and religious conviction in our schools, churches, laws, elected officials and government, not a matter of telling anyone who to vote for or what party to espouse.

The important issue is the principles and Christian values in the moral makeup of our leaders. The well-being of our country is something that even our churches and ministers, our youth leaders and Bible study groups ***must*** address with courage and conviction and not shy away from. The ***erroneous*** assumption that Christians should simply wait for the end, accept the separation of church and state, and not be accountable by abdicating their responsibilities is wrong. Christ fought and died for us. God fought and sacrificed for us. Isn't it time we fought and sacrificed to retain the gifts God gave us of liberty and freedom which we received because we based our very foundation on Godly principles and fought for them?

Christians and politics do mix and it is our Christian duty to serve our country. Fighting for its Christian principles with courage and conviction is what defines us as those who stand up for our God and our future. God clearly hates the slothful, the lazy, the timid, and the lukewarm and provides dire warnings to those who have desiccated our freedoms and our faith. We must *fight* for our faith and our values, and the beauty of our God-given Constitution or we too will be consumed by the terrors of evil. Ministers *must* have the courage to teach that sin is sin no matter how politically incorrect it is to say so. They must lead by addressing the responsibility we have to care for what God has given us. They must teach their parishioners to appreciate the freedom God has provided and admonish them to do their part and vote for those with Christian values.

Bullet Points

Loving God requires following His word.

Scripture tells us to render unto Caesar but not give place to the devil.

Loving is to teach and rebuke.

The privilege to vote is a gift from God.

Evil attacks by instilling godlessness in politics, government, textbooks, and children.

Supporting Scripture

Colossians 2:8,	Matthew 22:39,
Ephesians 4:26,	1 Timothy 6:11,
Matthew 11:29,	Ephesians 6:13,
11 Corinthians 4:4,	Mark 4:15,
1 Chronicles 21:1,	Acts 18:9,
Ephesians 5:11,	11 Timothy 2:7.

Chapter Nine

COUNSEL, COMPASSION & HUMAN NATURE

We often feel guilty when we cannot overcome the pain and fear which our life circumstances can create. Because we are children of God, we want to control these emotions through our trust in God. Thus, living with negative emotions can make us feel guilty and unworthy of God's help...and even wonder if we lack sufficient faith.

It helps if we understand that we are born with a survival mechanism which uses pain and fear to protect us from harm. Just as we fight Satan more wisely when we understand his nature, and why and how he seeks to harm us, and utilize the power of prayer because we know what God can do, we can fight our human nature more effectively when we understand how it works. By learning about our natural emotional make-up we can assess what is happening to us and why, and find the resources with which to fight.

Our human nature is built into our psyche, is an innate need to protect and survive, and uses emotion to warn us of danger or draw us to happiness. Even Christ felt fear and fought this part of His human nature before He could submit to the will of His Father. As children of God we know that with every difficult circumstance we overcome, we grow stronger spiritually and emotionally. Understanding what we feel and why, and how to move from pain to trust and acceptance, changes the way we react to circumstances and makes them easier to bear. Learning how to deal with our human nature helps us become successful in our spiritual life. Both have to be understood for them to grow stronger.

Grief is a debilitating emotion and is the result of loss; even a perceived loss. It can be triggered by the death of a child, spouse or parent; the end of a romance or marriage; the loss of a home, a job, our savings; the loss of one's health or the health of a loved one; or anything else which we deem of great importance to us. A study of the effects of grief was conducted by a Swiss-born American psychiatrist named Elisabeth Kubler-Ross. During her study she discovered that the reactions to grief included denial, anger, bargaining, depression and acceptance and that most of us must experience all of these conditions before we can heal. She determined that when we sense a potential loss, our human nature places us into a state of denial where we unconsciously ignore or deny the first signs of a problem. Our psyche decides that everything will work out, what we feel will somehow be resolved, and allows us to remain in denial until reality is unavoidable.

The second stage of grief is anger. Anger can be directed inward, toward the circumstance, toward the person we believe caused the loss, or even toward those who counsel us. Satan is delighted to have us remain in this stage of grief and even more delighted if we blame God for our loss and then live with guilt. But God knows that we battle not only Satan, but the very nature with which we were born. He wants to help us recognize these truths and understand why we feel as we do and how we can move through and away from those feelings. He wants to turn our loss into a victory of faith.

Once we move past anger, we move into the stage of bargaining. We bargain with whomever we believe can change our circumstance, including God. We promise to do better, to work harder, to make up for every wrong thought or action if only the circumstance would be removed. As children of God we hope that by going to church more often, praying more often, tithing more and working harder in the vineyard, we will garner the favor of God who may then remove our cross.

When these three stages fail to help, we may move back and forth between them once again or fall into the fourth stage of grief which is depression. Depression creates great internal sorrow, and is the result of an inner decision that the pain we feel is too difficult to fight. Depression destroys our hope for future joy. But once this stage is successfully navigated, we move into the healing stage of acceptance where the energy for everyday tasks returns and we live with our loss. When we understand our human nature, we can move through the stages of grief more quickly. When those who counsel us also understand that these stages of emotion are a natural part of the make-up of mankind, they counsel with greater compassion and effectiveness. This understanding allows us to recognize the stages of grief and why the pain and fear is not easily and immediately overcome. It also prevents us from innocently heaping guilt on an already battered soul which believes that if they continue to experience pain and fear, they are not trusting God.

While the soul and the spiritual make-up of that person knows this to be true, the pain to their physical make-up is too great for them to utilize this information. But with compassion, patience and an explanation of what is happening internally and why, the soul can move away from the pain, guilt and isolation, and into the love, compassion and advice of their faith.... and heal. The end result is a stronger child of God and a stronger, more compassionate counselor. This understanding creates a bond between the two, and creates souls who can then reach out with that same understanding to help someone else. Satan does not want us to understand human nature, wants us to feel guilt and give up trying. He wants us to feel that because we continue to experience pain and fear, and even anger, we are not a true child of God.

But God wants us to know that our human nature is a part of us and with His help we can move through these stages quickly and overcome their negative effects. Satan wants to block our understanding, while God wants to increase our understanding and create a blessing from it. With God's help, a child of God does not have to bow before their human nature, but can begin to understand its process and use the power of their faith and the love and support of their bearers of blessing to overcome it.

Bullet Points

Grief is an emotion which moves through five stages before it can heal.

The stages of grief are denial, anger, bargaining, depression, and acceptance.

Christ felt grief. God offers us comfort.

The promise of life after death also brings comfort.

God assures us that all things happen for the good of those that love God

Supporting Scripture

Luke 12:6,

1 Timothy 2:4-6,

Hosea 4:6,

Revelation 21:7,

James 5:7,

1 Corinthians 15:58,

Revelation 20:12,

Isaiah 53:3,

Jude 21: 11

Peter 3:9,

Hebrews 9:16,

Revelation 14:13,

Jude 22.

Chapter Ten

SACRAMENTS AND PASSPORTS

Societies have instituted rules which keep order and civility. These include stopping at an intersection with a stop sign, moving with a green light, and turning with a green arrow. These rules help us arrive at our destination without mishap. There are also rules we must follow if we wish to travel to another country such as the prerequisite that we obtain a passport. As we adjust to the rules of society, we begin to understand that it is easier to reach our goals when we know what is required, and how we can best obtain what we need to be successful. Yet, we balk at the idea that there could be prerequisites for entering heaven.

The requirement that we obtain a visa or a passport to travel to another country is an excellent example for understanding why we need to meet a certain criteria to enter the Kingdom of Heaven. While many feel that believing Christ died for us is enough, those who know scripture understand that there are prerequisites, taught throughout scripture, for becoming the Bride of Christ and the overcomer who Christ will take when He returns.

The parable of the five foolish and five wise virgins warn us that among believers, only half will be prepared to be taken at the First Resurrection and thus half will not be prepared and will be left behind. All ten of these virgins were believers and were waiting for the bridegroom, yet only half had prepared properly.

Rules, like a passport, act as tools which help us reach our goal. A driver's license, a viable vehicle, and roadmaps are tools which allow us to navigate to unknown area. Similarly, a visa or passport is the tool used by a non-citizen of a country to gain permission to enter that country. Without a passport we cannot enter countries we might wish to explore, nor even board a plane or ship to leave our own country. God too requires certain things of those who will be the Bride of Christ and these include a certain code of behavior and obtaining the sacraments which create a covenant with God.

A sacrament, or covenant with God contains certain rules for receiving the gifts we are offered from such a bond. Holy Baptism, Holy Communion, and Holy Sealing are the three sacraments. They are prerequisites to becoming a part of the Bride of Christ. Scripture tells us why they are necessary and how they provide us with the means by which we can escape the captivity of Satan and return to God. Sacraments allow us to obtain God's protection, avoid the traps laid by Satan, escape the consequences of both our sins and the sins of our forefathers, and become pleasing in the sight of God.

The sacrament of Holy Baptism is given to break the captivity of inherited sin inflicted upon mankind by the sin of Adam and Eve which had denied us access to God. Holy Communion offers us the forgiveness of sin through the sacrifice of Christ, requires a true acknowledgement and repentance of our sins, and provides strength for striving to avoid those sins in the future. Holy Sealing is the gift of the Holy Spirit which is bestowed on us to teach us, guide our steps and protect us from spiritual harm.

These are precious gifts which must not be grieved by our lack of knowledge and lack of obedience to the word of God. Hosea 4:6 clearly warns: *"My people are destroyed for lack of knowledge; because thou hast rejected knowledge, I will also reject thee……"*

2 Corinthians 2:11 warns: *"Lest Satan should get an advantage of us: for we are not ignorant of his devices."* And Matthew 12:31 clearly warns: *"Wherefore I say unto you, All manner of sin and blasphemy shall be forgiven unto men; but the blasphemy against the Holy Ghost shall not be forgiven unto men."* Thus, those things which God tells us through scripture are provided to help us return to God and remain with Him for all eternity.

Church, prayer, tithing, fellowship, and learning to love are some of the tools which guide us to our spiritual destination and are inspired in us through the work of the Holy Spirit. Scripture, another tool, is a map which guides us through the maze of Satan's playground by the safest route possible. The path to God can be navigated by knowing God's words. Without this knowledge and the covenants or sacraments God offers, we cannot be free of sin nor understand godly love and cannot become the Bride of Christ.

Scripture gives us direction and information which is amazingly applicable to our modern world. We face different concerns than our grandparents may have faced; a different grief, a different joy, and a different worry, but we are engaged in the same spiritual warfare and we hope for the same outcome. We are striving to learn how to make our life better and our spiritual future secure. If we do this through scripture and by utilizing the "passports" God offers, we can learn what we need to do and why. Then, the sacraments of our faith will not be taken unworthily because we will understand their importance, realize why they are necessary and how we can use them.

Following the rules which exist to keep us safe, developing as Christians through the word of God, and obtaining the passport which enables us to travel with Christ at the First Resurrection is essential. The rules for obtaining a "passport" to heaven help us avoid doing the very things which keep us from all that God wants for us.

Bullet Points

Rules help us follow the laws of the land and keep society safe.

There are also rules for living as God asks us to live.

We cannot know how to live as God asks if we do not know His words.

Scripture teaches us God's words and direction.

A passport is an excellent analogy of the requirements for travel with Christ when Christ returns.

The parable of the five wise and five foolish virgins warn us to be prepared.

<u>Supporting Scripture</u>

Matthew 25:3, 5,	2 Corinthians 2:11,
Matthew 12:31,	Mark 6:8, 12,
Matthew 25:10,	Mark 10:17,
Matthew 25:21,	Luke 8:15,
Mark 10:19,	Mark 10:21.

Chapter Eleven

WHY GOD ALLOWS HEARTACHE

It is difficult to live through heartbreaking circumstances especially when it seems that God does not hear nor answer our prayers. When difficulties continue with no end in sight we can become discouraged and may even question our faith or our worthiness to have our prayers heard. We may wonder what we did wrong to deserve what has befallen us. These are normal human reactions, but they are not godly; they come from Satan.

Satan wants us discouraged by heartache and wants us to blame God, feel unworthy of His help, and question His lack of intervention. When Satan succeeded in causing Adam and Eve to sin and opened the door to sin, we became subject to battle not only our own sin, but the inherited sin which scripture defines as the sin of our ancestors which is visited upon the third and fourth generations. This clearly shows us that the weaknesses of our forefathers may be the source of addictions and other tendencies which are so difficult to fight.

But God factored this into His plan of salvation and provided us with a way to overcome this difficulty. He offers His comforting presence during that struggle and through scripture teaches us what we need to know. Further, our Heavenly Father is both omnipotent and omnipresent and tells us in Romans 8:28, *"And we know that all things work together for good to them that love God, to them who are called according to his purpose."*

He shows us that there is a reason why we live through heartache and when we understand why God allows our struggles, those struggles are easier to bear, and the blessing we can derive from the experience may become evident to us more quickly. Our job is to believe that a blessing will come, and to believe that good will result from what transpires in our heart as we go through our difficult circumstances. When we know what scripture tells us about this phenomena we can place our faith in God's help and wisdom. Scripture tells us that God does not bring our heartache, but that Satan does, and that God in His perfect righteousness must allow it. However, God will take that heartache and turn it into a blessing for those who are faithful. Just as God went with Shadrach, Meshach and Abednego into the furnace (Daniel 3:20), and with Daniel into the den of lions (Daniel 6:6), and with David when he faced Goliath (1 Samuel 17:49), He goes with us.

The blessing God creates is, in part, also a way to establish our trust in, and loyalty to Him. When we trust in His decisions He is able to strengthen us when we go through our heartaches. But, when we are not aware that it is Satan who brings our heartache and that God creates a blessing from it, and thus cannot trust God, our heartache is more difficult to bear, and the blessing harder to recognize. We often remain in that heartache longer than necessary had we understood what we needed to do.

The Biblical account of Sodom and Gomorra teaches us about God's compassion. As we read that He agreed to Abraham's plea (Genesis 18:32) to save Lot and his family from the destruction of the city, we know He answers prayers. We learn of God's patience when Jonah ran from Him (Jonah 1:3), we understand His gentleness through the beatitudes Christ spoke (Matthew 5:3-11), we see His longsuffering in all His references to us as children rather than adults, and we see His love throughout the beauty of the creation which He fashioned just for us. We see that those strong in faith are gifted with courage, patience and the capacity to love.

When we have an intimate relationship with our Heavenly Father, His words touch a chord in our heart which allows us to internalize His loving, gentle nature. With these facts in our heart and mind we change our inner nature and we develop a trust in God which grows stronger over time. We muster our strength to wait patiently for our circumstances to change and learn to dismiss our anger, fear, anxiety, and doubt. Most importantly, we can thank God for our circumstances because we know that they bring valuable changes to our heart to create in us one who can become a part of the Bride of Christ.

Fellowship with other believers can help us. If we share our worries and our triumphs with one another and bear one another's burdens we will uplift one another in times of sorrow. We can pray for one another, remind one another of the various verses in scripture which may pertain to our circumstance, bask in the promise that God never leaves us, and provide love, forgiveness and encouragement to one another.

Our Heavenly Father is loyal to us and expects us to be loyal to Him and to one another, especially during difficult circumstances. God loves us. He teaches us through the difficulties Satan brings into our lives. He works miracles through what we go through and is pleased when we use our experiences to help others move through their difficulties. He wants us to grow from children to the Bride of Christ which can only be accomplished if we ourselves develop in love and understanding, compassion and strength. We will bring those qualities with us as we work side by side with Christ during the thousand year reign of peace when we return to earth after the wedding feast at the end of the tribulation.

However, most of us have asked the question, "Why, God, why?", or perhaps "How long do I have to suffer?" Sadly, asking these questions can make us feel guilty; feel that we have failed God by not trusting Him or believing that what we go through is known by Him. Many have felt this same despair and asked these same questions even knowing that their troubles are not instigated by God but by Satan. Satan's power is so all-encompassing that he not only challenged God but also engaged in a war with God which he believes he can win. We tend to forget that Satan would never have begun such an effort if he thought that he would lose. That alone should tell us that Satan is a formidable enemy. Further, if we have not had troubles we must examine our heart to see why Satan leaves us alone.

Our Heavenly Father has a far greater power than the power of evil and will win the spiritual war in which we are all engaged. His plan of salvation will prevail despite Satan's efforts. We, however, do not have a greater power than Satan, nor do we have an equal power, and are thus pawns in Satan's hands except for God's protection and direction. The Biblical story of Job demonstrates how Satan can do with us as he pleases……. except for the limits placed on Satan's power by God. This story also demonstrates that what Satan is allowed to do cannot destroy those who seek and love God.

Therefore, when we tire, when we become discouraged and when we question God, He understands. He has witnessed…and allowed….what we must go through. He uses our sorrow to our benefit and always brings from it a blessing. God suffered greatly as He witnessed the pain and sorrow which Christ endured and remembers that even Christ said in His agony, *"Let this cup pass from me."* Our Heavenly Father suffers when we do as well. Christ understood that He must endure His pain and suffering for a greater purpose. Despite His human fear, He held firm to His purpose and said to God, *"Not My will, but Thy will be done"*. When we follow Christ's example and demonstrate our loyalty to and trust in God during difficult circumstances, it is not the questions we ask or the agony or anxiety we feel, or the weakness and failure we exhibit which God counts, but the final submission to His will that He looks for, and which will produce the miracle of transformation in our soul.

As Christians, we must remember that if we never felt pain, we would not know that God is our healer. If we never had to pray we would not know that He delivers us from our difficulties. If we never felt sadness, we would not feel His comfort. If we never had a trial to go through, we could never call ourselves overcomers. If we never suffered, how would we understand the suffering of others, or what Christ suffered on the cross? And if we were never broken, how would we learn that God can make us whole? If our life was perfect, we might not have the opportunity to know God and recognize how much we need Him and how much He does for us.

We should marvel at how profound it is that God turns evil into good so that all things work for the good of those who love the Lord. And, we should marvel at how much this can comfort us as we go through our trials and tribulations. We have the incredible promise of Revelation 2:10 which tells us: *"Fear none of those things which thou shalt suffer...."* And Revelation 21:4: *"And God shall wipe away all tears from their eyes; and there shall be no more death, neither sorrow, nor crying, neither shall there be any more pain...."*

Bullet Points

Heartache comes from Satan, not from God.

We realize that we need God when we endure difficult circumstances.

God uses our heartache to mold us into His children.

Our suffering is easier to bear when we know why it is occurring.

Faith increases when we see God helping us through our difficulties.

Satan flees when we do not lose our hope or our trust in God.

God always creates a blessing from our difficulties.

<u>Supporting Scripture</u>

Romans 8:28,	Matthew 24:21,
John 14:27,	Genesis 18:32,
Chronicles 19:11,	Psalm 27:14,
Jonah 1:3,	Psalms 31:24,
Matthew 5:3-11,	Acts 20:29.

Chapter Twelve

GOD'S PLAN OF SALVATION

As we read scripture, the beautiful plan which begins and ends with God's desire for mankind is unveiled for us. God, knowing that man would sin, arranged for him to learn of good and evil so he would have the opportunity to freely choose good, to repent of all evil, and to seek the forgiveness of his sin and a life with God. Scripture teaches us that God longs to fill His kingdom with souls who will truly love one another, and love His Son and Him above all things. Matthew 22:37-39 says, *"Jesus said unto him, Thou shalt love the Lord thy God with all thy heart, and with all thy soul, and with all thy mind. This is the first and great commandment. And the second is like unto it, Thou shalt love thy neighbor as thyself."*

God wants these souls to understand the value of love, trust, and loyalty, and to practice these attributes voluntarily. (John 14:23) God began His plan by creating the earth in its limited universe. Then He created Adam and Eve to live happily in the Garden of Eden, walking and talking with Him. But the angel Lucifer, later known as Satan, rebelled against God because he was jealous of Christ, and of the new being, man, who God planned to elevate above the angels. (Isaiah 14:12-15) As a result of his rebellion, Satan was thrown to earth with the angels (Revelation 12:9) who followed Satan and thereby also disobeyed God. These numbered one-third of all the angels.

Satan knew God's plan and understood that when the plan was completed, and God had obtained the number of faithful loving souls He longed for, Satan would be thrown into Hell for what he had done and with him all evil would be forever bound. To prevent God's plan from moving forward and thus forestall his own destruction, Satan destroyed God's relationship of trust and loyalty with Adam and Eve by enticing them to sin through disobedience. Satan knew that sin would automatically separate man from God because of God's perfect righteousness. Thus, God then banished Adam and Eve as he had banished Satan. (Genesis 3:1 and Genesis 3:23) But God, knowing what Satan would do, provided a way for Adam and Eve, and the generations to follow, to escape the captivity of Satan through the forgiveness of sin and return to God.

Christ offered Himself as the perfect sacrifice by which the sins of man could be forgiven. (John 1:29) At every turn, Satan interfered with God's plan, trying to destroy those who tried to follow God, because when God collected the number of souls He desired for His new creation, Satan would be bound forever. Thus Satan is fighting for his life when trying to draw us into sin.

However, because of God's love many of those tested by Satan are strengthened through his attacks, becoming like gold refined in the fires of tribulation. From these faithful, God is building what the Bible calls The Bride of Christ. God also provided for those who died in sin both before and after Christ provided His sacrifice by creating a means of testimony in eternity while grace is still available on earth. Christ entered hell after His death to give testimony of His triumph to those who had died in their sins before He could bring His perfect sacrifice. (Luke 24:46) He told them that now they too could find forgiveness. (1Timothy 2:4)

A specific amount of time has been allotted in God's Plan of Salvation for His chosen ones to be made ready. (Acts 1:6-7) When that time is up, God will send His Son back to earth for the First Resurrection (Revelation 20:5) when He will take to heaven both those from eternity who have obtained forgiveness and those alive who have remained faithful. (11 Peter 3:10) When they are gone, grace will also be gone, and the final destruction of the end times will begin on the earth where, among other things, one-third of all the people on earth will die. When the destruction ends, God will send His Son back to earth with those He had taken at the First Resurrection. They will have celestial (perfect) bodies, and will reign as kings and priests for one thousand years of peace to bring testimony to everyone living or dead who was not taken in the First Resurrection.

Satan will be bound during this time, unable to influence mankind, so all mankind will learn about and accept God. But, after the one thousand years of peace, Satan will be loosed again for a little while so those who have now accepted God can be tested. (Revelation 20:7) Satan will wreak havoc on those not firm in their faith and many will follow Satan. (Revelation 20:2) Then the Day of Judgment will arrive when everyone, except those taken by Christ for The First Resurrection, will be judged. Some, which the Bible calls the "goats", will be cast into hell with Satan forever, while others, called the "lambs", will inhabit God's new kingdom where there will be no sorrow and no tears. The goats, and Satan and his angels, will be cast into the lake of fire and brimstone and tormented day and night forever. (Revelation 20:10 and 15)

Those who are taken for the First Resurrection will continue to reign as kings and priests in the new kingdom. They will never have to be judged because their sins were forgiven, and entirely wiped away by God. Also important for us to know is that God wants a specific number of souls to be a part of the Bride of Christ. This is mentioned in scripture and also mentioned in the Apocrypha. 11 Esdras 2:40-41 says, *"Receive they number O Sion, and embrace those of thine that are clothed in white which have fulfilled the law of the Lord. The number of thy children whom thou longest for, is fulfilled: beseech the Lord that thy people, which have been called from the beginning, may be hallowed."* Our desire as Christians is to work toward the completion of God's work here on earth, labor in faith, love, and charity to make ourselves worthy to be a child of God. We learn God's words, put on the armor of God, seek forgiveness, strive to be an overcomer, and wait patiently for the completion of God's Plan of Salvation and the return of His Son. We carry the hope in our hearts that soon God will find the last soul. Romans 8:25 tells us, *"But if we hope for that we see not, then do we with patience wait for it."*

Bullet Points

A series of events, God's Plan of Salvation, has been placed into the physics of our world to develop a people who will become the Bride of Christ.

Christ will be sent back to earth for the First Resurrection when those souls are developed.

Satan knows he will be cast into the Lake of Fire forever when this series of events ends thus seeks to prevent God from gathering the number of souls He desires.

As God's plan nears completion Satan works havoc to break the faith of God's children.

Evil and goodness will be forever separated after Judgment.

Supporting Scripture

Romans 8:25,	Matthew 22:37-39,
Revelation 20:2, 5,	John 14:23,
Isaiah 14:12-15,	Revelation 12:9,
11 Esdras 2:40-41,	Genesis 3:1,
Revelation 20:1,	Genesis 3:23,
John 1:29,	Luke 24:46,
1 Timothy 2:4,	Acts 1:6-7,
11 Peter 3:10,	Revelation 20:10, 15.

Chapter Thirteen

LIFE AFTER DEATH

Christians are united in the belief that there is life after death. They also agree that there is a hell for unbelievers and sinners who also must await the return of Christ before their fate is sealed. However, Christian doctrines differ about what freedoms immediately or later exist for those who have died. Some believe that after death one enters into a deep sleep, others believe that there is a heaven and a hell in which souls simply wait. Others believe that there is continuing activity and some believe that this activity includes the opportunity for grace after death.

Scripture however, provides us with a great deal of information about life after death. Isaiah 5:14, 15 addresses hell and says, *"Therefore hell hath enlarged herself, and opened her mouth without measure: and their glory, and their multitude, and their pomp, and he that rejoiceth, shall descend into it. And the mean man shall be brought down, and the mighty man shall be humbled, and the eyes of the lofty shall be humbled".*

These verses tell us that those who were pompous, mean, or mighty will enter hell and because there would be so many, hell would have to be enlarged to accommodate them. Isaiah 14:9 also addresses hell saying, *"Hell from beneath is moved for thee to meet thee at thy coming: it stirreth up the dead for thee, even all the chief ones of the earth .. .. "* Isaiah 14:15 warns:*"Yet thou shalt be brought down to hell, to the sides of the pit."* Matthew 10:28 comforts believers with the words, *"And fear not them which kill the body, but are not able to kill the soul: but rather fear him which is able to destroy both soul and body in hell. . . ."* And John 11:25 provides the reassuring words, *"he that believeth in Me, though he were dead, yet he shall live.* These are the areas in which all Christians agree.

When Jesus received word that his friend Lazarus had died, He was with his disciples a far way from Bethany where Lazarus had lived and died. (John 11:14) Jesus journeyed the long distance to Bethany and arrived when Lazarus had already been dead for four days. As Jesus approached Bethany, Martha came out to meet Him, terribly distraught over her brother's death. Jesus went with her to the grave where Lazarus had been buried. There He prayed, thanking His Father in Heaven for hearing Him and for helping the people to believe. Jesus twice called Lazarus by name and Lazarus rose from death back to life again. Through this miracle Jesus demonstrated His power over life and death, not only here on earth, but also after we enter into death.

John 14:19 explains what Christ said about his own death. *"Yet a little while, and the world seeth me no more; but ye see me: because I live, ye shall live also."* But there are many other areas of scripture which tells us that where the soul goes after death is an active place. For example, 1 Peter 4:6 says, *". . . for this cause was the gospel preached also, to them that are dead, that they might be judged according to men in the flesh, but live according to God in the spirit."* These verses coupled with many others indicate that when Christ died, he brought the testimony of his sacrifice and the grace He offered to those in all realms of hell before ascending to heaven. Here are a few of the verses from scripture which further support this statement:

Ephesians 4:8-10, *Wherefore he saith, When he ascended up on high, he led captivity captive, and gave gifts unto men. (Now that he ascended, what is it but that he also descended first into the lower parts of the earth? He that descended is the same also that ascended up far above all heavens, that he might fill all things.)"*

1 Peter 3:18-20, *For Christ also hath once suffered for sins, the just for the unjust, that he might bring us to God, being put to death in the flesh, but quickened by the Spirit: By which also He went and preached unto the spirits in prison; Which sometime were disobedient, when once the longsuffering of God waited in the days of Noah . . ."*

John 8:56, *"Your father Abraham rejoiced to see my day: and he saw it, and was glad."*

John 5:25, *"Verily, verily, I say unto you, The hour is coming, and now is, when the dead shall hear the voice of the Son of God: and they that shall hear shall live."*

Luke 16: 19-31, *"There was a certain rich man, which was clothed in purple and fine linen, and fared sumptuously every day: And there was a certain beggar named Lazarus, which was laid at his gate, full of sores, And desiring to be fed with the crumbs which fell from the rich man's table: moreover the dogs came and licked his sores. And it came to pass, that the beggar died, and was carried by the angels into Abraham's bosom: the rich man also died, and was buried; And in hell he lift up his eyes, being in torments, and seeth Abraham afar off, and Lazarus in his bosom. And he cried and said, Father Abraham, have mercy on me, and send Lazarus, that he may dip the tip of his finger in water, and cool my tongue; for I am tormented in this flame. But Abraham said, Son, remember that thou in thy lifetime receivedst thy good things, and likewise Lazarus evil things: but now he is comforted, and thou art tormented. And beside all this, between us and you there is a great gulf fixed: so that they which would pass from hence to you cannot; neither can they pass to us, that would come from thence. Then he said, I pray thee therefore, father, that thou wouldest send him to my father's house: For I have five brethren; that he may testify unto them, lest they also come into this place of torment. Abraham saith unto him, They have Moses and the prophets; let them hear them. And he said, Nay, father Abraham: but if one went unto them from the dead, they will repent. And he said unto him, If they hear not Moses and the prophets, neither will they be persuaded, though one rose from the dead."*

From these verses we can deduce that when Christ died he descended into hell to bring his testimony of grace to all souls. If everyone in hell, the prison for sinners, were beyond help, He would not have offered them salvation.

In Noah's day, God brought the flood because the earth was filled with so much sin. Christ had not yet appeared, so sin could not be bridged, could not yet be forgiven. Thus, God made the decision to save only the few in Noah's family who were faithful to Him, and destroyed all others. This was to slow the rampant growth of sin which was occurring at that time and to preserve the line from which Christ would come. But when God saw the destruction and the multitudes of sinners who entered Hades, He made a covenant not to destroy mankind again until the end times. Thus sin again grew unfettered on earth until Christ came to pay the price of man's redemption.

Christ came to earth to sacrifice His life for the living. We also know that before Christ made that sacrifice there was no grace available, only the Law of Moses. Thus, unless Christ offered salvation to those who had lived under the Law of Moses none or only a few of these souls from this era could be saved. This would include the entire 5,000 years during which mankind lived before Christ appeared and made His sacrifice.

While many believe that Christ's sacrifice has covered only those who have lived *since* His sacrifice, scripture indicates that His sacrifice was for all who had ever died and would want forgiveness. Scripture also indicates that when Christ died on the cross, He went to the *dead* for three days and then to the Apostles still here on earth *before* ascending to God. His mission was to tell the dead of His sacrifice and offer them salvation. He also spent time to instruct, convince and comfort His Apostles before He ascended to God so they would continue His work of salvation.

However, just as on earth where some accepted and others did not, some in hell listened and others did not…and this still holds true today. Abraham had been faithful to God, but not alive when Christ brought the sacrifice which could free those who had died in sin. Scripture tells us that Abraham rejoiced when he saw Christ…. after Christ had died.

Further, the parable of the rich man and the beggar tells us that Abraham comforted the beggar…. after the beggar had died at the gates of the rich man's house. Scripture depicts the beggar as resting in Abraham's bosom. The rich man, who died at the same time, went to Hades where he was tormented. He was "across a gulf" from Abraham and the beggar Lazarus; in a different place. This passage in the Gospel of Luke is one of the Bible's most descriptive insights into death and clearly describes two places occupied by the dead, with a chasm between them which could not be bridged. This parable, spoken to the Pharisees, illustrates the chasm in eternity between those who in life pursued God and those who pursued material gain. Under the laws of Moses, this rich man would have to be condemned for all eternity.

However, when Christ brought the sacrifice which bridged the gulf between the Law of Moses, and the Law of Love, those who had been condemned by the law, but then accepted Christ….. those who believed and repented…. could obtain grace. God clearly tells us in scripture that He wants all men to be saved and has provided the way for them to do this despite their sins.

Thus Christ became the mediator for mankind when He gave His life and paid the price for the sin of mankind and even those who die in sin will have the opportunity to be forgiven and be taken into heaven.... *if they truly repent and follow.*

The keywords in John 5:25 are: "and now is" indicating that the time is here that the *dead* can hear the words of Christ. They will, in other words, receive testimony. Further, the words "shall hear", which mean, "are willing to listen" appear to indicate that not all of them will listen, believe, and repent to be saved. *("Verily, verily, I say unto you, The hour is coming, and now is, when the dead shall hear the voice of the Son of God; and they that hear shall live.")*

Another verse which supports the fact that Christ brought testimony to the dead is in the words of Christ's Apostles found in 1Peter 3:19. *"By which also he went and preached unto the spirits in prison."* The word prison as used here refers to those who died under the captivity of Satan because of their sin and entered hell.

Our prayers of intercession can help those who die in their sins to repent and seek forgiveness through Christ. Grace, through Christ, is the major difference between the Old Testament and the New Testament. To be right with God during the time of the Old Testament, man was required to live by the Law of Moses and, if he didn't, he was automatically condemned.

But in the New Testament, Christ came to earth heralding in an era of love, forgiveness, and compassion which bridged *both* eras. Sins could be forgiven through Christ if the heart was repentant and man sought God. God made sure that all men would have the same opportunity whether alive or dead to hear, at some time, what Christ had done for them and learn of the gift of redemption which was being offered to them.

Understanding these two eras, one of unrelenting laws, the other of love, make us thankful that we live in the era of love. However, God has provided for all men in both eras to be saved if they will accept what God offers them. 1Timothy 2:4-6 tells us: *"Who will have all men to be saved, and to come unto the knowledge of the truth. For there is one God, and one Mediator between God and men, the Man Christ Jesus; Who gave Himself a ransom for all, to be testified in due time."* This tells us that all men (*all men to be saved*) will receive testimony of the ransom (*ransom for all*) which Christ provided for them at some point in time (*testified in due time*). However, many will not accept or leave their evil ways and will not be found worthy.

1 Corinthians 15:17, 18 tells us, *"And if Christ be not raised, your faith is vain; ye are yet in your sins. Then they also which are fallen asleep in Christ are perished."*

These beautiful verses tell us that every person living or dead will eventually receive testimony. Sadly however, not every man will accept the offer of salvation. Thus we also read in scripture about those who will be lost and thrown into the Lake of Fire with Satan for all eternity.

Bullet Points

Many who died in sin before Christ came can still have their sins forgiven.

Christ entered into hell for three days before He ascended to heaven.

The gospel was brought to those in hell by Christ before He ascended.

God wants all men to be saved.

Everyone will learn of God and have the opportunity for grace before the second death.

Not all men will accept God's offer and will have to enter hell with Satan for all eternity.

Supporting Scripture

Isaiah 5:14-15,

Isaiah 14:9,

John 11:14,

John 11:25,

John 14:19,

1 Peter 3:18-20,

John 5:25.

John 5:25,

Matthew 10:28,

Isaiah 14:15,

1 Peter 4:6,

Ephesians 4:8-10,

John 8:56,

Chapter Fourteen

SATAN'S NEEDS AND HELPERS

Scripture clearly tells us that all men are sinners and that all men are susceptible to temptation. Therefore it is important for Christians to fully understand that Satan and his helpers are alive and well and running rampant in their quest to bring harm to all Christians.

Sadly, many of us never think in terms of an evil entity which is capable of invading man, nor of us being so weak as to succumb to such beings. We may not realize when we are battling such an entity and we do not always recognize when another person is battling a satanic spirit. We respond to what people say and do with little understanding that we should respond instead to what these spiritual entitles may cause them to do.

Our misunderstanding allows us to become the pawns or playthings of these spirits as we struggle against situations which we don't understand as evil at work. Scripture warns us in Hosea 4:6: *"My people are destroyed for lack of knowledge; because thou hast rejected knowledge, I will also reject thee, that thou shall be no priest to me: seeing thou hast forgotten the law of thy God, I will also forget thy children."*

This verse and many others throughout scripture clearly explain that without an understanding of what scripture tells us, we cannot know how to do battle with evil. However, if we do learn God's words, we find that God tells us what evil is, how to fight against it, and to love all souls even those being influenced by evil. God knows and teaches through scripture that mankind can be owned and directed by satanic influence and once free of that influence would gladly change their lives. For this reason, we grieve God when we waste our time and energy fighting the wrong battles against a soul and therefore losing the real battle against the entity which directs them.

First and foremost Christians must understand why Satan does what he does and what power he employs to work his evil. In John 8:44 we are told, *"…… for he is a liar and the father of it."* And in John 8:44, *"……..He was a murderer from the beginning, and abode not in the truth, because there is no truth in him……"*

This clearly indicates that we must be on guard against the lies evil tells us which distract us from the real issue we must face. Satan loves the anonymity of working in secret to keep Christians from God. He wants us to hate and judge and condemn… not Satan but the soul. He is so subtle that many cannot believe that he exists. Genesis 3:1 tells us, *"….. the serpent was more subtil than any beast……"*

The three prior verses alone teach that Satan is a liar, a murderer, and is subtle in his attacks. Matthew 4:1 adds that Satan also tempts us. He is actually called "the tempter". *"Then was Jesus led...... to be tempted of the devil."* And in Matthew 4: 3 *"and when the tempter came to Him, he said....."*

Additionally, Satan can move men to do his bidding (1 Chronicles 21:1), can walk back and forth on the earth (Job 1:7), cause illness (Job 2:7), can take God's word from men's hearts (Mark 4:15), can enter man (Luke 22:3 and John 13:27), can blind the minds of them which believe not (2 Corinthians 4:4), can transform himself (2 Corinthians 11:14), can send messengers to hurt man (2 Corinthians 12:7), can hinder people (1 Thessalonians 2:18), and can produce signs and has powers (2 Thessalonians 2:9).

It is especially important for us to acknowledge that Satan is capable of producing signs and has supernatural powers, *"Even him, whose coming is after the working of Satan with all power and signs and lying wonders.* Signs and wonders support false doctrines and a belief in certain practices, symbols, or people. To safeguard us from being misled in this manner, God warns us not to embrace the occult and to test all doctrines to be sure that they are based on the true gospel of Christ.

When Adam and Eve sinned by disobeying God, they opened the door to the curse which required mankind to learn about evil. But God arranged that by learning of evil, mankind could also learn to appreciate what is good. The curse which resulted from the disobedience of Adam and Eve separated man from God and is called inherited sin for which God provided the sacrament of Baptism. God also provided the forgiveness of sin and the Holy Spirit to help mankind overcome the influence of Satan. Thus all men are sinners and only through the sacrifice of Christ can those sins be forgiven and thus again allow man fellowship with God.

Scripture also speaks of the sins of our forefathers which is similar to inherited sin because it too is passed from generation to generation. Some claim that generational sin causes a change in our DNA which is passed to future generations and can only be corrected through forgiveness and future abstinence. This may be why some families never escape certain patterns such as the alcoholism which may occur in a grandfather, a father and a son.

Only when we ask and allow God to cleanse us and then we take on the fight to overcome those patterns or tendencies can we break free and set our children free. This is why God speaks over and over again in scripture about being an overcomer, fighting the good fight, watching for our enemy and praying for and loving one another. Keeping God first and foremost in our lives is paramount to freeing ourselves from satanic ownership and passing that ownership to our children through *our* sins.

For example, we've always been blessed as a country because we've kept God in everything, from school prayer, to the décor of our government buildings, to our currency. Now, we are losing that blessing because a few are banning this form of thankfulness to, and acknowledgement of, God. What had been passed down as a *blessing* from our ancestors is turning into a *curse* to future generations because we are taking God out of the equation. We are witnessing the *generational sins of the forefathers* quite clearly as we witness the loss of faith, abuse, alcoholism, corrupt government and a myriad of other problems going from grandfather to father to child and some of these actions now being accepted as a "disease". But the truth is that Satan is the father of abuse, alcoholism, drug addiction, homosexuality, hatred, and a host of actions and attitudes which rob us of our faith, our peace and our relationship with God. Without God's protection and what we must learn which will help us fight evil, we could lose our future with God.

Matthew 23:33 warns, *"Ye serpents, ye generation of vipers, how can ye escape the damnation of hell?"* Ezekiel 31:16 warns, *"I made the nations to shake at the sound of his fall, when I cast him down to hell with them that descend into the pit . . ."* This verse tells us that not only will Satan be cast into hell but others with him as well. These include the evil spirits who were thrown from heaven with Satan because they too rebelled against God. Also included will be the "goats" who scripture describes as those who would not accept what God both offered and required.

It is almost impossible to know what God asks of us, or develop the kind of heart God loves if we do not know the word of God and thus understand what we must beware of, and how we can fight the forces which work to keep us from God. And if we have an enemy who has the power to keep us from God and the power to cause us to behave in an ungodly manner, why would we not want to learn how to do battle with this enemy? Can we fight an enemy we don't know exists?

Our enemy is a strong, powerful, supernatural entity who was once sitting next to God. He must destroy us to stay free and has minions of helpers to do so. He knows scripture and God's plan of salvation and therefore fully understands that when God finds the number of souls He longs for, he will no longer have a reason to tempt mankind, and that he will be bound for one thousand years.

When Satan left heaven, he took one third of all the angels God originally created with him to work against us. They have the power to enter and dwell in us and prevent us from seeking God. We must realize that this is something to be feared, and in that fear we must learn of this enemy and how to protect ourselves and our loved ones.

Satan and his helpers want to destroy the faith of the children of God, thus God warns us in Luke 11:26, *"Then goeth he, and taketh to him seven other spirits more wicked than himself; and they enter in, and dwell there: and the last state of that man is worse than the first."*

This is a clear warning that the spirits of evil can enter our hearts and dwell there causing incredible havoc in our lives and separation from God. But if we are faithful, if we learn God's words and direction, we find that no matter what we face, God provides for us. God comforts us with the words from Luke 11:11-13 which tell us, *"If a son shall ask bread of any of you that is a father, will he give a stone.......how much more shall your Heavenly Father give the Holy Spirit to them that ask him?*

We need to know God, know what He tells us, what evil we face, and what God offers us…..and ask Him to help us. If ignorance of the law is not reason enough to be excused from error in our courts and judicial system, why would it be a reason to be excused for our sins and excused for our refusal to learn God's words and strive to please Him?

Bullet Points

We fight the wrong battles when we are unaware of God's words.

All men are sinners.

Sin allows Satan and his many helpers access to our soul.

We succumb to sin through our lack of knowledge about Satan, and God's plan of salvation.

Satan and his helpers have been endowed with many powers to entice and fool us.

The sins of our forefathers give Satan even further access to our souls.

God has provided help through Christ's sacrifice and by teaching us through scripture.

Supporting Scripture

John 8:44,   Genesis 3:1,

Matthew 4:1,

2 Thessalonians 2:9,

Luke 22:3,

2 Corinthians 4:4,

Mark 23:33,

1 Chronicles 21:1,

Mark 4:15,

John 13:27,

1 Thessalonians 2:18,

2 Corinthians 12:7.

Chapter Fifteen

THE OVERCOMER

Another of the many precious gifts God has provided for Christians is the promise that if they sincerely strive to learn and do what He asks, He will reward them immensely. In Matthew 25:21 God says, *".....Well done, thou good and faithful servant: thou hast been faithful over a few things, I will make thee ruler over many things: enter thou into the joy of thy lord."*

Scripture tells us that God refers to us as His children, and also tells us that He wants us to become the bride of Christ. These descriptions present an expectation of an expanding maturity as we grow from child to bride. Scripture further supports this expectation of development in 1 Corinthians 13:11 where we are told, *"When I was a child, I spake as a child, I understood as a child, I thought as a child, but when I became a man, I put away childish things."*

As we study scripture, we find the word "overcomer" often used in reference to God's children. Revelation 2:11 tells us *"....He that overcometh shall not be hurt in the second death."* And Revelation 2:26 promises, *"And he that overcometh and keepeth my works unto the end, to him will I give power over the nations."* Revelation 3:5 tells us, *"He that overcometh, the same shall be clothed in white raiment; and I will not blot out his name out of the book of life, but I will confess his name before my Father, and before his angels."* Revelation 21:7 says, *"He that overcometh shall inherit all things; and I will be his God, and he shall be my son."*

In Revelation 7:13 we read, *"......What are these which are arrayed in white robes? And whence came they?"* Revelation 7:14 answers saying, *"....These are they which came out of great tribulation, and have washed their robes, and made them white in the blood of the Lamb."*

A white robe is the symbol of an unblemished soul, one which has had its sins forgiven and strives to do as God asks. The blood of the Lamb is the sacrifice which Christ made so those sins could be forgiven. The word "washing" is indicative of two processes which go hand in hand. The first requires the act of acknowledging one's sins, feeling remorse for having committed them, striving to overcome the tendency to commit them again, and succeeding in much of that striving. The second part of the process is accepting and partaking of the sacrament of Holy Communion provided by the sacrifice of Christ. This is the actual washing or cleansing of our sins which can take place worthily only through the actions mentioned in part one of this process.

Perfection cannot be attained while we are in the flesh and living in Satan's territory. But God rewards us for our contrition and our diligent striving to apply His words to our lives, and for our thankfulness for the forgiveness of sin. In time, these help develop us into the overcomer who has grown in faith and made changes whereby our former ways and former temptations have been laid aside and we work toward behavior which is godly.

God tells us in Romans 12:2, *"Be not conformed to this world; but be ye transformed by the renewing of your mind, that ye may prove what is that good and acceptable and perfect will of God."* But we are also told that we must be careful not to become entangled in evil. Galatians 5:1 warns, *"Be ye not entangled again with the yoke of bondage."* This indicates that it is possible for us to become entangled again even after we break away from sin and even after God himself frees us.

Thus, to be an overcomer, we need to protect ourselves from the traps which might once again engage us, and even in this God provides us with how we can reach our goal. The armor of God is mentioned often throughout scripture and tells us that God, aware of our fragility, offers us protection. Ephesians 6:11 clearly says, *"Put on the whole armour of God, that ye may be able to stand against the wiles of the devil."*

This tells us that without the armour God provides we may not be able to stand against evil. Further, Romans 13:12 teaches, *"The night is far spent, the day is at hand; let us therefore cast off the works of darkness and let us put on the armour of light."* Here we are told that it is imperative to denounce all former errors, begin making changes in our life, and obtain this armour quickly. We are warned that there is not much time left before Christ returns and that when He does return, it will be too late.

The armour itself is righteousness. However, righteousness cannot be obtained without faith. Faith comes from our relationship with God. And that relationship is developed by learning of God, knowing what He asks of us, striving to do what He asks, developing a close relationship with Him and having our sins forgiven. The word "darkness" is indicative of all things evil and the word "light" represents Christ and all He taught and all He sacrificed for us. To obtain the armour or protection of God, we must denounce all things which are the works of darkness and embrace all things which Christ brought us.

When we have done our best toward this goal, God will empower us to withstand evil even when it is at its peak of strength. 1 Corinthians 6:7 says, *"By the word of truth, by the power of God, by the armour of righteousness on the right hand and on the left."* And if we have done our due diligence and we have obtained the armour God offers, He promises that we will withstand the evil at the end of days. Ephesians 6:13 tells us, *"Wherefore take unto you the whole armour of God, that ye may be able to withstand in the evil day, and having done all, to stand."*

Bullet Points

Scripture describes those that Christ will take at the First Resurrection as the overcomers.

An overcomer is someone who has overcome temptation.

Temptation and sin are overcome by wearing the armor God provides.

The armour of protection is made up of a number of different actions.

Scripture describes what the armour of God is and how to attain it.

To become an overcomer or obtain the armour God offers we must know scripture.

Supporting Scripture

Matthew 25:21,	Revelation 2:26,
1 Corinthians 13:11,	Ephesians 6:11,
Revelation 3:5,	Romans 13:12,
1 Corinthians 6:7,	Revelation 2:11,
Galatians 5:11,	Revelation 7:13,
Ephesians 6:13,	Revelation 21:7,
Romans 12:2,	Revelation 17:14.

Chapter Sixteen

LITTLE SINS AND LARGE SINS

Most of us view some sins as inconsequential and other sins as heinous. We feel that overcoming little sins is an easy task if we put our mind to it, while the larger sins may be more difficult to overcome. But few of us view sin, especially the "little" sins as a captivity with which a spirit of this world can imprison us, keep us from God, and further impel us to repeat our sins. Few of us understand that the white garment we must wear to the wedding feast following the First Resurrection represents the total absence of sin and does not excuse even the smallest stain of the smallest sin.

However, scripture tells us in Romans 5:12 *"Wherefore.....for that all have sinned."* And 1 Timothy 2:2-4 tells us *"....that we may lead a quiet and peaceable life in all godliness and honesty. For this is good and acceptable in the sight of God our Savior; Who will have all men to be saved, and to come to the knowledge of the truth."* Through these verses we understand that not one among us is without sin and that each of us must individually find our way to Christ to obtain the forgiveness of our sin. We also learn that it is through the truth of God's words that we can find what we are seeking, and in full and true remorse for our sins that we can find forgiveness.

Ephesians 4:14-15, explains, *"That we henceforth be no more children, tossed to and fro, and carried about with every wind of doctrine, by the sleight of men, and cunning craftiness, where they lie in wait to deceive. But speaking the truth in love, may grow up into him in all things, which is the head, even Christ."*

These words show us that God is aware of our status as children who make mistakes, but these words also show us that God expects us to mature and put aside those inclinations and do so by learning what He asks of us, and placing His words into our hearts and actions. 1 John 3:8 clearly says, *"He that committeth sin is of the devil; for the devil commiteth sin from the beginning. For this purpose the Son of God was manifested, that he might destroy the works of the devil."*

11 Corinthians 5:17, explains, *"Therefore if any man be in Christ, he is a new creature; old things are passed away; behold, all things are become new."* 11 Corinthians 5: 21 instructs, *"For he hath made him to be sin for us, who knew no sin; that we might be made the righteousness of God in him."*

Romans 5:20-21, tells us, *".....where sin abounded, grace did much more abound; That as sin hath reigned unto death, even so might grace reign through righteousness unto eternal life by Jesus Christ our Lord."*

Without the sacrifice of Christ all men would be bound forever with Satan in the second death of eternal torment and none would have eternal life with God. Through Christ however, grace has been offered to those who will follow Christ through both their belief and the works which that belief inspires. Throughout scripture the requirement to learn of God's words is tantamount. Without knowing these words we cannot know God and without that knowledge we cannot please God. It is not just a matter of faith, but a "doing and working" which our faith requires and which creates in our hearts the strength and desire to grow into the Bride of Christ.

John 14:21 explains, *"He that hath my commandments, and keepeth them, he it is that loveth me....and I will love him, and manifest myself to him....."* John 14:23-24 tells us, *"....if a man love me, he will keep my words, and we will come unto him, and make our abode with him. He that loveth me not keepeth not my sayings; and the word which ye hear is not mine....."* John 14:26 says, *"But the Comforter, which is the Holy Ghost, whom the Father will send in my name, he shall teach you in all things, and bring all things to your remembrance, whatsoever I have said unto you."*

James 2:17 emphatically states that *"Even so **faith, if it hath not works, is dead**, being alone."* James 2:26 tells us, *"For as the body without the spirit is dead, so **faith without works is dead** also."* It follows that if we need works to accompany our faith we cannot *know* what works we need to do without knowing God's instructions about *how* we should work. Works of faith include how we should treat one another, how we should instruct, exhort, rebuke ourselves, our family, and our neighbors and how we can utilize the sacraments God provides. We also learn that some of these works include prayer, tithing, keeping the Sabbath holy, listening to and learning the word of God and fully understanding and utilizing the sacraments. We must understand evil, why we are stalked, how to fend off temptation, and become teachers of all these things.

All sin is unacceptable to God. If we acknowledge this and seek forgiveness for every sin, we please God. But when we study His word and become enlightened by the incredible scope of what true love shows us, we become even more aware of what sin is and how we can make changes in our lives. What was once a sin of no consequence soon becomes a sin of great consequence because we have been enlightened by the love we learn through knowing God. We are born with the ability to love but only selfishly, whereby we seek only personal reward. But as we bask under the perfect love of Our Heavenly Father and His Son, we begin to see love in an unselfish light and learn how to serve others and appreciate their service. When we experience the perfect love which Christ and our Heavenly Father so freely give us, we cannot help but want to emulate that love by doing what is pleasing to them. A miracle of transformation occurs as we shed the selfish love of our Adam-like nature for the perfect love of the Christ-like nature.

Bullet Points

Many classify sin as small sins of no consequence and larger sins requiring forgiveness.

We cannot know the full scope of our sins without knowing God's words.

The forgiveness of sin requires faith.

Faith is dead if no works accompany our faith.

To know what works of faith will please God we must know what He asks of us.

God saw us initially as children, but expects us to grow into a Bride for His Son.

Perfect love provides the desire to please those we love.

<u>Supporting Scripture</u>

Romans 5:12, 1 Timothy 2:2-4,

Ephesians 4:14-15, 1 John 3:8,

11 Corinthians 5:17, 11 Corinthians 5:21,

Romans 5:20-21, John 14:21,

John 14:23-24, John 14:26.

Chapter Seventeen

THE RIGHT TO BE ANGRY

We live in a busy world filled with tension, anxiety, jealousy, and perceived wrongs. These breed a strong anger which many release on the nearest, least dangerous object. Often someone's anger is surprising because we saw no need for it and no manner in which it served to solve a problem.

Most of us feel anger from time to time and many of us feel guilty about the ease and immediacy with which our anger surfaces. Sometimes it is the little things which add up and cause our anger, but more often it is something sudden which surprises us and is the immediate reaction to real or perceived pain, loss, rejection, fear or tension. Today's world is filled with anger because so many have lost the peace which knowing and trusting God can create in our hearts. Road rage is one such example.

However, we should feel righteous anger in certain situations, and even express that anger in some cases. But it is the control, the letting go, and the action of that anger which Christians need concern themselves. Anger is natural, but the hate or harm which stems from anger is satanic. Satan uses many avenues to produce anger, using it to reach his goal of creating disharmony.

As we grow, we mature and we presumably learn self control. While self control does not mean that we cannot feel anger, it does mean that we must express that anger in a limited fashion. As we learn what God tells us about expressing anger, we learn how to counteract its negative influence with something positive. God can open our understanding of temporal things, but we will never find a permanent solution to our problems until we understand and apply the spiritual aspect to our use of and reaction to our anger.

In today's world, anxiety is a part of everyone's life, but it's the control of that anxiety which can limit our anger and which comes from trusting God with our life thus not giving in to our fears. Understanding our psyche is helpful as well. The study of psychology teaches that anxiety attacks are from continuous tension which occasionally explodes into intense panic and can cause irreparable harm, thus its progression needs to be limited.

Anxiety or panic attacks can last a few minutes or a few hours. Sweating, apprehension, a pounding heart, or a feeling that you have lost control, can't breathe, are having a heart attack, or are fearful of dying are all symptoms. These can be very frightening. A conversion reaction can also occur where anxiety is converted into more severe physical symptoms resembling disease or disability. This is another symptom of anxiety which can encourage the quick response of anger. We "learn" to react to anxiety and evil, and can unlearn that reaction if the old causal conditions are removed. God can help us "unlearn" reactions by removing our fear and increasing our trust through the safety of our relationship with Him. Sadly we often carry anger which we have suppressed, and transfer it to the only acceptable emotion we are "allowed" to have, which is depression.

Studies indicate that the act of reconciliation often dissipates anger and depression, but the question which plagues the Christian is "how does one reconcile if the same harmful acts are committed over and over again?" Matthew 5:25 says, *"Leave there thy gift before the altar, and go thy way; first be reconciled to thy brother, and then come and offer thy gift"* but how is this done when someone does not have remorse and will behave in the same manner again and again? Can one of two parties reconcile?

If someone does ask for forgiveness it is much easier for us to forgive. If we love the soul yet are "allowed" to openly hate the actions, we can be honest about our feelings and work toward resolving the negatives our feelings create. But when we bury what has occurred, allow it to fester for a long period of time, there is a lingering infection. This occurs when there is a lack of remorse on the part of those who brought us harm. Thus, there was and is no closure in the *natural* sense.

While we understand that Satan is the real cause of all hurtful behavior, we face a dilemma because if we *excuse* someone's actions based on our belief that Satan directed that person, we can easily feel that we have compromised our principles. Additionally, excusing inappropriate behavior causes us to transfer the anger or the fear we experience from that behavior to someone else, possibly even to ourselves. For example, those who are afraid to confront an abuser will often blame the abused because it is safer to transfer anger to someone who would not respond by causing them harm. Thus a father's abuse is often blamed on the mother, which is a classic case of transference and occurs quite often in families. The directive here is to acknowledge the problem, assess it accurately for what it is, openly place the anger where it belongs, condemn the sin, and *don't stay where the sin is occurring*....yet be willing to forgive the soul for sinning. That way there's no baggage to carry.

God often gets angry when we sin. He forgives us when we repent, but is angry again when He sees us continue in those sins, especially when we know better. Yet He always forgives us when He sees that we are repentant and that we want to overcome these tendencies. He warns us to run from sin and this means from the sin of other's as well as our own. We can lay aside anger if we understand anger, and understand that it is often misdirected. If we don't understand this, nor recognize our personal shortcomings, we can't acknowledge them.

If we don't seek the right relationship with God where He can direct us to the truth, teach us about evil and rebuking the spirits which seek to harm us, we never really change. Nor can we heal from the harm others have done to us if we don't acknowledge their actions as sin inspired by evil and, if it occurs repeatedly, to leave. Once we leave, we can work to let our anger go. If that person seeks us again, we can rebuke their sin, admonish them and forgive, but not remain for further abuse. If we don't take these steps, then the problem will always be lurking in our lives and also in our subconscious waiting to resurface again, waiting to cause us anger and anxiety, and pushing us toward living in an ungodly atmosphere.

The Bible tells us *how* we are to handle the sin of others. Christ always acknowledged sin when he saw it and He was angered by it. Often we sweep it under the table and enable it to flourish by not rebuking it. But Christ utilized God's protection and the angel service to keep His anger in a Godly perspective. He never used his anger to bring harm to anyone. He prayed, He testified, He rebuked, and then He forgave.

Evil spirits can cause a person to be cruel and Christ recognized those spirits in those with whom He interacted. When Christ called a spirit by name, acknowledging it and rebuking it, the spirit could no longer hide, thus when Christ demanded the spirit leave, it did. The Bible describes this in Mark 9:25 where it says, *When Jesus saw that the people came running together, he rebuked the foul spirit, saying unto him, Thou dumb and deaf spirit, I charge thee, come out of him, and enter no more into him.* Perhaps we cannot make a spirit leave someone, but we can call it out so it knows we see it, and we can rebuke it. Further, we can pray that the hold the spirit has will be weakened.

Scripture and psychology books both reinforce similar conclusions for dealing with the pain others bring to us. Words like projection, rationalization, transference, displacement, suppression, and denial and what they describe are similar to much of what is described in scripture in the attitude of the Pharisees, the accusations of those who persecuted Christ, the actions of Judas.

For example, projection occurs when someone transfers one's own shortcoming onto someone else. Many abusers and alcoholics blame everyone but themselves for what they do. They choose a scapegoat for their displaced aggression and project their own shortcomings on that target, denying they are taking their aggression out on an innocent person. If they were not in denial, the abuser would have to see himself as a coward. He rationalizes his behavior, offering excuses, blaming others, and feeling justified in his cruel acts. He suppresses and consciously puts his actions out of his mind. He is too cowardly to deal with his problems.

The word "anger" in the concordance shows us many verses throughout the Bible which indicates God's anger. In Exodus 32:22 Aaron said, *"....Let not the anger of my Lord wax hot . . ."* In Numbers 11:10 scriptures tells us, *".....and the anger of the Lord was kindled greatly . . ."* And in Deuteronomy 4: 25 we are told, *"....and shall do evil in the sight of the Lord thy God, to provoke him to anger;...."*

Further, it is interesting to note that scripture also tells us that God is sometimes comforted by His anger. Ezekiel 5: 13 says: *"Thus shall mine anger be accomplished, and I will cause my fury to rest upon them, and I will be comforted . . ."* However, God has the right to judge, punish, and be angry at both the soul and the deed because He is without sin.

We, on the other hand, have sinned and have no right to judge others. We cannot be angry with the soul, but *can* and should be angry at the deed. The expression of anger toward the deed is a rebuke against evil. This is important to understand because if the Bible tells us we *can* express anger at the sin and acknowledge the sin, and this admonition agrees with the psychology books which say that when we suppress anger it can be detrimental to our personal well being, we can rest in the fact that expressing anger even if only at the deed itself is important for avoiding what could harm us both spiritually and physically.

God brought the wrath of His anger to those with whom he was angry, but *we* can't do this because it is not our right. Even God holds back His full anger. Jeremiah 30:24 tells us that God is holding back His anger now: *"The fierce anger of the Lord shall not return, until he have done it, and until he have performed the intents of his heart: in the latter days ye shall consider it."*

Through this verse we know that not only is God holding back, planning the right time to vent his anger for the evil which has been done, but also that this "right time" will be the latter days, the end times which we have now entered. Genesis 6:6 says *"....and it grieved him at his heart"* and Genesis 8:21 says, *"...behold I will destroy them with the earth"* and in Genesis 9:15, *"...And the waters shall no more become a flood to destroy all flesh"*. The story of the flood teaches us that God was so angered by the sinfulness he found on earth that He sent the flood to destroy the perpetration of sin by destroying the sinners. But after they were destroyed, God felt grieved and didn't want to express His anger in destruction again until the very end days. God sent the rainbow to mark the covenant He then made with man not to destroy unrepentant sinners again until the bride of Christ was removed from the earth.

The New Testament also addresses anger. The words of Christ in Mark 3:5 tell us, *"And when he had looked round about on them with anger, being grieved for the hardness of their hearts, he saith . . ."* Christ was perfect. He did not sin. He went to the cross completely unblemished, free from sin. Therefore when the Bible shows us that Christ was angry, it also shows us that *justified* anger, correctly *checked* and understood, is acceptable.

The Bible also addresses the grief which Christ felt as he was subjected to disloyalty, disbelief, and outright hatred. Isaiah 53:3 tells us, *"He is despised and rejected of men; a man of sorrows, and acquainted with grief:..."* And Proverbs 29:27 tells us, *"An unjust man is an abomination to the just: and he that is upright in the way is abomination to the wicked".* As believers in Christ, we are also hated by many. We are also forewarned that we have enemies in this world and that those who are wicked will seek to harm us.

The wicked are ruled and inspired by Satan and we must walk in God's words so we can have His protection and direction and we must not respond with hatred, but trust that God will avenge the harm others bring us. Romans 12:19 tells us, *"Dearly beloved, avenge not yourselves, but rather give place unto wrath; for it is written, Vengeance is mine; I will repay, saith the Lord.".*

Bullet Points

Today's world is filled with satanic provoked anxiety, tension and perceived wrongs.

These emotions breed anger, and uncontrolled anger causes sin.

Biblically and psychologically, those who intentionally bring harm to others are impaired.

Self control and mental health come from knowing and implementing God's words.

Scripture teaches us how to quell anxiety and anger and replace them with good will.

Righteous anger toward a deed but not the soul is acceptable to God.

Supporting Scripture

Matthew 5:25,	Mark 9:25,
Exodus 32:22,	Numbers 11:10,
Deuteronomy 4:25,	Jeremiah 30:24,
Genesis 6:6,	Mark 3:5,
Genesis 8:21,	Isaiah 53:3,
Proverbs 29:27,	Genesis 9:15,
Romans 12:19.	

Chapter Eighteen

IS FORGETTING NECESSARY TO FORGIVING?

Much of what some term "Christian Guilt" stems from the acknowledgement that we do not and cannot always live up to the very principles we espouse. We simply cannot be perfect in the practice of all the aspirations set before us as Christians no matter how hard we try. And, we often commiserate over our failures even when we repent our mistakes and strive to do better in the future. Yet it is our failures which keep us humble, remind us of how much we need God, and how blessed we are to have been brought into our Christian faith. Our failures also impel us to appreciate the unconditional love so evident in the sacrifice God made for us when He provided us with the forgiveness of sin.

God tells us that when we have sinned and we have repented with remorse and the hope that we will not repeat that same sin, and have received Holy

Communion worthily, He remembers that sin no more. In other words, our sin is forgotten. Hebrews 8:12 tells us, *"For I will be merciful to their unrighteousness, and their sins and their iniquities will I remember no more."* Hebrews 10:14, 17 also tell us, *"For by one offering he hath perfected for ever them that are sanctified. And their sins and iniquities will I remember no more."*

When our children act in ways which are not pleasing to us, we may reprimand them but when they ask for forgiveness and strive to make corrections, we forgive them and easily forget the indiscretion. But sometimes, situations arise which require us to remember what occurred in order to protect ourselves and others from future harm.

In general, forgetting past indiscretions helps us move on and helps us find the peace we need in our lives. But, as in all good things, sometimes we expand one good point into 'rules' which bring more harm than good. We misunderstand the proper meaning and context of the original thought. We increase our anxieties by an unnecessary ideology which we find difficult to fulfill.

God gave us our memories for a reason. When we remember, for instance, how badly it hurt when we touched a hot stove, we would be careful not to touch a hot stove again. We use our memories to keep us from those things which may bring us harm, and to draw to us those things which bring us joy. Our memories also enhance our faith and help us make the tough choices when we must act out of our faith. Faith is actually the *memory* of (trust in) what God has done for us.

Hebrews 11: 7, 8 reminds us, *"By faith Noah, being warned of God of things not seen as yet, moved with fear, prepared an ark to the saving of his house; by the which he condemned the world, and became heir of the righteousness which is by faith. By faith Abraham, when he was called to go out into a place which he should after receive for an inheritance, obeyed and went out, not knowing whither he went."* This tells us that faith brings us the strength to act as God asks rather than as our inclinations might momentarily suggest.

When someone acts not as God has asked and harms one of His children, He remembers those acts and, if they do not repent, tells us that *He* will take vengeance. In fact, the only time God forgets is when those He loves and who love Him make mistakes, repent, and ask for forgiveness. Then he gladly forgets their sins and remembers them no longer. But He also remembers the remorse He felt after he'd sent the flood and is thus slow to act and longsuffering in the hope that those who sin will eventually have regrets.

However, for the child of God, misplaced Christian guilt demands that when we forgive someone we are to also forget what they did to harm us *despite the fact that there is no scripture to support this statement* and there is danger in practicing this misconception. God wants us to have peace and joy in our lives. He also wants us to be armed at all times to fight the wickedness we face from Satan. To have peace, we cannot carry guilt, especially when that guilt is misplaced and a result of remembering the harm we received at someone's hands. Remembering danger is a protective measure and a healthy practice as long as we have forgiven the soul for committing that deed. The keywords here are, 'if we have forgiven them.' God wants us to forgive, but He has not asked us to forget.

When God tells us to arm ourselves so we can fight the spiritual wickedness which seeks to devour us, the armour He speaks of is His words, His instruction, and His protection. When our heart is right with God and we continue to seek to learn and do what He asks of us, His direction and protection is ours. He protects us from dangers, but warns us that we have a responsibility to be prudent, to be aware of evil, and to 'watch' for evil.... and flee it. We cannot watch for what is forgotten.

1 Peter 4:7 tells us, *"But the end of all things is at hand; be ye therefore sober, and watch unto prayer."* 1 Peter 5:8 says, *"Be sober, be vigilant, because your adversary the devil, as a roaring lion, walketh about, seeking who he may devour."* False prophets will come and we must watch for their errors so we do not fall prey to their teachings. Evil circles us and tempts us and we must remember their end, so we are not tempted. Even family members may denounce God and as we are told in Matthew 10:21, *"....children shall rise up against their parents and cause them to be put to death."*

Thus we must remember just as we must forgive. We must be watchful and careful just as we are forgiving and loving. We must not let our guard down as these end times are fulfilled, for God clearly warns in Mark 13:20, *"And except that the Lord hath shortened, those days, no flesh should be saved; but for the elect's sake, whom he hath chosen, he hath shortened them."*

Bullet Points

We can never attain spiritual perfection, but we must continually strive for it.

Occasional failure keeps us humble.

Failure brings an appreciation for the sacrifice of Christ and the forgiveness of sin.

It is easier to overcome future temptation when we remember the shame of our past sins.

It is not necessary to forget when we forgive.

Remembering past harm helps keep us safe from future harm as long as we can forgive those who brought the harm.

Supporting Scripture

Hebrews 8:12,

1 Peter 5:8,

Mark 13:20,

Hebrews 10:14, 17,

Matthew 10:21,

Hebrews 11:7-8,

1 Peter 4:7.

Chapter Nineteen

FORGIVING YOURSELF

One of the most difficult things for a truly loving Christian to learn is how to forgive themselves. While they easily forgive others, mistakes made either before they became a Christian or as they were growing in faith often come back to their thoughts and cause sleepless nights and anguish. Retracting past actions and words is not possible and these can be replayed in our minds wishing that those circumstances had not occurred.

Securing the forgiveness of those we hurt helps toward resolving this problem. Making restitution also adds to the resolution of the concern we feel. But often, the person we hurt may have died, may have relocated, might have refused to provide the forgiveness, or would use the opportunity to bring harm again. This precludes the closure so helpful in resolving guilt and forgiving ourselves. However, there is another element to this dilemma which Christians should consider.

We know that Christ died for our sins and that His death was the perfect sacrifice through which our sins were not only forgiven but wiped from all record spiritually. If scripture teaches us these truths and if we believe what scripture tells us, then from where does our continued anguish originate? It surely cannot come from God.

Satan's job is to destroy our faith. He believes that by doing this he can prolong his freedom… and to destroy a Christians faith requires a personal attack on our hope, our courage, and our ability to trust. If Satan can successfully attack a Christian on these fronts, he may break an otherwise strong faith. If he can cause us to be depressed, filled with guilt, tired and exhausted from our thoughts of the past, he can wear us down. We need, then to ask ourselves why Satan would have this power over us and what we need to do to thwart this type of spiritual attack.

The first thing we can do is pray. Christ provides one of the most wonderful offers to counteract this type of dilemma in John 14:27 where He says, *"Peace I leave with you, my peace I give unto you: not as the world giveth, give I unto you. Let not your heart be troubled, neither let it be afraid."* This is very powerful. What these words tell us is that when we pray, we can thank God for the peace He has provided for us, but also remind Him that Christ promised that we could also have His peace. We can ask for this in our prayers and ask that it work to still our troubled heart and mind.

If this approach is not sufficient, then we need to be introspective and take a good look at ourselves so we can search for what might be holding us back from finding that peace. If we have asked for forgiveness from God, if we are truly remorseful, if we are striving to never commit that act again, and if we have partaken of Holy Communion... and still have no peace, then we must look inward. Satan has looked into our heart and found something which he is using to his advantage. 2 Corinthians 2:11 warns: *"Lest Satan get an advantage"*.

Many of us are perfectionists. We work hard, do our best, and push ourselves to perform at a high level of achievement. This can be a very good trait. However, sometimes the gifts we have been given which allow us to perform at this level become mixed with pride. We are proud of our achievements and proud of the hard work we willingly placed into those achievements. But pride has no place in our Christian life. God has said in Proverbs 29:23, *"A man's pride shall bring him low...."* And 1 John 2:16 tell us, *"For all that is in the world, the lust of the flesh, and the lust of the eyes, and pride of life, is not of the Father, but is of the world."*

Pride comes from Satan and can easily cause us to put so much of ourselves into our achievements that we no longer take time for God. We can also begin to believe that it is our own efforts which created the achievement rather than God's blessing. Loving the achievement excessively can be devastating if it is taken from us.

When we have great pride we also begin to view ourselves as exceptional and want others to do the same. Thus when we are forced to admit that we have not been perfect in the eyes of God, our pride is hurt and subconsciously this creates the need to feel good again about ourselves. This need causes us to enter into a never ending cycle of thoughts which are made up of fear, guilt and concern over our personal failures. Rather than keep us humble they make us angry at the situation which forced us to become imperfect. Satan wants these emotions to create a barrier to the love, protection and forgiveness of our Heavenly Father.

But once we know to watch for pride, to acknowledge that all we have comes from God and not through our own achievement, we can overcome. We can free ourselves of the pride, anger and guilt which creates the inability to forgive ourselves. Thus there can be a multitude of lessons in our struggles and we can be thankful that God so patiently brings us into an awareness of those things which we need to address so we can grow into the bride He wants for His Son. We can also see how a blessing is created from our heartaches.

Sadly, many young people dwell on the hurt caused by a broken relationship. This not only exacerbates their emotional and physical pain, but it also brings them a great deal of guilt, anger and distrust which compounds their pain. They must move on, but must also examine the underlying causes for the broken relationship. To avoid a repeat of the situation which could bring that same harm to them again in the future, they must begin to understand and recognize the selfish nature, the ungodly nature, and the indiscriminate nature in self and others to learn how to build better future relationships.

If one feels that they have been a part of the problem, they must do as much for themselves as they do for others by forgiving themselves, by not carrying guilt, but by doing better in the future by remembering the lesson. One must bring the problem to God and then trust Him to help. To make the pain of a perceived loss subside one must forgive the soul and forget the incident but carefully consider and remember what to avoid in the future. God wants us to forgive, but has not asked us to forget what should become a protective measure or learning experience for us. He may have allowed a broken relationship to make us a better and wiser person in the future, or to protect us from a relationship which would not have fostered the growth of our spiritual life.

Satan uses people to harm people. Some of these people are good people who fall prey to the mistakes Satan inspires. Others are not concerned about what God wants of them. If we remember this, we can work to discern what lives in our heart and in the heart of others to avoid those situations in the future. Evil circles and tempts us as well, thus remembering the lessons attached to our mistakes as well as the mistakes of others warns us not to be tempted to engage them again. Further, if our relationships are with souls who do not seek God, and never will we become unequally yoked whereby one or both who share that yoke will inevitably fall.

We each have a responsibility to be prudent, and to be aware of evil, and to 'watch'. 1 Peter 4:7 tells us, *"But the end of all things is at hand; be ye therefore sober, and watch unto prayer."* 1 Peter 5:8 says, *"Be sober, be vigilant, because your adversary the devil, as a roaring lion, walketh about, seeking who he may devour."* We cannot watch, nor be vigilant if we forget our lessons or if we never grow from them.

When Scripture teaches us to arm ourselves with the word of God it does so to help us become aware of the spiritual wickedness which seeks to devour us. The armour it speaks of is God's words, His instruction, and

His protection. When our heart is right with God and we fully understand what He asks of us, what dangers we face, and what our future will be, and we strive to please Him, we will have His guidance and protection. When we have the wisdom, courage and self-esteem to learn and overcome, to seek others willing to do the same, we have matured enough to have something of value to offer. But if we remain complacent in godly matters, and desperate in personal matters, and without introspection we cannot grow and may make the same painful mistakes over and over again.

The end time is a dangerous era for all Christians. It is a time of great power for Satan and if we are not spiritually prepared, his anger and desperation can bring us great harm not only spiritually, but also emotionally, and physically. Thus we must remember just as we must forgive. We must be watchful and discerning just as we are forgiving and kind. We must not let our guard down as these end times envelop us and we must remember that God clearly warns in Mark 13:20, *"And except that the Lord hath shortened, those days, no flesh should be saved; but for the elect's sake, whom he hath chosen, he hath shortened them."*

Bullet Points

Committing a hurtful or damaging action cannot be retracted.

God's forgiveness is available if we have remorse.

Forgiveness must be sought from the person one hurt.

Forgiving oneself is sometimes difficult.

Pride and one's need to appear perfect is a stumbling block to self-forgiveness.

Satan is the instigator of pride which is often why we continue to be hurt.

We will make the same mistakes again if we do not learn the lesson in a broken relationship.

Supporting Scripture

John 14:27,	Proverbs 29:23,
1 John 2:16,	Luke 15:7,
Proverbs 16:18,	11 Corinthians 7:10,
Hebrews 6:6,	11 Peter 3:9,
Psalm 36:11,	Proverbs 11:2.

Chapter Twenty

FROM ANGER TO BLESSING

Everyone, good or bad, gets angry. God even gets angry. Christ too, once became so angry that He overturned the market tables inside the gates of the temple. There are differences however between feeling anger, expressing anger, and maintaining anger. Anger is a natural consequence of the Adam-like nature and as we move from the Adam-like nature to the Christ-like nature we learn…and desire… to control our anger.

Initially, we *feel* anger, but feeling anger can move into expressing anger which comes in two forms; one is productive and the other negative. Productive expression is when we calmly acknowledge, and explain why we felt anger over a certain situation, and what we believe should be put into place to prevent the cause of that anger in the future. This helps us avoid circumstances which *cause* anger and helps us communicate our feelings and needs to those with whom we interact.

Negative expression occurs when we openly express our feelings in a manner which angers others and we offer no constructive explanation of, or methods for, preventing the cause of our feeling or expression. A negative reaction demonstrates that we have not controlled our anger, have not directed it toward solutions based in love and respect, and that we do not actively seek resolution. This is detrimental to those around us and detrimental to our soul salvation.

The act of maintaining our anger is encouraged by Satan and must be overcome. The memory of what caused our anger may serve to keep us from harm, but the maintenance or harboring of anger works to cloud our judgment, prevent change and growth, and robs us of love. It also robs us of the ability to maintain the fruits of the Holy Spirit which strives to guide us toward the godly love expressed by Christ. Harboring anger can also make us ill because it destroys our peace and creates anxiety, hate, and other detrimental emotions. It also means that we have not forgiven.

Forgiving others is necessary to obtaining our own forgiveness through Holy Communion. Our worthiness when taking Holy Communion is *dependent* upon either our forgiving others or sincerely *striving* to forgive others for the harm they caused. When Christ was asked what the most important commandment was, he said that we should love God with all our being and love our neighbor as ourselves. God has granted grace to us **on the condition** that we take the sacrament of Holy Communion **worthily.**

God understands that sometimes we continue to feel the hurt, even labor under the harm, brought to us by a word or deed. He therefore accepts our honest efforts to work toward forgiveness knowing that this effort may not produce results overnight but will eventually be fruitful. We can promote forgiveness in our heart through the powerful tool of prayer asking God to help us forgive, and asking for the peace which Christ said He gladly gives us. We cannot condemn and judge the person who brought us harm because God has clearly stated that He will take vengeance *for* us and that our job is to forgive. Our worthiness depends on us doing so because the Bride of Christ will have a loving, forgiving nature.

Further, we don't know what conditions may have existed in or for the person who brought the harm. They may not yet know God, they may be pawns in Satan's hands, they may have suffered abuse themselves, or they may be laboring under the captivity of jealousy from which they cannot escape. It is also possible that we may have misinterpreted what was said or done. Thus God asks us to wait, to trust that He will handle their indiscretions, and asks that we forgive so *we* are not burdened by *their* faults and failings. Furthermore God tells us that **He will bless us** for striving to behave in this manner. It is up to the other person to seek their own forgiveness from God and those they harmed, and make restitution for the harm they caused. If they don't seek forgiveness or try to make restitution, God will deal with them; He does *not* forget the harm brought to His precious children and His Son's bride.

Christ brought His message in love and gentleness and then allowed His message to take root as men took that message home with them. We too can bring a message, but it must not be presented in a manner which will evoke anger. Scripture explains that in time the power of love and prayer, and of our personal example, can cause our message to take root. Psalm 133:1 tells us, *"Behold, how good and how pleasant it is for brethren to dwell together in unity!"* Therefore, if we provide a subtle message through our personal behavior, thus our reaction to an unkindness, that may carry a far stronger and more positive impact than would our anger. Being angry with someone who caused our suffering, when God offers us a blessing for handling it correctly, makes no sense. We receive something incredibly valuable by handling our anger correctly. Satan may inspire someone to hurt us, but God can turn it into a blessing for us. This is one of the most magnificent miracles of our life of faith, and ***those who harm us have no idea of the gift that the harm they brought us can provide for us!*** God works in mysterious ways!

If we learn how this process works, we can overcome a great deal. We can help ourselves and we can help others. We can stand firm when we are attacked knowing that God loves us and will create a miracle from our experience. Even if we fall prey to fear or anger temporarily, we can work out of it, rise above it and bring joy to the heart of God in the process.

Colossians 3:21 tells us: *"Fathers, provoke not your children to anger, lest they be discouraged."*

Hebrews 13:6 tells us: *"So that we may boldly say, The Lord is my helper, and I will not fear what man shall do unto me"*.

Hebrews 13:16 tells us: *"But to do good and to communicate forget not; for with such sacrifices God is well pleased."*

Matthew 7:12 tells us: *"Therefore all things whatsoever ye would that men should do to you, do ye even so to them...."*

And Proverbs 16:24 tells us: *"Pleasant words are as a honeycomb; sweet to the soul, and health to the bones."*

Proverbs 8:32 tells us: *"....for blessed are they that keep my ways."*

Anger has its place and sometimes we must be angry. But in most cases we become angry over something that doesn't really matter. Scripture teaches us that the bottom line is to flee from evil, but love the soul, and where possible, keep peace with one another. We must work together to learn and teach God's words so we can be a part of the First Resurrection, and we must overcome the traps Satan lays for us. In fact, God can and often does replace what someone took from us.

Some people however, are governed by evil. Some are so arrogant that they would never consider that what they do is wrong. Some have no concept of what it means to take Holy Communion **worthily**. But we must consider that there is the possibility that if we refuse to forgive someone and retain our anger toward them, it could be that God has answered *their* pleas for forgiveness and **they will have our place at the wedding feast** because of our refusal or inability to forgive. Thus, those who bring us harm are best left to God to handle.
What is imperative is that we overcome the tendency to make a blanket judgment about what others do.

Scripture teaches us to love one another, care for one another, and forgive one another, but not to judge one another....that is up to God alone. Our job is to continually examine with honesty if we are doing what God asks of us. We are to let our anger go and to forgive all harm even if we must remember that harm to protect ourselves in the future. We are ***not*** asked to remain in the company of those who enjoy hurting others.

Thus, while we might be better served to avoid interaction with those who are governed by evil, God asks that we always forgive the soul because only He... not we... know what causes that soul to sin. The spirits of jealousy, competitiveness, pride, or arrogance may abide in the person who is hurtful and they will continue to bring harm until God helps them recognize those spirits and they consciously work to exorcise them or... they are cast into the Lake of Fire where they can no longer harm a child of God. But if we strive to do as God asks, and pray for those who have brought us harm, He promises to look after everything else.

"For God shall bring every work into judgment, with every secret thing whether it be good, or whether it be evil." Ecclesiastes 12:14

Bullet Points

Everyone, good or bad, gets angry even God, and once, Christ too, became angry.

Anger can be productive when we calmly acknowledge, and explain, why we felt anger and what can prevent the cause of that anger in the future.

Negative expression occurs when we openly express our feelings in a manner which angers others, offer no constructive explanation for preventing future anger, and demonstrates that we have not controlled our anger, nor directed it toward solutions based in love.

God tells us that He will bless us for striving to behave correctly.

Those who harmed us and caused our anger actually bring us a blessing when we handle the situation correctly.

Supporting Scripture

Psalm 133:1,	Colossians 3:21,
Hebrews 13:6,	Hebrews 13:16,
Matthew 7:12,	Proverbs 16:24,
Proverbs 8:32,	Ecclesiastes 12:14.

Chapter Twenty One

ADDICTIONS AND SPIRITS

Today's world is fraught with activities which cause unintentional pain and suffering, and is a result of us not teaching our children and youth the meaning of one of the most important verses in the Bible. This verse is from Matthew 12:45 and says, *"Then goeth he, and taketh with him seven other spirits more wicked than himself, and they enter in and dwell there; and the last state of that man is worse than the first"*.

Two of the spirits of which this verse warns, are those causing drug and alcohol addiction for which society puts forth two philosophies. One philosophy claims that addictions originate from a pre-birth disposition, and another claims that illness is their driving factor. Both philosophies remove the onus from the individual, imply the need for a greater tolerance and also implies that *all* addictions be regarded in a similar manner. However, while society excuses some, there are others it does not excuse such as kleptomania, pornography, anorexia, and pedophilia, to name a few. Adam and Eve's sin was the initial act which caused all men to sin, but scripture also tells us that we can inherit, and suffer from, the sins of our forefathers. Jeremiah 11:10 says, *"They are turned back to the iniquities of their forefathers, which refused to hear my words;.....".* Exodus 20:5 says *".....visiting the iniquity of the fathers upon the children unto the third and fourth generation...."* And in Numbers 14:18, we are told *"....and by no means clearing the guilty, visiting the iniquity of the fathers upon the children unto the third and fourth generation."* This indicates that what our parents, grandparents, great-grandparents, or even relatives further back in time, engaged in could impact us. Accepting these passages at face value, the question which follows is: "At what point do we excuse a behavior on the basis that it occurs because of the sin of an ancestor?" The answer must be: "At no point". We are and must remain individually responsible for what we do, for God teaches that we must strive to overcome everything within us which He cannot allow to enter His new kingdom.

Scripture teaches that we are to strive to escape the captivity which Satan exercises over us in *all* matters if we want to be found worthy…and that God will help us overcome them. Further, being aware of what scripture tells us becomes an incentive and a comfort to those engaged in, yet saddened by their activities. While the world accepts, condones, and sometimes encourages certain behaviors, our duty is to learn what God tells us, avoid what displeases Him, and help others escape from that captivity. While many know of Adam and Eve and the inherited sin they brought to mankind, few understand the sin of our ancestors. If these create a gene, pre-disposition, or illness which causes an addiction, we must learn what God says about how to overcome what He, in His righteousness *cannot* allow into His kingdom. Evidence indicates that drug users and alcoholics have overcome these addictions through programs which use the faith based approach of abstinence. Why then should we succumb to the belief that we cannot overcome all addictions? If we can free ourselves of one destructive spirit, why should we not be able to free ourselves of any spirit through God's instruction? If, as some say, we inherit a kind of DNA change which allows a specific spirit to cause a thirst for something which is displeasing to God, and if we accept that the sin of Adam and Eve allowed Satan access to man, we should also accept that the sin of our forefather's also allows a satanic spirit access to us. Matthew 8:16 explains that there were many possessed by evil spirits in Christ's time and that when Christ cast these spirits out, the people were healed. *"When the evening was come, they brought unto him many that were possessed with devils: and he cast out the spirits with his word, and healed all that were sick."*

Luke 8:29 says, *"(For he had commanded the unclean spirit to come out of the man. For oftentimes it had caught him: and he was kept bound with chains and in fetters; and he brake the bands, and was driven of the devil into the wilderness.)"* Therefore, it appears that these spirits can be made to leave just as they appear to leave when a drug addict or alcoholic finds success through a twelve-step abstinence program. The Bible clearly tells us that some spirits are more difficult to remove, but by prayer and fasting they can be made to leave. "Fasting" in this context means to "stay away" from, abstain from, the activities they require for their existence. When the apostles complained that they were unable to cast out a certain spirit, Christ told them that only by prayer and 'fasting' could they be cast out. Matthew 17:21: *"Howbeit this kind goeth not out but by prayer and fasting."* And Mark 9:29 says, *"And he said unto them, This kind can come forth by nothing but by prayer and fasting."* These verses address the spirits and the authority by which they must leave those they invade. We associate the word fasting with denying ourselves food, but here it means to deny the spirit what it needs to live whether it is drugs, alcohol, pornography, or any other lust (spirit) we wish to be free of. While some spirits are easily rebuked, others cling to those whom they have invaded with incredible tenacity. But, by not "feeding" them, by abstaining from what they want and need to live, they have no choice but to leave! This requires that we run from temptation when it presents itself, and stay away from that temptation. When that spirit finally starves because it cannot obtain what it wants, it will leave for a more satisfying experience through a more easily directed person.

The bottom line is that some must fight a very powerful and tenacious spirit to become all that God wants them to become. But, God is willing to help; He knows the power of those spirits and He knows the striving of the heart. **Failure does not mean defeat; it means that we need to fight again,** and that each time we fight we become stronger **and more beloved of God**. Therefore we should strive to overcome and believe that, in time, those spirits can be broken. Failure doesn't mean someone can't be forgiven or loved, or nurtured through the process of change, but it does mean that they cannot keep believing that what they do is acceptable to God because of a predisposition, the sins of their forefather's, an illness, a specific DNA, or even being "wired" a certain way. Proverbs 3:5 tells us, *"Trust in the Lord with all thine heart; and lean not unto your own understanding"*. God's words will always tell us the truth and always work to bring us into freedom. As children of God we need to understand the incredible connection between original sin, generational sin, and the spirits which attack, and seek a home, in mankind.

We need to discuss this subject and learn what scripture tells us. We need to explain this concept to others so we can **all** help those who desire to free themselves from those spirits which keep us from God. We must unite in this godly position, rather than fall into the complacency and acceptance of those things which may prevent us or someone we love from being one of the five wise virgins rather than one of the foolish, and lose their place in Heaven. If we do not understand what position we must take, we can't teach our children its importance and many may believe they can 'dabble' in what is potentially incredibly dangerous to them. They need to understand that the spirits which enjoy certain activities can enter them and cause them to want more. Eventually that spirit will control them and force them to feed that spirit. They need to be taught that with *each* encounter with any of these addictions, the spirit will garner a stronger hold over them and become increasingly difficult to remove… and could cost them their soul salvation.

God leaves no question unanswered. Sadly, when parents don't have the answers, they can't teach their children, and without this knowledge children will succumb to these spirits. Many children…and adults….are not aware of what their children face in today's culture, and therefore are not aware that they must protect their children from these perils. This is why God asks us to know His words and to remain in constant fellowship with one another. Talking with one another about God's admonitions is crucial. If we don't know the power of Satan and his cohorts, or how easily we can become trapped, we cannot make an informed decision, understand the choices we have, nor the consequences of our actions nor the actions of these spirits. We must help our children and youth understand why they must say "NO" and *flee* from what has become acceptable in the eyes of the world despite being displeasing to God. The world is too dangerous to our spiritual well-being for us not to be armed with God's warnings and have the courage to stand up and fight for those principles. However, as we do this, we must continue to exercise unconditional love and compassion, patience, instruction, and prayer for those who are trapped. When we stand firm in rebuking these spirits yet act with love and patience, the spirits which have trapped so many begin to weaken. If we remember the words, *"There but by the grace of God go I"*, we will find that providing love, compassion, prayer, and exhortations about what God tells us in scripture will be the path to understanding where we stand and how to help. But most importantly we must understand and teach as Matthew 12:45 warns, *"Then goeth he, and taketh with him seven other spirits more wicked than himself, and they enter in and dwell there; and the last state of that man is worse than the first"*.

Further, this same philosophy applies to homosexuality. This proclivity also claims a pre-birth disposition which removes the onus of action from the individual. Again however this argument will not withstand the question of which addictions one must excuse on this basis and asks that if we consider homosexuality, alcoholism, and drug addiction acceptable on the basis of a pre-disposition or an illness, then why do we not remove the onus of responsibility from those engaged in kleptomania, pornography, gluttony, anorexia, and pedophilia, to name a few? Yet all these spirits can be made to leave.

The Bible very specifically addresses homosexuality. Romans 1:27, 32 says: *"And likewise also the men, having the natural use of the woman, burned in their lust toward one another; men with men working that which is unseemly, and receiving in themselves that recompense of their error which was meet. Who knowing the judgment of God, that they which commit such things are worthy of death, not only do the same, but have pleasure in them that do them."* Leviticus 18:22 says: *"Thou shalt not lie with mankind, as with womankind: it is abomination."* And Leviticus 20:13 tells us: *"If a man also lie with mankind, as he lieth with a woman, both of them have committed an abomination: they shall surely be put to death...."* 1 Corinthians 6:9 tells us, *"Know ye not that the unrighteous shall not inherit the kingdom of God? Be ye not deceived..... nor effeminate, nor abusers of themselves with mankind."* And, 1 Timothy 1:9-10 states: *"Knowing this, that the law is not made for a righteous man, but for the lawless and disobedient, for the ungodly and profane......for them that defile themselves with mankind....and if there be any other thing that is contrary to sound doctrine...."*

Further, Genesis 19:1-13 addresses the proclivities of the men of Sodom, the city God destroyed because of their sin and which is the basis of the word sodomy. There are additional passages in scripture which describe homosexuality as a sin before God and even tells us that this activity will increase as we near the First Resurrection. The bottom line is that we must strive to overcome all things which are displeasing to God. If we fail, we must have remorse for that failure, and try again to overcome. We need to understand that if we do not do our part to teach God's words and help others, especially those who are trapped, to overcome... we fail too. We need to talk about this subject at church, during fellowships, during Bible studies and learn what scripture tells us. We need to unite to fight against the complacency and acceptance that today's political correctness embraces and which may prevent us or someone we love from being found worthy.

If we do not proclaim what is sin and rebuke it, we can't teach our children its importance and thus many children may believe, under peer pressure that they can simply experiment with drugs, alcohol, homosexuality, or pornography. They may not understand the power of the spirit or spirits which enjoy those activities and can enter their hearts and cause them to want more. If this occurs, *that spirit will control them* and force them to feed that spirit and with *each* encounter into these addictions, the spirit will garner a stronger hold over them and become increasingly difficult to remove.

Matthew 12:45 says, *"Then goeth he, and taketh with him seven other spirits more wicked than himself, and they enter in and dwell there; and the last state of that man is worse than the first"*.

Bullet Points

Many in today's society assign certain behaviors to illness or an inherent proclivity.

Neither of these assignations consider those behaviors a sin.

Scripture designates that certain behaviors arise from inherited sin and satanic influence.

Scripture addresses both inherited sin and satanic influence as sinful.

God's words tell us how to remove and overcome both inherited sin and satanic influence.

"Fasting" means to eliminate the access, influence and temptation a spirit demands.

Supporting Scripture

Romans 1: 27, 32,	Leviticus 18:22,
Leviticus 20:13,	Jeremiah 11:20,
Exodus 20:5,	Numbers 14:18,
Matthew 12:45,	Mark 9:29,
Psalms 37:3,	Proverbs 3:5,
Luke 8:29,	1 Timothy 1:9-10,
Genesis 19:1-13,	1 Corinthians 6:9,
Matthew 8:16,	Matthew 17:21.

Chapter Twenty Two

WHY TOUGH LOVE IS REAL LOVE

The term "tough love" became popular when its attributes were discussed by Bill Milliken in his book *Tough Love* which was published in 1968. These words became popular again in the 1980's when David and Phyllis York developed a set of strategies for employing tough love. These arose from the needs of those coping with the addictions of people they loved.

During these two eras, parents were surprised to learn that their children were using drugs and alcohol and falling into other addictions as well. Initially the parents covered the transgressions of the child. But as children fell further into their addiction and lost touch with what they had been taught about Biblical principles and could no longer serve God, many parents recognized the need to intervene on a greater level.

Over time, studies were conducted and books written about how to overcome these addictions, and strategies were developed for those who sought help. Christians understood that indifferent disregard for right and wrong would damage one's soul salvation and sought assistance from their church by requesting counseling and intervention from their ministers.

As the behaviors of the addicted were further studied, the passive behavior of those seeking to help was also studied and brought forth astounding information. Studies demonstrated that many of those who interacted with someone with an addiction had fallen into the trap of wanting to be their "friend", wanting to avoid confrontation and unconsciously seeking and needing their approval.

It became clear that this type of parenting and friendship, contributed to the addiction of those they wanted to help and was thus proclaimed to be an "enabling" personality. This personality is one where the enabler "feels good" by believing they are providing love when they allow, support, and champion those with an addiction and even believe that they are following biblical precepts by doing so. Yet they are actually helping themselves because the undying devotion and adulation of those they enable feeds their personal needs and creates a co-dependency. Through this co-dependency the enabler has his or her needs met, and the addicted exists in a relationship which comfortably contributes to their behavior. As long as the addict has their enabling devices in place, they can deny that what they are doing is wrong.

Newer studies determined that co-dependency is an addiction of its own and that the enabler has a fear of abandonment which causes them to become addicted to being needed and appreciated. They bask in what they consider their courage in standing up for others. They are often however, unconsciously acting out of an emotional wound or programming from childhood.

Real love is not selfish. It does not look for love in return. It looks for the well being of others and therefore to their relationship with God. Real love is willing to lose someone's adulation to help them understand what holds them back from being found worthy. Real love is supporting someone through their addiction *without* condoning it.

From a Christian prospective, *both* the addicted and enabling personalities need to be addressed. The captivity and destruction these behaviors produce must be acknowledged and broken. Destructive behavior is any behavior which is, or results in, displeasing God. Furthermore scripture tells us that anyone who causes or enables the stumbling of another is not pleasing to God and will be severely judged for doing so.

Matthew 18:6-7 tells us, *"But whoso shall offend one of these little ones which believe in me, it were better for him that a millstone were hanged about his neck, and that he were drowned in the depth of the sea. Woe unto the world because of offenses! For it must needs be that offenses come; but woe to that man by whom the offense cometh!"*

Further into this chapter God explains that He does not want these sheep to be lost, but that if an offense exists it must be "plucked out". It also tells us that the **"church"** must **explain their fault** and **help them overcome**. Thus by pretending that the "fault" is acceptable because it is an addiction is ungodly, and contributes to both parties failing to keep God's statutes.

Luke 17:1 also addresses this issue and says, *"....offenses will come; but woe unto him, through whom they come."*

Throughout scripture God tells us to rebuke the sinner, to overcome sin, and to seek forgiveness. It also teaches us that God looks for what lives in our heart, for our striving, and not at our failures. As we read about the sins of our forefathers and the "tendencies" one might have for any addiction, we know that God understands the struggle involved. God promises the strength to overcome, demonstrates that these spirits can be made to leave, and promises His grace for those who strive. His grace is extended to those who continue to fail but who have acknowledged their sin, hate their sin because of their love for God, and strive to the best of their ability to overcome it.

Nowhere in scripture does it say that God simply "excuses" sin or allows us to ignore, accept or justify it. Sin is sin, addiction or not, and can keep us from being found worthy. However, God forgives our sin and teaches us to forgive, not to judge, to love our brethren and bear their burdens as we rebuke the sin.

Romans 1:24 tells *us "Wherefore God also gave them up for uncleaness through the lusts of their own hearts, to dishonour their own bodies between themselves. Who changed the truth of God into a lie, and served and worshipped the creature more than the Creator...."*

Tough love offers a set of strategies which guide a parent or friend in setting boundaries with those they want to help. These include love, support, longsuffering, patience, and all the fruits of the spirit yet still rebuke and teach about the sin. This helps enablers move from their Adam-like fallibility of selfish need to the Christ-like nature which teaches to "go and sin no more". This also provides the sinner with help but never condones their sin, and in fact reminds them of God's help and their free will to choose to fight their sin... or lose their soul salvation. Harsh words, but true.

2 Timothy 4:2-4 tells us *"Preach the word: be instant in season out of season: reprove, rebuke, exhort with all longsuffering and doctrine. For the time will come when they will not endure sound doctrine; but after their own lusts shall they heap unto themselves teachers, having itching ears; and they shall turn away their ears from the truth, and shall be turned unto fables."*

Sadly, the world in which we live has become a world of enablers under the guise of "political correctness". Many are afraid to stand against sin and many have such a strong need to be loved for their tolerance that they unknowingly enable so they can feel noble, kind, appreciated, and needed. Further, justification reigns in today's world and causes even Christians to tell themselves that they must never judge therefore must support those who cannot stop their sin. This however is enabling... and while real love does not judge or condemn, it does recognize sin and rebuke it with gentleness, kindness and by example.

Malachi 2:8 tells us, *"But ye are departed out of the way; ye have caused many to stumble at the law; ....."*.

Luke, 22:32 tells us, *"But I have prayed for thee, that thy faith fail not; and when thou art converted, strengthen thy brethren."*

God wants us to help one another, but to do so under His will and according to His precepts. The bride must be worthy of Christ and no evil or evil spirits can or will be allowed in God's kingdom. Our job is to strive to overcome *all* sin and to preach this to our brethren. All Christians, enabler or not, must learn how to stand strong for Biblical principles and reach out to teach those principles making no excuses for sin. Offering tough love does not mean being cruel. The real cruelty is to enable and condone the sin, and thus mislead those who come to us for support.

Further, God will hold each of us accountable if we know His precepts and do not share them with others or do not reach out to help them acknowledge their sin and work toward overcoming. God will also hold His ministers accountable for this inaction as they are held to an even higher standard.

Bullet Points

Tough love offers a set of strategies which guide a parent or friend in setting boundaries.

Enablers must move from their Adam-like fallibility of selfish need to the Christ-like nature which provides the sinner with help while rebuking the sin.

It is important not to condone the sin and to teach what scripture tells them about that sin.

Enablers have a co-dependency which is an addiction of its own.

Offering tough love does not mean being cruel.

The real cruelty is to enable and condone the sin, and thus mislead those who seek support.

Ministers will be held to an even higher standard and held accountable if they condone and do not rebuke the sin of those for whom they are responsible.

Supporting Scripture

Matthew 18:6-7,	Luke 17:1,
Romans 1:24,	2 Timothy 4:2-4,
Malachi 2:8,	Luke 22:32.

Chapter 23

WHEN TO HOLD AND WHEN TO FOLD

When we witness the subtle control evil exercises in the captivity which causes blindness and stiff-necked resistance to God's words in the heart of someone we love, it is easy to become frustrated and allow our well intentioned testimony to become a seemingly unproductive argument. When our prayers appear unanswered and we tire from the constant struggle of an interaction which seems to bears no fruit, we wonder if we should give up or increase our effort. But our effectiveness lies in knowing when to hold and when to fold, and why we should exercise both options. These are important factors to consider.

As children of God we desire to be kind, empathetic, and compassionate while also being strong, firm and have no fellowship with evil. Ephesians 5:11 tells us: *"And have no fellowship with the unfruitful works of darkness, but rather reprove them."* Yet in Galatians 6:2 we are told, *"Bear ye one another's burdens."* On the surface these verses seem contradictory, but other parts of scripture demonstrate that each has their place in how we are to bring testimony. Our life as children of God requires us to care for our spiritual life, the spiritual life of our family and to bring others testimony of God's plan of salvation and the sacrifice of Christ. To be effective we have to utilize God's teaching through scripture in word and deed, and to pray specifically about each situation we encounter. But we also have to act within the parameters of God's direction. This requires the understanding that we are dealing with the power of Satan as well as our own Adam-like nature. When we fully understand that we battle powers and principalities which are the spirits of this world, we are not as easily discouraged by the unkind or ungodly words and deeds which our testimony might evoke nor of the appearance of a failed testimony. Scripture teaches us that when we bring testimony to someone under satanic control, we are not dealing with only the person to whom we speak, but also with the spirit which holds them captive. That spirit considers the child of God who brings their testimony a danger to its existence, and is aware that their words and deeds have the power to remove them from the heart it has entered. That spirit will put up a fight to thwart all testimony and will direct its venom toward the person bringing that testimony. But the greater the attack, the more impact we are making on the soul. Ephesians 6:10 tells us, *"....Be strong in the Lord, and in the power of his might."*

When we acknowledge that we are not dealing with the person to whom we bring the testimony, but with the spirit which is determined to remain comfortably in their heart, we must ask God to help us discern when it is time to hold and hammer away, or time to fold and come back another day with our testimony. It is imperative for the children of God to understand that by providing constant assistance to a soul, we may be aiding, abetting and enabling that spirit to thrive, rather than helping the soul rid itself of the spirit which impels the behavior which is displeasing to God. This is a very important point for all children of God to consider when engaging in testimony. To be effective against these spirits we must understand the term "tough love" discussed in an earlier chapter. The tough love approach advocates that we carefully assess the assistance or interaction we provide to determine whether or not our intervention is aiding and abetting *the spirit* causing the harmful behavior of that soul. If so, we have become an "enabler".

These terms are often used when addressing those burdened by a drug addiction but work for all behaviors which are not pleasing to God and especially those which are the work of a spirit. Neither action of holding or folding indicates that we are winning or have given up. Both actions have a time and a place in our testimony, and both actions are godly. It is not an either or situation when we hold and fold, but a combination which allows us to bring our testimony through word and deed (hold) while firmly refusing to enable (fold). The term to "hold or fold" is used in the card game of Poker to describe the decision to increase a bet in the hope of winning, or withdraw from further betting because one feels that they cannot win. Similarly, the child of God deciding to hold or fold is making the decision to provide testimony to the person in need while being careful to walk away before providing assistance or sustenance to the spirit in control. The spirit in control knows and fears those who recognize it and know its needs. When the child of God "holds" by identifying, rebuking and "starving" the spirit they are addressing, it will eventually look for greener pastures where it will not be identified and challenged. However, we must walk away or fold when the soul allows the spirit to abuse us in word or deed or demand that we help it meet its needs. Once our point is made and the spirit is identified and rebuked, it can be told that we recognize its venom of evil, know that it comes from the spirit and not the captive soul, and that we will return at another time to speak to the goodness of the soul which belongs to God. This disallows the spirit the freedom to use the soul to dispel its wrath. In time the soul recognizes the work of the spirit and begins to desire freedom.

Amazingly, scripture tells us how a soul can cause an invading spirit to leave. Mark 9:29 tells us: *"This kind can come forth by nothing, but by prayer and fasting."* In this context the word fasting means denying or starving the spirit of what it desires. Once we have developed a full understanding of what God teaches us about invading spirits, we will no longer feel guilty when denying certain forms of assistance, nor be angered when meeting with resistance. We will no longer lose heart or think of giving up our testimony. We will understand that attacks come from the spirit. While this infuriates the spirit, lets it know that it has been recognized, rebuked and will no longer be "fed" what it desires, it also lets that spirit know that we will not give up.

When we face a spirit and know what scripture tells us about these spirits we are better armed to teach its victim to recognize it and thus understand why they are separated from God and how they can obtain their freedom from that spirit. Once the soul acknowledges the spirit, the spirit knows its days are numbered, and our testimony begins to bear fruit even if we cannot see the progress which is being made. The spirit in control does not want the soul it has invaded to recognize it and rightfully fears those who do. If that spirit sees that the child of God has identified it and wants to "starve" its needs, and sees that those who are helping that soul are exercising tough love, it fears that the soul in which it lives will begin its fight against that spirit and, with God's help, will overcome it. Thus it attacks the child of God bringing their testimony to that soul, and does so vehemently because it is fighting for its home and its freedom to obtain what it wants. However, if we offer help as an enabler, that spirit will use the child of God and not budge from its hold on the soul. It has no reason to leave, because you, the one who seeks to help, are enabling the spirit as you enable the one you are seeking to help.

We must offer our help yet remain firm in our faith and in testifying of God's laws and the precepts required to attain our soul salvation. We want to be good teachers and good role models while standing firm in our conviction. If we reach out with understanding to those who suffer and we fully support our faith by bringing them God's words...both the admonitions and the promises....we become a role model to them. We demonstrate love despite the captivity which causes them to fail, and consistently teach about the sin, the spirits which bind them to that sin, and what God offers them… and gain respect for our stedfastness.

Once we have developed a full understanding of what God teaches us about invading spirits, we will no longer tire of the failure of our testimony, nor tire from the failure of the invaded soul to fight that spirit. We will have the patience to persevere, and the wisdom to fight effectively. We also have to pray specifically about the situation and have the soul which is in captivity also pray. These efforts combine to help us connect to the power of the Holy Spirit to obtain God's gifts of direction, and to act within the parameters of those gifts. We are bringing the power of the Holy Spirit to the captive soul. When we have initiated these actions and trust God to do the rest we will not become discouraged by the unkind or ungodly words and deeds which our testimony might evoke nor of the failure which our testimony might appear to be.

We must also be ready for the spirit to put up a fight and direct its venom toward us. That spirit can attack the child of God in many ways and be a danger both to the one bringing testimony and to the one receiving that testimony. However, once we are aware of this we can ask God for His protection and His help to stand firm through it. The spirits we face can see this determination and begin to understand that they cannot attack us with guilt or fear, or by convincing us that we will lose the fight or give it up. They can see that are not afraid to face them and that we will expose them to those we wish to help. That spirit also sees that we are applying God's words with Christian courage and perseverance and that God is providing us with protection against its' evil. That spirit is then forced to acknowledge that we know when to walk away and when to return to fight another day when God has again prepared that soul for further testimony and weakened that spirits hold on them just a little bit more.... and will do so until it leaves!

Bullet Points

Christians seek to help others and to bring testimony.

Tough love is a term used to teach an enabler not to aid and abet.

Sometimes help and testimony is brought to someone with an unclean spirit.

An unclean spirit will resist and attack the Christian because it fears the testimony.

We are not discouraged when we know the that it is the unclean spirit, not the soul, which responds with vehemence to our testimony.

The Christian should both hold and fold but not give up.

Supporting Scripture

Ephesians 5:11,	Galatians 6:2,
Mark 5:16,	1 Timothy 2:4-6,
Mark 5:8,	Ephesians 6:10,
Hosea 4:6,	Matthew 18:18,
Mark 5:2,	Mark 5:9.

Chapter Twenty Four

DEBATING THE UNBELIEVER

It is a strong temptation to enter a heated debate over doctrine. It is even more tempting when we know scripture well, are deeply convinced of our interpretation and zealous in our desire to share what we have learned. Sometimes such a debate can be fruitful, but often it ends in anger. We can be frustrated when our point of view is rebuked. The person with whom we speak may also be frustrated because their point of view is rebuked. Should we therefore avoid these debates and if not, what can we do to make our point and bring our testimony without causing anger or frustration?

While Christians find great joy in their faith and in spreading the gospel, not everyone understands the nuances of personal interaction and communication. There are specific rules when engaging in a debate and specific rules which should be implemented to keep the communication open. Once someone feels personally rebuffed or rebuked, they tend to withdraw either physically or mentally. This ends the potential for further discussion and creates a closed mind.

There are many rules put forth about the nuances of good communication, but the rules which are most important are to *never* argue, to always be polite, to always be patient, to admit what we don't know, and be willing to postpone a conversation until we find the answer. It is imperative to ask, and then listen to, the other person's position. It is also important to speak in terms which those with whom we engage can understand, and to think about how they will interpret and receive our words. It also helps if a conversation is opened by addressing topics of interest to the other party. Success requires an ethical standard, an emotional tie, and a logical progression. How we ask questions and how we react to the response to our question reflects our ethical standard. How we engage someone, arouse their interest, and demonstrate our own interest in their responses creates an emotional tie which slowly builds our case. Finding a way to use their responses to support what we say creates a logical progression which is helpful in controlling and framing the debate.

If a child of God asks, for instance, "What do you think causes so much evil to exist in the world?" And if the answer is: "I believe that all evil stems from the personal lusts of man.", rather than jump into our personal opinion, we should continue to draw them out by asking "Why do you believe this?" Thus the response might be, "Because I have seen some of those lusts in action and witnessed the harm they cause to others." You might then ask, "Is there any impetus or influence other than selfishness which you believe might drive someone to cause this harm?"

By asking questions, listening to the answers and offering **no** immediate opinion, rebuttal or rebuke, we learn how to engage the person with whom we are communicating. In terms of the questions described above, by following these rules, we have already learned that the person with whom we are speaking may not know about Satan's power or his purpose. When our response is not, "No, you're wrong", but is instead, "I can understand that the actions you witnessed must be pretty appalling and the plight of man rather dismal, but have you ever considered whether or not there could be an evil influence such as Satan to push men into those actions?"

This response would not close the conversation, but open it again because we have expressed our interest in that persons opinion. Continuing this conversation might provide this answer to our question: "No, I haven't, mainly because I don't think there is a Satan and also because it's unlikely that some entity could influence the will of men." We might respond with: "I read two passages in the Bible which touched on this subject and fascinated me. I'd like to know what you think of them, so let me tell you what they are. Acts 5:3 says, *".....why hath Satan filled thine heart to lie.......and to keep back part of the price of the land?"* And 11 Corinthians 2:11 says, *"Lest Satan should get an advantage of us: for we are not ignorant of his devices."*

Initiating a conversation in this manner piques the curiosity, and engages the other person in a conversation which does negate their opinion. As a Christian, we have opened the door to exploring an otherwise taboo subject. We may even have opened the way to enlarge the exploration of this single subject into a full blown testimony. It is *not* the debate, nor the faith of those involved, but *the manner* in which the debate is carried forth that matters.

If the conversation begins to feel stilted, leave it for another day rather than create an unpleasant experience. Evoking someone's defense mechanisms will preclude a healthy, open conversation and must be avoided. But by being patient and sensitive to their feelings and their long held beliefs we can, with God's help bring our testimony and meet with success. Romans 14:1 warns us, *"Him that is weak in the faith receive ye, but not to doubtful disputations."* Thus we must remain positive, and flee any debate before it becomes an argument by returning to a more neutral communication so we can bring our testimony again another day.

Bullet Points

A debate is not always productive communication.

There are numerous nuances to good communication and interaction… which we should try to learn.

How we engage others is more important than what we want to tell them.

Always listen to another's position before stating your own.
Never provoke or anger when testifying.

The testimony must be ethical, bind by touching the heart and through logical progression.

Supporting Scripture

Acts 5:3,

2 Corinthians 2:11,

Titus 2:15,

1 Corinthians 13:5,

Titus 1:9-10,

Titus 2:1.

Titus 2:7,

Romans 14:1,

Proverbs 20:2,

Galatians 5:26,

Ephesians 6:4,

Chapter Twenty Five

RULES FOR CHRISTIAN PARENTS

Proverbs 20:11 warns: *"Even a child is known by his doings, whether his work be pure, and whether it be right."* Thus, instruction in scripture is necessary and instruction regarding hearth and home and interaction with others should also be provided by parents. We read in Proverbs 23:12: *"Apply thine heart to instruction, and thine ears to the words of knowledge. Withhold not correction from the child."* And 11 Timothy 4:2 tells us, *"Preach the word; be instant in season, out of season; reprove, rebuke, exhort with all longsuffering and doctrine."* Many areas of scripture admonish children to heed the instruction their parents provide and assumes that such provision *will* be made by the parents. Ephesians 6:1 says, *"Children, obey your parents in the Lord; for this is right."* Proverbs 4:1-2 says, *"Hear ye children the instruction of a father, and attend to know understanding. For I give you good doctrine, forsake ye not my law."* The Bible also tells us what will occur when children are *not* taught of spiritual matters and of personal interaction. Without knowledge of God's words and the love and respect for others this teaches, evil can overtake the heart. Matthew 10:21 warns: *"And the brother shall deliver up the brother to death, and the father the child: and the children shall rise up against their parents and cause them to be put to death."*

The Bible also tells us about the joys for the parent and child when the family unites in faith, and interact with the respect wrought by love. When the child has received godly instruction, Proverbs 3:13 explains: *"Happy is the man that findeth wisdom, and the man that getteth understanding."* And Proverbs 23:24 says, *"The father of the righteous shall greatly rejoice: and he that begetteth a wise child shall have joy of him. Thy father and thy mother shall be glad, and she that bare thee shall rejoice."*

With proper instruction as a child, those who fall from their faith often return with a greater faith because they realize what they lost when losing God's blessing despite Satan working to separate a child from the parent, and thereby from instruction. Ephesians 6:4 reminds Fathers, *"And, ye fathers, provoke not your children to wrath: but bring them up in the nurture and admonition of the Lord."* And Proverbs 22:15 says, *"Foolishness is bound in the heart of a child; but the rod of correction shall drive it far from him."* Scripture teaches that children are to obey their parents in all things, not just those things relating to their spiritual instruction. Colossians 3:20 states, *"Children, obey your parents in all things: for this is well pleasing unto the Lord."* This includes proper etiquette, activities of daily living, and the dangers of the outside world. We know that society demands specific rules of etiquette when engaging in a formal setting such as a black tie dinner and that this would preclude dressing in jeans and a tee shirt. Talking with our mouth full, chewing food with our mouth open, using the salad fork for the entree, or using a toothpick in public is not considered good etiquette. But how do we learn the rules of etiquette?

Our expertise in many areas is most easily learned, retained, and automatically employed if learned when very young. Without being taught proper etiquette when engaging in a formal activity our children are vulnerable to embarrassment and possible censure. They may learn from their experience and make changes, or they may not recognize what changes are required and forfeit opportunities which could have been of benefit to their future. Good manners are important in business, in relationships, and for self-esteem, and can make a difference in one's level of achievement… and in the testimony they might offer. Change can be effected quickly and easily once one recognizes what is lacking and is determined to master what they require. But those who are taught at a young age use their faith, and their good manners automatically and thus with ease, and become more thoughtful about the impression they make. A spiritual education allows one to become aware of sin and evil, what steps to take to avoid those pitfalls and how to be a role model for their family and community.

While parents recognize the benefits of teaching children how to make their bed, wash the dishes, wash their clothing, and perform a variety of chores necessary to running a household and caring for themselves and others, many neglect that child's spiritual education. The child who has been taught these skills will enter into adult life better equipped to marry, to run a household and perform the daily tasks. Adding spiritual knowledge to this mix creates a future role model and future generation who will know God and strive to do as He asks. What parents teach their children impacts every aspect of that child's life. The children of God understand that when a parent does not teach their children about God, it can be deadly to the soul of both the parent and the child, but sometimes they miss how important good housekeeping and good manners and the respect this creates can be. Thus teaching on many levels makes one a better parent. Also important to understand is that today's world is filled with a huge array of social networking opportunities which our youth use to interact with others. They rarely understand the incredible impact this can have on their future or that Satan sees that future and wants it to align with his ways; not God's ways. Children must be taught that whatever they write or post on these social networks is *forever* imbedded on the Internet even if it is eventually deleted. Employers search these networks to learn about potential employees and do not hire those who post venom, sexual innuendo, foul language, or even use bad grammar or speak badly of others. Photos can be retrieved and predators can predict patterns of behavior and travel paths.

Satan is alive and well and targets our children. We must teach our children that they will face a battle for their soul every day of their lives and only through God and proper instruction can they survive what this world will bring them. Satan wants them but so does God who offers them an incredible future which must be sought today and everyday and not put off until tomorrow. Ephesians 6:11-12 warns, *"Put on the whole armour of God, that ye may be able to stand against the wiles of the devil. For we wrestle not against flesh and blood, but against principalities, against powers, against the rulers of darkness of this world, against spiritual wickedness in high places".* If parents will not teach this to their children, who will? And how will parents respond when God asks them about the fulfillment of their stewardship.

Bullet Points

Parents should provide the teaching of table manners, house chores, courtesy and the dangers in social networking.

Teaching children about God is a parent's responsibility. Scripture admonishes children to listen to their parents.

Father's are given stewardship over their children's spiritual instruction.

Without instruction children will fall prey to the devil.

Children without a knowledge and belief in God will rise against their parents in the end times.

Supporting Scripture

Proverbs 20:11,	11 Timothy 4:2,
Proverbs 23:12,	Ephesians 6:11-12,
Ephesians 6:1,	Proverbs 4:1-2,
Colossians 3:20,	Proverbs 23:24,
Matthew 10:21,	Proverbs 22:15,
Ephesians 6:4.	

Chapter Twenty Six

KIDS AND COLLEGE

We live in an era of unrest spiritually, physically, emotionally, and politically. Danger stalks Christians from every angle of life and even more so our children. Satan desires to break the faith of our children so that he can create a generation of ungodliness. He knows God's Plan of Salvation, knows his future, and knows that during the tribulation many will lose their faith. Thus, not only must *we* hold fast to what is good, but we must teach our children to hold fast. 11Thessalonians 2:15 tells us, *"Therefore brethren, stand fast, and hold the traditions which ye have been taught whether by word or by epistle."* 1 Thessalonians 5:21-23 advises, *"Prove all things; hold fast that which is good. Abstain from all appearances of evil. And the very God of peace sanctify you wholly....."* 1 Thessalonians 5:12 tells us, *"Wherefore comfort yourselves together, and edify one another, even as also ye do."* These verses advise us to hold onto what we have been taught and to teach and be taught by both the spoken and written word of God and comfort one another through those teachings.

However, what a parent can do in the face of the contemporary dangers which encompass their children remains blaringly unanswered because we cannot keep our children confined to the walls of our homes hearing only things of God. They must gain an education to earn their daily bread and must learn the consequences of evil. They, using their free will, will be required to choose good or evil for themselves. Parents do however have a number of clear responsibilities regarding their children.

First and foremost they must teach them about God's Plan of Salvation, about evil and why it will attack them, and what will happen if they succumb to evil. They must teach their children about spiritual warfare and how a spirit can inhabit their hearts and *demand* behavior which is displeasing to God. If parents neglect this teaching, they themselves will be displeasing God and they will become those mentioned in Malachi 2:8: *"But ye are departed out of the way; ye have caused many to stumble at the law....."* and in Matthew 18:6: *"But whoso shall offend one of these little ones which believe in me, it were better for him that a millstone were hanged about his neck, and that we was drowned in the depth of the sea."*

Secondly, parents must carefully vet the colleges which their children will attend and examine the policies of its instructors. Many colleges support and encourage their tenured professors in teaching social justice, socialism, communism, Marxism, godlessness, religious doubt, and a psychological freedom in opposing Christian tradition. Many have eliminated God and the religious writings of our forefather's from the history books they require their students to purchase. Nevertheless, there have been a large number of colleges rising to the needs of Christian children by claiming to offer an education which retains, supports and encourages accurate history, and a godly life and atmosphere. Liberty University in Virginia, Taylor University in Indiana, Heritage Christian University in Alabama, Florida Christian College in Florida are but a few one might consider examining. However, no college education can take the place of what parents must instill into their children's hearts at a young age nor provide the example of godliness, proper communication and respect.

Children need to be taught what to watch for so they can guard their Christian beliefs. Sunday Schools, Vacation Bible Schools, Christian youth groups, and even Conservative Political Youth Groups such as YAF can help our children maintain their faith and grow in the ability to make tough choices on their own. For many parents, the act of effective communication has not been their forte. None of us are perfect in all things. But what we must do if we suspect that we are lacking in these skills, is to find through fellowship those willing to pick up where we leave off. Perhaps an aunt or uncle, a minister or a neighbor, a coach or a teacher, a best friend or someone willing to be a role model will step in. God will provide what we need if we ask Him for help and then work to utilize that help. Communication during fellowship with our brothers and sisters in faith can fill in the gaps and not only teach our children, but teach parents as well. Friendships for our children with other believing children and making plans to room at college with a believer may be options to consider. Most importantly parents need to understand that in today's world and in most instances, Christian kids and college campuses don't mix. Most campuses are a danger to our children. But when we recognize the dangers, watch carefully, pray, and we have done our best to teach and guide our children, we must sometimes simply let go. If we must concede to this action, we must nevertheless watch and listen, visit, communicate well, and constantly assess so we are ready to step in if something seems awry.

Additionally, it is wise to locate a church in the town or city where the child will attend college, visit the Rector and ask him to visit the child, perhaps even take them to church to receive Holy Communion and the word of God…..and ask them to alert you if they notice a problem. Some ministers are willing to arrange for a child to be visited in their dorm every six weeks or so as a part of their outreach program. Today's world is especially difficult because our young people encounter a biased education, the subtle seduction of drugs and alcohol, and are faced with many difficult decisions. Evil is alive and well and even more determined to destroy our children's faith as it is ours. But by being watchful, using the gifts of the Holy Spirit, cherishing our faith, and sharing our experiences of faith with one another, we will touch the heart of God and learn how to be protected and make ourselves ready.

The bottom line is that parents must recognize that danger exists today more vehemently and deadly than ever before for our children, and steps must be taken to avoid those dangers by learning what options are available, developing a plan of action and teaching children properly. Ephesians 5:6-11 tells us, *"Let no man deceive you....be not partakers with them.....walk as children of light....For the fruit of the Spirit is in all goodness and righteousness and truth: Proving what is acceptable unto the Lord. And have no fellowship with the unfruitful works of darkness, but rather reprove them."*

Bullet Points

Satan is especially active on the college campus.

A generation of ungodly people can result if our children fall.

Scripture admonishes parents to teach their children about God, Satan, and the end times.

Parents should choose their children's college carefully.

A strong upbringing in, and knowledge of scripture protects children from satanic attack.

Parents will be held accountable if their lack of instruction is the cause of their child's fall

Supporting Scripture

11 Thessalonians 2:15,	Malachi 2:8,
1 Thessalonians, 5:12,	Ephesians 6:11,
1 Thessalonians 5:21-23,	Matthew 18:6,
1 Corinthians 13:11,	Ephesians 6:13.

Chapter Twenty Seven

HUSBANDS, WIVES AND ROLE MODELS

God gave men the toughest role, the one which only a man of faith and strength can properly execute. Christ was the ultimate role model, the ultimate man of strength, courage and love. He laid down His life for us. God asks that we strive to become Christ-like in our nature by laying aside our ego, killing our old nature and placing the well being of others above our own. This is difficult to achieve yet it increases love, respect and trust, and creates a bond in our relationships. It gives credence to what one might teach or suggest and creates a person whom God can trust and use to help others. When interacting with others, we must have that person's respect to be effective. We can't demand from others what we won't give, and can't expect loyalty when we have not provided loyalty. But when we are recognized as a person who is firm in faith, honorable in all deeds, forgives mistakes, remains loyal, and does not easily take offense, over time we gain the trust and the respect of others. When we've earned respect, others will trust us enough to follow our lead, and listen to what we teach.

God has given husbands the responsibility to see to the spiritual well being of their family and to create a household which is godly, orderly and happy. But to lead, not demand, one needs to earn respect by demonstrating his own consistent principles. Once this is achieved at home, it will fan out to other areas of our lives and, as scripture tells us, brings us a great blessing. Sometimes our self-righteousness makes us angry with those who have failed us in some manner. This is related to ego, and makes it difficult to be the one to make peace or to be the first to apologize. Yet often it is a comedy of errors or one impulsive moment or angry word, which one may even wish they could take back, which escalates into a resentment which is difficult to overcome. Thus we face many challenges when trying to fulfill those responsibilities which God asks of us. While we are to teach and admonish one another and love and forgive one another, God understands that no one is perfect. He tells us that love covers mistakes, never brings them up in front of others, causes us to regret unkindness, and encourages us to strive harder in the future. When we receive these gifts from someone, it creates an atmosphere where we desire to return the love and respect to the person who provides this example. It also produces a tenderness which is often expressed in open affection. If each of us took the responsibility to make things right when they go wrong, we would seldom hold onto anger and would begin to receive a greater expression of love and appreciation from those we love. This is the blessing God provides when we strive to be that example.

God has charged husbands with the responsibility of his family's faith... even in today's world where husbands and wives now work outside the home and share parental and household responsibilities. Thus, it is easy to understand why confusion reigns about what role God may want husbands and wives to assume and who should carry the dominant role. Yet, scripture is clear about the role of husbands and wives. At first glance, scripture appears outdated and untimely because of the role husbands and wives must now accept to meet the demands of today's world. However, as we examine what this scripture means to each spouse, we begin to understand why the advice is still valid and valuable for today and can being a blessing to the Christian family. God is orderly and He would like us to live in an orderly manner which encourages the growth of love, peace, scriptural wisdom, and godly integrity. His direction protects us from harm both naturally and spiritually, and creates an example for our children, keeps doubt and confusion at bay, promotes forgiveness and provides godly self-esteem. By having a specific path to follow, we avoid the anxiety of not knowing what to do. We are also becoming a worthy bride for the Lord Jesus.

When wives are asked to be subject to their husbands in everything, it is understandable that they may balk. They do so only when they do not understand the deeper meaning of the scripture which asks this of them. For example, Ephesians 5: 23-25 says, *"For the husband is the head of the wife, even as Christ is the head of the church; and he is the savior of the body. Therefore as the church is subject unto Christ, so let the wives be to their own husbands in everything. Husbands love your wives even as Christ also loved the church and gave himself for it."* The true meaning of these three verses make it easy for a woman to subject herself to the conditions mentioned and difficult for the husband to live up to those conditions. God is telling the husband to literally give his life for his wife as Christ did for us...the church. To protect her, love her, care for her, teach her, forgive her, and help her prepare herself and those she loves for an eternity with God. If a husband were to provide these incredible gifts to his wife, a wife would bask in the subjection the Bible requests of her. However, even if a husband does not live up to the ideal which scripture asks of him, 1 Peter 3:1 tells the wife, *"Likewise ye wives; be in subjection to your own husbands; that if any obey not the word, they also may without the word be won by the conversation of the wives."* Here the wives are asked to conduct themselves as an example for their husbands and pray that by their behavior, God's word will soon be placed into the husband's heart and they will become all God asks them to become. The reward, should this occur, is excellent for the wife. Ephesians 5:33 tells husbands and wives, *"Nevertheless, let every one of you in particular so love his wife even as himself, and the wife see that she reverence her husband."* Loving another as well as we love ourselves is not always easy. Further, reverencing someone who we feel has acted badly can be a difficult task. Thus, the struggles to put away the Adam-like nature, seems to be quite equally dispensed between husband and wife. Another contentious verse can be found in 1 Peter 3:7: *"Likewise ye husbands, dwell with them according to knowledge, giving honour unto the wife, as unto the weaker vessel, and as being heirs together of the grace of life; that your prayers be not hindered"*. Today's women consider themselves to be strong physically, mentally and spiritually, and are not pleased to note that scripture considers them the weaker vessel. Yet if a man becomes strong in the eyes of the wife through his diligent application of scripture, his fairness, his honorable behavior and his love and respect toward his wife, it becomes easier for a woman to accept the husband as the stronger one *because* of his example. In fact, he becomes someone upon whom she can fully rely. Again while the onus seems to fall upon the husband, the wife is forced to see the husband as the stronger vessel when he works diligently to fulfill the direction of scripture. However, the wife is asked to love her husband and to submit in body and in instruction. Colossians 3:18-19 says, *"Wives, submit yourselves unto your own husbands, as it is fit in the Lord. Husbands, love your wives, and be not bitter against them."* Perhaps as God sees us strive to follow His words, he strengthens us and rewards us for that striving. If our heart's attitude is to fulfill God's wishes, and both husband and wife make the effort God asks of them, what can come of those efforts but a happy and peaceful home blessed by God? When we pray together as a family, and listen to what lives in the heart of a faithful and godly spouse, any anger or resentment one might have felt can be washed away. Hearing a plea during our family prayer from a spouse asking God to help them be a better help-mate, to be more loving and understanding will touch and soften our heart and push away our anger or resentment…the bitterness mentioned in Colossians 3:19. Further, we can trust that God will re-direct all things for the good when a heart is humble enough to acknowledge a fault and ask for help. Proverbs 8: 10-11 tells us, *"Receive my instruction, and not silver; and knowledge rather than choice gold. For wisdom is better than rubies; and all the things that may be desired are not to be compared with it."* And Proverbs 8:21 says, *"That I may cause those that love me to inherit substance, and I will fill their treasures".*

When children are a part of the household, both husbands and wives are given instruction to teach the children God's words. Proverbs 13: 1 tells us, *"A wise son heareth his father's instruction."* Proverbs 15:5 says, *"A fool despiseth his father's instruction"*. Proverbs 2:11 tells us: *"Even a child is known by his doings, whether his work be pure, and whether it be right"*. Proverbs 23: 26 says: *"My son, give me thine heart, and let thine eyes observe my ways."* Husbands and wives are asked to teach and to become a role model of God's instruction for children. This behavior will bring a great blessing upon the household and also to future generations. God is not concerned with our daily squabbles or differences of opinion, nor of our desire to have our way as long as we do our best to keep peace, show love, learn God's words, want them to be a part of our domestic life as well as our spiritual life and we teach them to our children. God blesses us and keeps love alive when He sees our effort to do those things which He asks of us.

Bullet Points

Few marriages survive in today's ungodly world.

Scripture provides instruction to husbands and wives.

Respect is the key to having others look up to you.

At first glance, scripture seems to favor husbands, but wives are actually the beneficiaries of God's instruction.

Christ laid down His life for His church and husbands are asked to do the same for their wives.

Integrity and trustworthiness are required to be a Christian leader.

Respect grows when integrity and trust is constant. Self-sacrifice is the example Christ gave us.

Our own self-sacrifice pleases God and begins in our family circle.

God can keep our love alive if we ask Him and are striving to do His will.

Supporting Scripture

Ephesians 5:23-25,	1 Peter 3:1,
Ephesians 5:33,	1 Peter 3:7,
Matthew 5:25,	11 Corinthians 2:11,
Ephesians 6:4,	Titus 1:9-10,
Colossians 3:18-19,	Proverbs 8:10-11,
Proverbs 8:21,	Hosea 4:6,
Proverbs 29:23,	Matthew 19:6,
Ephesians 5:33,	2 Corinthians 6:14-18,
1 Timothy 4:16,	1 Corinthians 15:58,
Ephesians 5:23-25,	1 Peter 3:7,
Colossians 3:19,	Proverbs 13: 1,
Proverbs 15:5,	Proverbs 2:11,
Proverbs 23: 26.	

Chapter Twenty Eight

WHEN WE ARE UNEQUALLY YOKED

Rules and laws must be established for a society to function in an orderly fashion. Organizations adopt rules for its operation and to guide the conduct of its members. Churches do the same. Most rules are established for the good of the group, emanate from its mission or doctrine, and employ basic courtesies. Christians also follow rules based on the Gospel of Christ, although different doctrines require slightly different rules. While all Christian doctrines emanate from the teaching of Christ, many apply interpretations to scripture which can create varying ideas. For example, the doctrine of the Catholic Church does not allow divorce and bases that rule on passages similar to Luke 16:18 which says, *"Whosoever putteth away his wife, and marrieth another, commiteth adultery: and whosoever marrieth her that is put away from her husband committeth adultery.* And in Matthew 19:6, *"....What therefore God hath joined together, let not man put asunder."* However, other denominations allow divorce and base their decision on scripture gathered from *all* parts of the Bible which address both husbands and wives and the child of God who finds himself surrounded by evil. Allowing divorce is based on delineating scripture which provides advice and admonition for a *faithful couple*, from scripture which advocates for a child of God who is yoked with someone ruled by Satan.

While the conduct, example and prayers of the child of God may turn the heart of the unbeliever and should be given a chance to work, there are instances when the unbeliever succumbs to and relishes in abusing the child of God. There are also situations where the unbeliever regularly abandons the tenets of marriage through adultery and harms the child of God through the hurt and neglect this creates. Further, such neglect may cause even the child of God to abandon the tenets of marriage as they mistakenly employ the wrong approach to meet their own need for love. Difficult experiences are a part of life and a part of our growth process, but can also cause our fall from grace. While heartache, failure, and mistakes are a learning experience which creates a better Christian, a more compassionate counselor and a more loving bride for Christ, Satan works to destroy relationships in an effort to destroy faith. In addition to the temptations he brings, he also uses guilt, ego, pride, lust, fear, depression, hopelessness and the mistaken belief that we are required to remain in an ungodly relationship. Satan keeps us bound through these emotions. If we accept the premise that we can learn from our mistakes, that God forgives, and even that scripture indicates that God is a circumstantial God, perhaps we should examine scripture more closely for how the spiritual addresses the natural to learn how we should view this matter.

If the admonition not to *"putteth away his wife"* was issued for the benefit of believers, it teaches us to view our marriage as a lifetime commitment and *work* at loving, respecting, and forgiving one another. Scripture teaches us that the arranged marriages of early times did not always begin with love, but through respect, honor and commitment, love emerged and grew *from God's blessing.* In this we see a promise for the children of God who are *both* willing to keep their commitment despite their difficult circumstances. Instilling love into our hearts is how God blesses those who strive to keep His words. However, when there is *no* attempt to love and *no* commitment, *no* respect, and when evil rules one of the two who have married, scripture tells a completely different story. When all efforts have failed to bring the sinner to repentance, the spouse who finds themselves in the midst of constant satanic attack is advised to flee.

Being "unequally yoked" are the words used in the Bible to describe this phenomenon. Ephesians 5: 33 says, *"....let everyone of you in particular so love his wife even as himself; and the wife see she reverence her husband."* This verse describes the *equally yoked* couple. However when this does not occur, one may be **un**equally yoked. A yoke is a heavy wooden or leather neck harness worn by two oxen or horses. It joins them together, holding them in a side by side position. It forces them to work in synchronization to pull a heavy cart or plow. The yoke requires that they match their gait through the placement of their feet and body and synchronize their movements so the power of their weight and muscle will help them pull the load and equally share the burden. If their gait were not synchronized one would pull when the other did not and the load could tilt to one side causing them both to stumble. This is an excellent analogy of marriage. If one spouse is pulling properly and the other is not, both can fall as a result. Thus, it is important to marry someone with whom one is "equally yoked". In the *natural* sense they share the work, the burden and the joy of a home and family. In a *spiritual* sense, they have greater strength to serve God through that work, fight Satan through those burdens and share the joy of God's blessing on their union. They also have greater strength to maintain and protect their relationship.

When the going gets tough and Satan attacks, the yoke can be most effective. When we face difficult circumstances, and we pull together our character is proven to us, to those around us and to our Heavenly Father. However, when we are unequally yoked with an unbeliever or with unrighteousness, scripture clearly tells us to *"come out from among them and be separate"*. Thus, the faithful child of God who has made a valiant effort to be a good example and to help their spouse spiritually is *not* required to *stay* in an ungodly marriage. 2 Corinthians 6:14-18 tells us, *"Be ye not unequally yoked together with unbelievers: For what fellowship hath righteousness with unrighteousness? And what communion hath light with darkness? And what concord hath Christ with Belial? Or what part hath he that believeth with an infidel? And what agreement hath the temple of God with idols? For ye are the temple of the living God; as God hath said, I will dwell in them, and walk in them; and I will be their God, and they shall be my people. Wherefore come out from among them, and be ye separate, saith the Lord, and touch not the unclean thing; and I will receive you, And will be a Father unto you, and ye shall be my sons and daughters, saith the Lord Almighty"*

Bullet Points

There are many varying doctrines in the Christian faith.

The doctrine of the Catholic Church forbids divorce.

Scripture seems to indicate that there are exceptions to this rule.

God warns throughout scripture to flee from evil.

Being unequally yoked with darkness is not pleasing to God.

Scripture admonishes that one "come out from among them".

Supporting Scripture

Luke 16:18,	Matthew 19:6,
Ephesians 5:33,	2 Corinthians 6:14-18,
Titus 2:7,	Romans 14:1,
2 Corinthians 2:11,	Ephesians 5:11,
Hosea 4:6,	Luke 8:15,
2 Corinthians 7:1.	

Chapter Twenty Nine

PRAYERS THAT TOUCH GOD'S HEART

We may not realize how many times each day we pray because we tend to think only of our more formal prayers. But many times each day we may say a quick sentence or two of thanksgiving, or one of intercession. There is also the prayer in which we simply and informally talk to God about our life, our goals, our problems and our love for Him because we want to have an intimate and personal relationship with Our Heavenly Father. This becomes our own one-on-one experience during which we often feel and express great emotion. Then there is the prayer which we may enter into with our spouse, or spouse and children and perhaps other family members.

During these prayers, each person prays aloud creating a bond of faith and sharing what lives in one another's heart. This teaches children how to pray. It is in this prayer, which occurs once in the morning and once at night, where we desire to cover all the parts of a prayer which we believe is important to a complete communication with Our Heavenly Father. Prayer helps us in all things. All of us know the pain of heartache; we may have endured a difficult circumstance or may have watched someone we love suffer its pain. As children of God we understand that our Heavenly Father can turn all heartache into a blessing by giving us an opportunity to learn, and grow in faith from what we experience. But we also understand that we can become emotionally exhausted as we live through the changes which are brought by our heartache. Sadly, sometimes we feel guilty when we give in to feelings of depression, or hurt, or emotional exhaustion because we fear that this indicates that we are not trusting God with the outcome. God knows however, that emotional pain can be debilitating, as can our fears, and because we are impatient by nature we long for the change and the lesson to be instantaneous. In time however, we learn that as we pray, and as we mature in faith, we increase our trust in God, and this in turn allows us to develop a peaceful heart no matter what our circumstances.

God gave Christ souls who would be faithful to Him and who would become what scripture terms, "The Bride of Christ". Loving these souls, Christ prayed for them asking that His Father help them develop the faith they would need to be with Him forever. The 17th chapter in John, (John 17:1-26) is devoted to the prayer Christ prayed for His followers and in John 17:24, 25 we can read, *"Father, I will that they also, whom thou hast given me, be with me where I am; that they may behold my glory, which thou hast given me: for thou lovedst me before the foundation of the world. O righteous Father, the world hath not known thee: but I have known thee, and these have known that thou hast sent me."* Through this prayer we see the love Christ has for us and how fervently He pleads for us. Through His prayers we can learn how to pray and how to touch the heart of God.

Scripture warns against repetitious and public prayers and tells us in Matthew 6:7, *"But when ye pray, use not vain repetitions as the heathen do: for they think that they shall be heard for their much speaking"*. Acronyms can help us remember what we need to know by breaking our lesson into parts represented by a single letter and creating a word from those letters. The letters in an acronym represent a word used to trigger our memory. Thus it is helpful to select a single word containing a letter for each part of a prayer to help us include everything necessary to the perfect prayer. These words are praise, accountability, petition, protection, intercession and thanksgiving. If we use these words to form an acronym; a single word which helps us remember the parts we wish to include in every prayer, we might form the word "PAPPIT". PAPPIT would represent the following:

1. Praise: Praise God for His goodness and power and mercy
2. Accountability: Recount our sins, repent and ask for forgiveness and mercy
3. Petition: Ask God for help in the matters which concern us
4. Protection: Acknowledge and ask for God's protection
5. Intercession: Pray for those, alive and dead, in need spiritually and physically
6. Thanksgiving: Specifically thank God for all He has and will do for us

A relationship with God means that we communicate with Him and share the joys and sorrows in our heart. Repetition by rote does not encourage a close relationship, or provide a sincere heart to heart communication. By recounting our sins and the remorse we feel we humble ourselves before God and recognize our need for His grace. Further, God promises wonderful things when we come to Him in prayer. Matthew 7:7 tells us, *"Ask and it shall be given you; seek, and ye shall find; knock, and it shall be opened unto you."* We should pray many times during the day. Our morning prayer should include our thankfulness for what God has done for us and should contain a humble request for His guidance and protection throughout the day. Evening prayer should again contain our thankfulness for God's guidance and protection throughout the day, acknowledgement of His amazing love, grace and power, an intercession for others in need, and a humble request for His continued guidance, love and protection. Before leaving the safety of our homes, we should pray and ask God to accompany us and guide our steps, make our outing fruitful and secure through His protection. We should also pray before we eat thanking God for His provision and ask that He remove the curse and bless our food. Other prayers can be short and quick and cover an instant need or thank Him.

We must teach our children that with and through prayer, and their faithfulness they need not worry about their life, for God is always with them. Teach them that prayer, in the morning, at night, before each meal, when they leave the safety of their home, and whenever need, concern or thankfulness moves our heart, also moves God's heart to look after us. Teach the scripture which assures us that just as God looks after the birds, He will always look after us. Matthew 6:26 says, "B*ehold the* *fowls of the air; for they sow not, neither do they reap, nor gather into barns; yet your Heavenly Father feedeth them.Look at the birds of the air, for they neither sow nor reap nor gather into barns; yet your heavenly Father feedeth them."* And Matthew 10:29, 31 tells us *""Are not two sparrows sold for a farthing? And one of them shall not fall on the ground without your Father....Fear ye not therefore..."* God does not want us to pray the same repetitious prayer over and over again because we rush through words so familiar that we don't hear or listen to their meaning. God wants us to have an intimate relationship with Him by talking with Him as we would with someone we love. Prayers that are short but from the heart are better than long memorized prayers. Neither does He want us to use these repetitious prayers publicly where we will direct our attention to how we sound to an audience. God is truly our Father in Heaven, He loves us like a father loves his children and tells us in Matthew 6:5, *"And when thou prayest, thou shalt not be as the hypocrites are: for they love to pray...that they may be seen..."*

Near the end of the prayer we pray each night, we can intercede even for those we have never met. We can ask our Heavenly Father to give a hearing unto all the pleas and petitions of His children all over the world. Then we can plead that if Our Heavenly Father cannot answer those prayers now, He nevertheless, will let His children know that He keeps them in the hollow of His hand; and offers them a peaceful heart. The power of prayer offers us the greatest rewards and can mean the difference between life and death, between hope and hopelessness, between foolishness and wisdom. James 1:5 tells us, *"If any of you lack wisdom, let him ask of God, that giveth to all men liberally, and upbraideth not; and it shall be given him."* And one of the most wonderful promises in scripture can be found in Deuteronomy 11:13-14: *"And it shall come to pass, if ye shall hearken diligently unto My commandments which I command you this day, to love the Lord your God and to serve Him with all your heart and with all your soul, that I will give you the rain of your land in his due season, the first rain and the latter rain, that thou mayest gather in thy corn, and thy wine, and thine oil."*

Pray for wisdom in God's ways and ask for the wisdom to understand scripture and to place our steps where we will be pleasing in the sight of God. Little by little our understanding and our faith will increase and our thoughts and actions will follow accordingly. Praying with sincerity and to communicate with God brings about change and results in a welcome and joyous peace and trust. Our prayers touch God's heart. He sees past our words and into our hearts. Nothing is hidden from Him. He knows whether or not we are truly humble, how thankful we are, and how sincere we are. He doesn't want us to pray by rote (Matthew 6:5-7) or to impress. He wants to hear a longing in us to be with Him, to serve him and those He loves. He wants to know that we desire to learn of Him and to do our best to follow that which He asks of us. But He also wants to show us that He listens, He hears us, He loves us, and that He has the power to change us, change our lives and create in us those who long to be the Bride of Christ. That is the wonder of prayer!

Bullet Points

Prayer is imperative to our soul life.

When our prayers are not repetitious we please God. PAPPIT is an acronym which can help us remember what to include in our prayers.

PAPPIT means praise, accountability, petition, protection, intercession, and thanksgiving.

It is important for all Christians to teach their children how and when to pray.

Praying for wisdom and understanding will help us learn and grow as Christians.

Supporting Scripture

Matthew 6:5,	John 17:1-26,
Matthew 6:7,	James 1:5,
Deuteronomy 11:13-14,	Matthew 7:7,
Matthew 6:26,	Matthew 10:29, 31.

Chapter Thirty

THE ELUSIVENESS OF SELF ESTEEM

Sadly, so many of us believe that to be a Christian means that we must not cause others to become angry and that we must be tolerant and forgiving in all things. This is a perversion of scripture and a misrepresentation of what God asks of us. The confusion this belief creates is the prime reason why we have little confidence, little conviction and low self-esteem.

What we have misunderstood is that much of scripture refers to how we are to interact with other **believers** and provides different advice when we speak with unbelievers who engage in actions which are displeasing to God. Titus 1:10 tells us, *"For there are many unruly and vain talkers and deceivers...."* And in Titus 1:16 *"They profess that they know God; but in works they deny him, being abominable, and disobedient, and unto every good work reprobate."*

Our response must be what Titus 2:7-8 tells us: *"In all things shewing thyself a pattern of good works: in doctrine showing uncorruptness, gravity, sincerity. Sound speech that cannot be condemned; that he that is of the contrary part may be ashamed, having no evil thing to say of you.* Titus 2:15 tells us, *"These things speak, and exhort, and rebuke with all authority...."*

However, we cannot speak with authority if we do not know God's words or what is meant by them, and sadly, when we find ourselves bereft of the information needed to successfully stand as a Christian, we retreat. This feeds the spirit of our lack of self esteem. We understand that we should know God's words. We understand that we should have stood up for our faith. We also know that we have no viable excuse for not doing these things which God asks of us. Thus we avoid the embarrassment which would demonstrate that we have been remiss and which would also demonstrate our failure to those who attack God or godly principles.

The psychological ramifications are great when we continue to brush aside our duty, especially our duty to God. And God clearly warns us in Hosea 4:6 that: *"My people are destroyed for lack of knowledge......"* This verse applies to every issue a Christian faces and is the core reason we fail and may not be found worthy.

Without self esteem, without a sense of who we are and what we stand for, we will never be effective in our faith. A lack of self-esteem, which grows out of a lack of understanding, can harm every aspect of our lives. Our relationship with spouse and children, our business aspirations, and most importantly, our faith are all adversely affected. Scripture even tells us that to know and acknowledge God is *"...health to thy navel, and marrow to thy bones."* (Proverbs 3:8)

Proverbs 3:3-6 tells us, *"Let not mercy and truth forsake thee; bind them about thy neck; write them upon the table of thine heart. So shalt thou find favor and good understanding in the sight of God and man. Trust in the Lord with all thine heart; and lean not to your own understanding. In all thy ways, acknowledge him and he shall direct thy paths."*

In scripture, the word truth refers to the word of God. Scripture teaches that unless everything we do and think and say is based on the word of God, we will be unable to discern between perverted doctrine and sound wisdom and without knowing the word of God we will stumble. Proverbs 3:23 tells us, *"Then shall thou walk in thy way safely, and thy foot shall not stumble. When thou liest down, thou shalt not be afraid: yea, thou shal lie down, and thy sleep shall be sweet.* Proverbs 3:26 *promises, "For the Lord shall be thy confidence, and shall keep thy foot from being taken."*

These words assure us that if we learn God's words, do our best to apply them, and speak them when we stand up for our faith, we will never have to be afraid, never lack confidence, or lose sleep. Further, Philippians 4:7 assures us, *"And the peace of God, which passeth all understanding, shall keep your hearts and minds through Jesus Christ."* Philippians 4:19 says, *"......God shall supply all your need......"* And 1 Peter 5:7 tells us, *"Casting all your care upon him; for he careth for you."*

We must also cast off all confusion and not overlook sin, nor be tolerant of sin unless there is remorse and the effort to change. We must as Christians stand up for godly principles and become a beacon of stedfastness without becoming withholding deserved forgiveness. We must be longsuffering and patient even when we feel or express anger, and not judge nor seek revenge. We can pray for guidance and seek direction in scripture. All these increase our self-esteem.

God has promised us His never ending help when we learn His words and apply them. No one can ask for better promises and no one can provide a better gift to their children than by teaching them these truths. Thus, as Christians, to gain self-esteem, to conquer self doubt and the psychological ramifications of fear and anxiety which today's society imposes on us, we need to immerse ourselves in the word of God. Then when we stand up in confidence to fight for our faith, using God's own words, He will reward us with the self-esteem we need to bring forth our strength and courage….and our loyalty. We can then express our joy and share the good news of being a Christian. Furthermore, we will have God's blessing and His protection.

Bullet Points

Fear, anxiety and confusion rob us of our self-esteem.

Lack of self-esteem can be overcome when we know God's words.

Using the authority of God's words to exhort and rebuke gives us confidence and protection.

God warns that we can be destroyed by a lack of knowledge.

Scripture tells us that we will be given health when we speak and apply sound doctrine.

We are promised peace, confidence, safety, sweet sleep, and favor when we know God's words.

<u>Supporting Scripture</u>

Titus 1:10,	Titus 1:16,
Titus 2:7-8,	Titus 2:15,
Hosea 4:6,	Proverbs 3:8,
Proverbs 3:3-6,	Proverbs 3:26,
Philippians 4:7,	Philippians 4:19,
1 Peter 5:7.	

Chapter Thirty One

WHEN DEVASTATING LIFE CHANGES OCCUR

There are times when a Christian finds himself laboring under a tremendous heartache which appears impossible to remedy. They may have reflected on their faith and done everything they know how to do to please God. They may have labored to change whatever mistakes once governed their lives, yet the situation in which they find themselves does not change. After months or years of struggle, of doing their best to learn and practice God's words, and of praying for help, and no help appears to arrive, they sometimes ask God why this has occurred, and may even ask where is God in their lives.

Satan will often use that sense of despair to rob us of our hope and our faith, and capture us with a spirit of depression to prevent our faith from being active. When we are about to be freed from one spirit, Satan will try to bind us with another. It is a classical part of spiritual warfare that when we are finally to overcome something which had been holding us back from becoming all that God sees in us, Satan brings us something else to keep us in captivity. Thus it can seem that we make no progress in our natural lives, nor in our spiritual lives.

What we need to understand is that during these difficult times, huge changes are taking place which we cannot see. We may have been under the control of a spirit which requires a great deal of time to remove, we may have harbored a secret desire to go back to the way things were before the start of our heartache, or we may need to rid ourselves of the influences of inherited sin which scripture tells us can be passed from generation to generation. God may also be preparing another person or event that will change our circumstance. What we need to believe is that if God has brought us to a crossroad, and we strive to be faithful, He will see us through it and that He *always* brings a blessing from it.

For countless souls, the breakup of a long term marriage is devastating to only one of the two in the relationship. Since it affects one's self-esteem and then also may demand a sharing, or even the loss, of a close relationship with children, former in-laws, common friends, a home and income, it is an excellent example of the trauma which can occur with a life changing event. It requires changes within every aspect of one's life. Its loss removes an existing support system from our lives and demands a greater and more complete reliance on God. It therefore requires the support of their bearers of blessing and fellow believers. It also requires that the bad behavior of others not become a personal need for revenge (Romans 12:19) and instead become a lesson in forgiveness. (Matthew 6:14) There are difficult tasks we face when we have been unfairly hurt by someone we once trusted. But God does know better than we what is good for us. While Satan may take something from us, God will allow it because *He can see* that what we had would have, in time, harmed us and harmed our soul salvation. He promises to comfort us as we go through the trial of fire which Satan may have brought but which God will use to purify us and lead us to greener pastures. Matthew 11:28 tells us, *"Come unto me, all ye that labour and are heavy laden, and I will give you rest."*

We face a similar heartache when we lose our job or home, or health. Each can be devastating. When we are exhausted from the struggle we face, if we know the comforting words of scripture we can find the help we need. Philippians 4:13 tells us *"I can do all things through Christ which strengtheneth me."* We will also understand that God will supply all our needs, even if they are supplied at the very last moment or not in the time or fashion we expected. Philippians 4:19 tells us *"But my God shall supply all your need....."* Even the fear we feel is addressed by scripture and we can read in 11 Timothy 1:7, *"For God hath not given us the spirit of fear; but of power, and of love, and of a sound mind."*

We will also accept the change we require more quickly *if we can believe* that God will use our heartache to teach us, make our future better, and bring us through and out of our heartache a better child of God than when we entered that heartache. Hebrews 13:5 tells us, *"Let your conversation be without covetousness; and be content with such things as ye have; for he hath said, "I will never leave thee, nor forsake thee."* It isn't easy to let go of the things we once cherished. It's even more difficult if we lost something which we did not care for properly and believe we lost because of our negligence. But God allows devastating life changes to occur to help us learn and change, and bring us into the fullness of His love and provision. This requires us to stifle our Adam-like nature and bring forth the new man, the Christ-like nature which God can bless and which He seeks for His new kingdom. It is not an easy task for us, but it is a task that once accomplished, will cause God to say of us, *"....Well done, thou good and faithful servant; thou hast been faithful over a few things. I will make thee ruler over many things; enter thou into the joy of the Lord".* (Matthew 25:21)

We cannot remain where we were, for if Christ came, we would be like the five foolish virgins of whom we are told, *"And while they went to bed, the bridegroom came; and they that were ready went with him to the marriage; and the door was shut. Afterward came also the other virgins, saying, Lord, Lord open to us. But he answered and said, Verily I say unto you, I know you not."* (Matthew 25:10-12) Thus when faced with difficulties, our strength lies in trusting that God is providing us with a new life through which we can become worthy and be ready when the bridegroom comes…and perhaps find much greater joy in what will be our new future!

If we can hold on during these times of great heartache, we can use the time to learn God's words and ask Him to let us use His words not only to learn and thereby mature in our faith, but also to comfort and be comforted. Then we can rest in the words of 1 Corinthians 15:58, *"Therefore, my beloved brethren, be ye stedfast, unmoveable, always abounding in the work of the Lord, forasmuch as ye know that your labour in not in vain in the Lord."*

Bullet Points

Sometimes the children of God suffer undeservedly at the hands of others.

Heartbreaking events are used by Satan to break our faith.

Heartbreaking events are used by God to create a faithful child of God.

The lessons for forgiveness are tantamount to recovery.

Spirits of this world do not want to let us go without a fight.

Scripture shows us what to do when we experience a devastating event.

Supporting Scripture

Romans 12:19,   Matthew 6:14,

Matthew 11:28,   Philippians 4:13,

11 Timothy 1:7,   Hebrews 13:5,

Matthew 25:21,   1 Corinthians 15:58.

Chapter Thirty Two

NO JOB, NO MONEY, NO GOD

The easiest way for Satan to break our faith is to take something from us and push us into despair over that loss. Whether rich or poor it is human nature to hate loss and wish for the return of what we had considered "ours". This attitude comes from the old Adam-like nature rather than the new godly nature which God wants us to have. Nevertheless, when we experience loss we expect that in time, with prayer, God will return what was taken from us.

Our response to physical pain is easily understood, but we don't always acknowledge that emotional pain can be just as difficult to bear. We tend to feel guilty when we express emotional pain, but somehow feel less guilt to admit to physical pain. Further, scripture tells us in Romans 8:28, *"All things work together for the good of those that love the Lord."* Thus we often feel that we must always wear a happy face regardless of how or why we suffer.

We understand, as children of God, that Satan brings us our heartache, physically, emotionally and spiritually, and that our Heavenly Father in His loving kindness and the righteousness under which He works, promises to turn those heartaches into a blessing. But we seldom acknowledge that our Heavenly Father has ordained that, because of sin, our lives have become our training ground whereby we learn how to become all that God hopes us to become. Therefore He allows our difficult circumstances to become a marker of our character development and the readiness required in those who will become the Bride He wants for His Son.

But there are times when we live through heartache or witness the heartache of those we love, when we ask ourselves privately how this promise of good from all circumstances could be possible. While we believe that scripture is God's personal, accurate and irrefutable instruction, seldom do we think to ask Him to unravel the mystery attached to His words and help us recognize their miracle and internalize how they are to be utilized. We suffer in silence and do not admit that inwardly we rail at what we face and then feel guilty about our private thoughts. The return of the happiness we have attached to what was lost becomes not only our new hope, but also our expectation. Yet the truth may be that what we want is not good for us.

Nevertheless, we argue that we were relatively good and faithful and will now become even better people and more faithful in the future and therefore, God being all powerful, will help us *by restoring* what we have lost.

As we lose patience with waiting or we begin to think that this time we may *not* obtain restoration, we immediately blame God and wonder why He has not helped. What we may have forgotten is that Satan is alive and well and his goal is to break our faith, while God's goal is create in us the worthiness to become the bride of Christ and…..that Satan uses people to harm people. What we may also have forgotten is that the reward which God promises His children may come only after great sacrifice and after being tried in the fire. Those who were not faithful may find this a time for reflection and a return to their faith while those who were faithful may not do this. The faithful may then be in greater jeopardy of wondering whether or not God is in control. This attitude can cause our anger and impatience to be directed toward God and not toward Satan or toward what we might be lacking. It is a terrible thing to suffer and to see that what we have worked for, hoped for, took for granted or expected, has suddenly disappeared and seems to be irreversibly gone. It is even more difficult when those who depend upon us also must suffer from our loss. Sometimes we must ask God "Why?"

As we move through our times of despair we may understand that we must strive to believe that God is with us and that we can trust Him to bring us through the difficulty we face. But to do this, we have to have a certain amount of peace in our hearts to function properly. Peace is a precious commodity and most of us try to preserve the peace we have, but sometimes we falter and our troubles take peace from our hearts.

Scripture tells us that both our Heavenly Father and His Son offer us their peace when we need help. Philippians

4:19 tells us, "*"And the peace of God, which passeth all understanding, shall keep your hearts and minds through Jesus Christ."*

John 14:27 tells us that Christ saud: *"Peace I leave with you, my peace I give unto you; not as the world giveth, give I unto you. Let not your heart be troubled, neither let it be afraid."*

And Philippians 4:13 assures us, *"I can do all things through Christ which strengtheneth me"*. But what do we do when we lose our strength and our peace? And why do we lose it? Scripture tells us that Satan attacks the children of God and that he knows where we are the most vulnerable. We also learn from scripture that God allows Satan to attack us because during that attack we are given the opportunity to grow in faith and be refined in the process. God would not offer strength if He did not know we would need it.

Further, we know that when scripture uses the word "world" it often means Satan or the evil which Satan inspires. John 15:18 tells us, *"If the world hate you, ye know that it hated me before it hated you. If ye were of the world, the world would love his own; but because I have chosen you out of the world, therefore the world hateth you."*

John 16:20 says, *"Verily, verily, I say unto you, That ye shall weep and lament, but the world shall rejoice; and ye shall be sorrowful, but your sorrow shall be turned into joy."*

If one substitutes the word "Satan" for the word "world" in these verses we can understand what God is telling us. While it will not take away the trials and tribulation we must endure, it does fill our heart with thankfulness that God comforts us through His words and gives us the assurance that we are His and that our sorrow will one day turn to joy. Once Satan sees that we understand what is occurring and that our heart is filled with thankfulness for the very thing which Satan thought would destroy us, he *leaves*. He's lost that battle!

As we examine scripture, we can also see that perhaps we are too hard on ourselves. What scripture really says about the expression of the fear, or pain, or sorrow we experience is best understood as we examine what Christ lived through and what He felt and expressed. His reaction can become our example. Christ spoke the words, *"Take away this cup from me"*, which clearly demonstrates that He did not want to go through what He knew He had to face. He asked God not to have Him have to endure what He knew was to be a terrible experience. While our pain cannot begin to emulate the pain Christ endured for us, we should not feel guilty if we wish, or ask God, to change our circumstances. But we can learn from the love in the heart of Christ and the trust He had in His Father. It allowed Him to submit to His sacrifice for us and produce the character in His soul which caused Him to utter the words, *"Nevertheless, not what I will, but what thou will"* ....after asking for it to be removed.

This is our example. God certainly allows us to express our fear, the pain we feel, and our wish that our circumstances were different. It is not that we are judged and found lacking when we ask God to take our troubles away, but that we end up *accepting* God's will and doing our best to *use* those circumstances to prove our character.

Our troubles will then become an indicator of the trust and acceptance which lives in our heart for the decisions of our Heavenly Father....no matter what the circumstances are. How we handle our troubles become, in essence, a marker of our spiritual maturity and our spiritual character. The miracle which occurs when we *adjust* our thoughts and actions, as Christ did when facing His heartrending circumstances, is that once we submit to God's will, our heartaches often become easier to bear, or simply disappear if the adjustment was accepted or the lesson was learned.

Once Satan realizes that he cannot break our faith, nor break our trust, there is no reason for him to continue his harassment. We then, are not only often released from Satan's captivity, but are also wiser and more trustworthy for having mastered the test which God arranged these circumstances bring to us.

Certainly it is difficult to experience heartache whether it comes from the death of a child, a debilitating disease, devastating betrayal, or watching someone we love suffer. Examining Christ's plea that God remove the cup from which He was to drink, and then His words of submission, we begin to understand what this effort cost Him. When we understand what Christ endured, and better appreciate His sacrifice, our own suffering is so much less because we recognize that it benefits us and perhaps those we love.

Mark 14:34 tells us of the emotional pain Christ suffered when we read Christ's words: *"My soul is exceedingly sorrowful unto death."* Mark 14:36 tells us that when Christ prayed, He said, *"Abba Father, all things are possible unto thee. Take away this cup from me, nevertheless not what I will but what thou will."* What few of us realize is that Christ later even repeated this plea a second time.

Asking God a second time was indicative of how much He was suffering as he thought of what was to come. Mark 14:39 tells us, *"and again He went away and prayed, and spoke the same words."* Therefore, if we are caught up in a circumstance which seems to have no end, or be unfair, we need not feel guilty when we ask God to let our circumstances pass, as long as our heart truly desires that God's will be paramount. This is indicative of the trust we place in God's design for our lives and perhaps the lives of those we love. Further, by trying to be more introspective and asking ourselves if we trust that which is occurring for our good, as scripture teaches, and whether or not we are willing to endure our circumstances in order to develop our character, we can grow into the Bride God desires for His Son.

Once we reflect on these questions and ask our Heavenly Father to help us learn from everything we experience, we can move with all our heart and with great sincerity from the words *"Take this away"* to the words, *"Thy will be done"*. This allows God access to our hearts and the ability to create the change in us which we require.

Christ dreaded the circumstances which He was to live through. He was afraid, He found Himself without any earthly support, and without a true and loyal friend. Christ's cup was a bitter one; it was the most bitter cup of circumstances we could imagine, yet because of His love for us, He stood firm and He trusted and obeyed what His Heavenly Father ordained.

Satan threw everything he had against Christ, but Christ remained stedfast. Thus, the Bride of Christ must remain firm in her trust and obedience to God and bring her sorrow and fear to God with honesty. She can be assured that God loves her, sees her tears, carries her through all circumstances, and creates a blessing from them

Our character, which is comprised of our ability to love and forgive, to have compassion and understanding, to submit to God's will, to be loyal and to trust God implicitly will be measured by how we deal with our circumstances. Those who have developed these attributes will be a part of the five wise, and not the five foolish virgins, and found worthy to go with the Lord when He takes His Bride. Our suffering, and our trials and tribulations, are for our greater good and how we handle them will be an example to those around us. How we approach adversity is a marker of our spiritual maturity. These are but a few of the blessings which God creates from our heartache and why all things work for the good of those who love the Lord.

Perhaps we have no job, no money and may have even thought for a moment that God does not hear us, but when we know God's words and take to heart the comfort of His words, we have defeated evil and we have come through the fire, and we know that soon God will bless us. Further, we will never fall to a point where we cannot be lifted up again and be better for the experience. The story of Job clearly shows us that God can restore all things and that if we remain faithful and trust Him He is bound in His righteousness to walk with us and carry us through all things.

Bullet Points

Suffering a serious loss can become a great spiritual opportunity.

Pain and heartache, worry and fear are natural consequences of loss.

Satan works through these senses to break our faith.

The word "world" in scripture often refers to Satan.

When we understand what Satan is doing and why, he loses his hold on us.

When we are thankful for what we learned by our loss, God blesses us.

Supporting Scripture

Philippians 4:19,	John 14:27,
Philippians 4:13,	John 15:18,
John 16:20,	1 Peter 5:8,
Proverbs 3:26,	2 Corinthians 2:11,
Genesis 3:1,	Hosea 4:6.

Chapter Thirty Three

PRETTY AND PETTY PRIDE

There are 49 verses in scripture which contain the word pride. Each of these verses condemns pride as an attitude displeasing to God, and defiling to man. Webster's Dictionary defines the word pride as "inordinate self-esteem, conceit, delight or elation with a position, possession or relationship, disdainful, and haughty". Roget's Thesaurus lists the words "egotism", "arrogant" and "regarding oneself with undue favor" as synonyms.

There are many reasons why we develop pride. Often it is because of an asset we project to others such as beauty, intelligence, wealth, talent, power, position or eloquent speech. Ironically, these are gifts which God gave us, not those we developed through hard work and perseverance. Being proud of an accomplishment toward which we labored and for which we thank God is very different than exhibiting pride to exalt ourselves above others. As we read the verses in scripture which address pride, we learn that in most of them God warns that those with pride will be brought down. Isaiah 25:11 tells us *"And he shall spread forth his hands in the midst of them, as he that swimmeth spreadeth forth his hands to swim; and he shall bring down their pride together with the spoils of their hands."* Daniel 5:20 warns, *"But when his heart was lifted up, and his mind hardened in pride, he was deposed from his kingly throne, and they took his glory from him."* Obadiah 2-4 tells us, *"Behold, I have made thee small.....thou art greatly despised....The pride of thy heart hath deceived thee....though thou exalt thyself as the eagle....I bring thee down saith the Lord."*

Yet, despite the foolishness of man and his fall from grace, God always gives us a second chance for redemption; a second chance to change our ways by learning His words, and from them, how we are to conduct ourselves, and what is pleasing or displeasing to Him. God graciously forgives our mistakes. But if we *enjoy* the evil which brings pride and arrogance into our lives, and do not know or heed God's words, the day will come when we can be overwhelmed by this spirit, no longer obtain grace, and may lose our soul salvation. The book of Proverbs provides the most comprehensive instruction about pride and how it will impact our spiritual life. Proverbs clearly tells us that pride is a spirit which is evil and must be exorcized from our heart. Specifically, Proverbs 16:18 tells us, *"Pride goweth before destruction, and a haughty spirit before a fall."* Proverbs 8:13 says, *"The fear of the Lord is to hate evil: pride, and arrogancy, and the evil way, and the forward mouth do I hate."* Proverbs 11:2 tells us, *"When pride cometh, then cometh shame...."* Proverbs 29:23 warns, *"A man's pride shall bring him low...."*

Zephaniah also makes reference to pride as emanating evil when it says that pride is from a "god of the earth". Zephaniah 2:10-11 tells us, *"This shall they have for their pride, because they have reproached and magnified themselves against the people of the Lord of hosts. The Lord will be terrible unto them; for he will famish the gods of the earth....."*

Further, defining pride as evil is addressed in Mark 7:20-23 where we are told, *"....That which cometh out of the man, that defileth the man. For from within, out of the heart of men, proceed evil thoughts...an evil eye....pride....All these evil things come from within and defile the man."* All of the warnings about pride can be summed up in two verses, one from 1 John and another from 1 Timothy. The verse from 1 John 2:16 tells us: *"For all that is in the world, the lust of the flesh, and the lust of the eyes, and the pride of life, is not of the Father, but is of the world. And the world passeth away, and the lust thereof: but he that doeth the will of God abideth forever."* And the verse from 1 Timothy 3:6 warns, *"....lest being lifted up with pride he fall into the condemnation of the devil."*

There are also a number of passages throughout scripture which provide insight into the progress we make as children of God. They are benchmarks by which we can gauge our progress as an overcomer and help us understand what we can and cannot accomplish. But what we sometimes forget is that without being humbled...often....we would not be brought back to the reality of our personal and deadly sin. Scripture tells us that not only are we sinners, but that our hearts are evil. Despite our struggles to become more Christ-like in nature, we fall far from that goal and can only make changes in our lives through Our Heavenly Father and by the grace He has provided through Christ. 1 Corinthians 12:7-11 tells us that even the Apostle Paul had to be reminded of his fallibility. He asked God to remove the thorn from his side and God answered by telling him to bear the thorn because God's grace would be sufficient to cover it. It was this "thorn" or "failing" which kept the Apostle Paul humble, kept reminding him that he was imperfect, and that without God's intervention he could never be found worthy. And Paul was then thankful for it! Scripture also tells us that what we see as a great fault in others pales in comparison to our own faults. Matthew 7:3-5 explains that there may be a speck in the eye of someone with whom we find fault and a beam in our own. Yet our human nature fights against acknowledging that this could be true. We easily rationalize and justify our faults, and maximize the fault in others. But the beauty of our faith is that once we begin to acknowledge our faults we begin to change. God steps in out of His incredible love to allow us to stumble, even to occasionally make fools of ourselves, so that we will experience embarrassment, sadness, remorse or even anger but we are then forced to acknowledge our imperfections and we lose the pride which can be so damaging to our soul.

When children witness the actions of those who are quick to acknowledge their mistakes, quick to forgive mistakes in others, and quick to give praise to God in all things, they learn… at an early age… those things which others struggle for many years to learn. Children are our future and sadly many are not being taught about Satan and what God wants us to learn. Children learn pride from prideful parents and learn humbleness by watching their parents remain humble.

Bullet Points

Scripture lists the word pride in 49 verses.

The word pride also means arrogance and conceit.

All verses containing the word pride condemn pride as evil.

Pride does not come from God.

Pride comes from a satanic spirit that enters the heart.

Everyone with pride will eventually be brought down.

Supporting Scripture

Proverbs 8:13, Proverbs 11:2,

Proverbs 16:18, Proverbs 29:23,

Mark 7:20-23, 1 Timothy 3:6,

1 John 2:16, Zephaniah 2:10,

Obadiah 2-4, Daniel 5:20,

Jeremiah 48:29, Isaiah 28:1,

Isaiah 25:11.

Chapter Thirty Four

SHOULD CHRISTIANS MAKE WAVES?

When writing this book, an incredible wave of patriotism and a return to Biblical principles began to flood this country. Ministers and Rabbi's from all across the country stood with incredible courage to speak to their members about the faith of the founding fathers and the Biblical references found in their speeches. Hundreds of thousands of people learned the history which had been removed from textbooks yet demonstrated the influence which the faith of the founding fathers had and used in the creation of our Constitution and our Declaration of Independence.

The founding fathers were people of faith who created a wave which resulted in an incredible patriotism, but also one which brought Christian/Judaic values into that patriotism. It was a wave heard across the country and across the oceans and began to influence everything from what parents taught their children to how parents planned to cast their political votes. It was and remains a wave which surely brought joy to the heart of God because it rose in defense and appreciation of the gifts He had provided for His people and for the nation they were establishing. And it took only a few people to start this movement. Thus, the answer to this question is an unequivocal "Yes, Christians should make waves." They should protect what God gave them.

If we look into Biblical history, we find that Christ made waves through the simplicity of His words and the unwavering doctrine of love He taught to the people of that time. As we follow the work of His Apostles, we also see the waves made by these men as they went forth with great courage to preach that same unwavering doctrine despite constant threats to their lives. Throughout history Christianity has flourished because a few men had the courage to fight against tremendous odds to keep faith alive and to spread the Gospel. Those who had the courage to make these waves understood the words of 1 Peter 5:1-2 where he said, *"The elders which are among you I exhort, who am also an elder, and a witness of the suffering of Christ, and also a partaker of the glory that shall be revealed: Feed the flock of God which is among you, taking oversight thereof, not by constraint, but willingly; not for filthy lucre, but of a ready mind:...."* They also believed the words in 1 Peter 5:8 which said, *"Be sober, be vigilant; because your adversary the devil, as a roaring lion, walketh about, seeking to devour whom he may devour."*

Because they were aware of the power of that roaring lion, the devil, they also knew that they would meet with resistance. Even today we must guard against false doctrine, greedy men, corrupt governments... and not be inspired and tempted by the devil who works to destroy a people and a nation "under God". We know from scripture, Acts 20:29 that Christ said, *"For I know this, that after my departing shall grievous wolves enter in among you, not sparing the flock."* This verse specifically warns that the danger will come from those "among" us and therefore be a subtle danger for which we must prepare and watch. Scripture warns about false doctrines, lukewarm attentiveness to God's words, and those who will deceive through vain talk. Titus 1:10 says *"For there were many unruly and vain talkers and deceivers....."* Revelation 3:16 tells us, *"So then because thou art lukewarm, and neither cold nor hot, I will spue thee out of my mouth."* And Mark 13:22 warns, *"For false Christ's and false prophets shall rise, and shall show signs and wonders, to seduce, if it were possible, even the elect."*

By learning God's words, through study, discussion and clarification when listening to our ministers and teachers, and by having fellowship with other believers, we keep from becoming lukewarm and learn to watch for false prophets and deceivers. Many have taken this one step further by writing, speaking, visiting, teaching and sharing God's words and warnings with others. Each of these children of God make small waves which extend further and further in a ripple effect as others pass on what they too have learned from their message. Those with the opportunity to reach many souls make larger waves which inspires even larger groups of people to remember God's admonitions for the end times in which we live. Sadly, many parents have not created a wave of faith and inspiration in their children, nor joined the revivals such as those which have so recently been sweeping our country. They have not worked to protect what God has provided for them through the founding fathers of this country. Some are simply lazy, and do not appreciate nor work to uphold the gifts they have received. Those who did not teach their children and whose children are now adults and also afraid to "make waves" thus do not stand up to protect those gifts from God, must begin to appreciate the liberties and freedoms they have been given... or they will lose them.

We all need to examine our Christian gumption and ask ourselves if we have made any waves of faith or have simply allowed complacency to rule our lives. Just as the Holy Ghost came upon thousands of people during the first Pentecost, so too has God answered the prayers of those intervening for the current unbelief and complacency and the current destruction of Biblical values by sending this new wave of faith and appreciation. God is giving us a second chance and warns in Revelation 3:3, *"Remember therefore how thou hast received and heard and hold fast, and repent. If therefore thou shalt not watch, I will come on thee as a thief, and thou shalt not know what hour I will come upon thee."*

We need to be thankful for any wave made by any true Christian, and become a part of that wave. For if we do not learn and listen now, and make changes now, we may come home to a house which is empty of faith and a country that is no longer free... and we may never have another chance to obtain it.

Bullet Points

Christians should definitely make waves to bring about a revival of faith.

Christians should definitely make waves to warn of false prophets and doctrines.

Christians should definitely make waves which will draw their children to God's words.

Christians are being given a second chance to get their house in order before the end times.

Christian's who are lukewarm in practicing their faith will be "spued" from God's mouth.

Christians should make waves themselves whether it is a small ripple or a large wave.

Making Christian waves applies to our country as well as our homes and churches.

Supporting Scripture

Acts 20:29,   Mark 13:22,

Revelation 3:16,   Revelation 3:3,

Titus 1:10,   1 Peter 5:8,

1 Peter 5:1-2.

Chapter Thirty Five
THE APOCRYPHA

The Bible is a divine record of God's plan of salvation and teaches God's children why and how they must strive to become a part of the Bride of Christ. The Bride of Christ consists of those souls who seek and practice God's word, remain faithful during great tribulation, and whom Christ will take to heaven at the First Resurrection. The Bible provides examples and stories, warnings and promises which instruct the children of God in what they need to do to protect themselves from satanic influence and to prepare themselves for the return of Christ.

The Bible consists of 17 historical books, 17 prophetical books, 5 doctrinal books, and 15 apocryphal books. Not all Bibles contain the Apocryphal books. The Apocryphal books are generally historic, but the Second Book of Esdras is prophetic and incredibly timely for what we are witnessing in the world today. As we read the second book written by the prophet Esdras, we see that God commands Esdras to reprove the people and preach the grace of God. In the course of his work, Esdras asks many questions of God and is provided with the answers. His questions are those which many Christians ask today and thus reading 11 Esdras provides us with both a warning and a comfort.

Many church hymns contain references to the words found in the Apocrypha as does many speeches given by early political figures. Thus we know that the Apocrypha was well read in earlier days. While the Apocrypha is not found in all Bibles, many Bibles do contain these books and place them in the center of the Bible between the Old and New Testament.

Herewith is a short synopsis of that which the second book of Esdras reveals throughout its chapters. It is formulated by gathering only a few words from its many chapters to provide an overall view of the communication between God and Esdras, and is therefore not entirely in context.

In 11 Esdras 6:19 God says, *"And I will call to account those who have caused harm with their unrighteousness...."* In 11 Esdras 7:21, *"For God hath earnestly commanded them who come into this world what they....shall do that they may live, and what they should observe to avoid punishment."*

11 Esdras 7:43 tells us, *"....the day of judgment shall be the end of this time....and the beginning of the time of future immortality, in which the temporal shall be past."* And in 11 Esdras 8:35, *"....and among the faithful there is none which hath not done amiss."* 11 Esdras

8:45 pleads, *"....be not wroth with us, but spare thy people....for thou art merciful unto thy creature."*

11 Esdras 9:7, 8, 10 says: *" ...everyone will be saved by his works, and by faith....preserved from the impending perils, and shall see my salvation... For such as have not acknowledged me....any my....law....must after death recognize it in torment."* 11 Esdras 10:21, 23 says: *" ....thou seest our sanctuary laid waste, our altar broken down, ...delivered into the hands of them that hate us."*

11 Esdras 12; 23-30 explains: *" ....in the last times, the Most High shall raise up three kingdoms with much trouble....that repeat...godless conduct....one shall devour the other and the other full of confusion and unrest".* And 11 Esdras 13: 23-24 tells us: *".... he that endure....have works, and faith towards the Almighty....are more blessed than they that be dead."* 11 Esdras 13: 37-38 says: *".... my Son...shall lay before them their evil thoughts, and the torments wherewith they shall begin to be tormented......"*

11 Esdras 14:11-13 tells us: *"For the time is divided in twelve parts and nine of them and half of the tenth part are all past. But the time after half of the tenth part remaineth yet, therefore set thy house in order......."*

And in 11 Esdras 14:17, *" .....more shall the evil be multiplied upon them that dwell therein."* 11 Esdras 15:9 says, *"I will avenge them speedily".* And 11 Esdras 15:37, *"Great fear and trembling shall be on earth"* and in 11 Esdras 15:19, *"A man should have no pity upon his neighbor...."*

In 11 Esdras 16:19 we read, *"....famine, plague, tribulations and anguish are sent as a scourge"* and in verse 54, *"Behold, the Lord knoweth all the works of men, their imaginations, their thoughts, and their hearts."*

11 Esdras 16:73 tells us, *"....then shall they be known who are my chosen...."* 11 Esdras 16:75 comforts us with the words: *"Be ye not afraid, neither doubt; for God is your guide."*

Few people have read the Apocrypha, but what Esdras relates is relatively easy to understand and compatible with the scripture found elsewhere in the Bible. It is an excellent way to better understand what Revelation describes about the end times and helps us see that we must continue to labor to produce the works which our faith must inspire both in ourselves and in others. Reading the second book of Esdras helps us understand that which is written in Revelation. All parts of Esdras are compatible with what we are taught in both the Old and the New Testament. It tells us that God sees all the works of men, even what lives in their imagination. It tells us about the end times and about God's chosen, and is thus a wonderful book to explore.

Bullet Points

The Bible is made up of 39 books when the Apocrypha is not included.

Not all Bibles contain an Apocrypha.

The Apocrypha consists of fifteen books and was once read only by priests.

The Apocrypha is mostly historical, but the book of 11 Esdras is prophetical.

11Esdras is a sixteen chapter easy-to-read account of the end times.

What Esdras writes is compatible with and supported by all other scripture.

It is an excellent way to better understand the end times.

Supporting Scripture

2 Esdras 6:19,   2 Esdras 7: 21, 43,

2 Esdras 8:35, 45,   2 Esdras 9:7-10,

2 Esdras 10:21, 23,   2 Esdras12:23-30,

2 Esdras 13:23-24,   2 Esdras 13:37-38,

2 Esdras 14:11-13, 17,   2 Esdras 15:9, 19, 37,

2 Esdras 16: 19, 54, 73, 75.

Chapter Thirty Six

DIFFERING DOCTRINES

There are approximately 38,000 different denominations within the Christian faiths some of which are Catholicism, Protestantism, Eastern Orthodoxy, Oriental Orthodoxy, Anglicanism, Nontrinitarianism, and Nestorianism and their two billion members the world over. These denominations differ in doctrine, some not very much and others quite a bit. Some differ on very minor points and others on major points and usually because of their varying interpretation of scripture. In general however, all acknowledge that Christ, and the sacrifice He made for mankind, is the basis of their faith and of their doctrine. Most differences occur on a point of Biblical rule rather than on the substance of the message of the Gospel. Human nature is such that we have a strong impulse to argue about these differences hoping to convince the other party that our interpretation is correct and draw them to our point of view.

Yet scripture warns us not to provoke one another to anger (Galatians 5:26) nor to enter into doubtful disputes. (Romans 14:1). Scripture tells an interesting story about just such a dispute. The Apostle Paul and Barnabas disagreed with others on a certain matter of law which was whether or not one needed to be circumcised to be a Christian. They decided to discuss their differences with other Apostles to determine the answer and fully expected the answer to be a yes or a no. After discussion however, they concluded that God would not want them to burden anyone with an issue which lay outside of the main message of the Gospel and that it was best if they made no distinction about whether or not this issue was important. Scripture defines their dispute in Acts 15:1-2 saying, *"And certain men said.....When therefore Paul and Barnabas had no small dissension and disputation with them......they determined....go up to Jerusalem unto the apostles and elders about this question."* Their decision is found in Acts 15:9-13 which says: *"...put no difference between us and them....why tempt ye God, to put a yoke upon the neck....believe that through the grace of Christ we shall be saved, even as they. Then all the multitude kept their silence.....And after they had held their peace....."*

This is an excellent example of how we should view similar disputes which scripture either does not clearly define or which we now know might have been something through which God protected the health and well being of His people. Scripture also tells us that when we speak of our faith we should be a pattern of good works and that we should use sound speech and uncorrupted doctrine. Titus 2:7-8 tells us, *"...shewing thyself a pattern of good works; in doctrine shewing uncorruptness, gravity, sincerity, sound speech; that cannot be condemned; that he that is of the contrary part may be ashamed, having no evil thing to say of you."* However, that said, scripture warns often and emphatically that false prophets and false doctrines will be on the rise as the return of Christ approaches (Mark 13:22) and that these false doctrines may cause many to fall.

Thus, Christians should rebuke and exhort one another with authority where needed (Titus 2:15) and to be careful that Satan does not gain an advantage over us. (11 Corinthians 2:11) Scripture teaches that we can test sound doctrine by comparing what we are told or how we interpret what we read or hear by the fruits of its teachings. (Matthew 7:15-20) If we test a doctrine against the fruits of the Holy Spirit and ask those with whom we debate to do the same, scripture itself can determine whether or not the debate is of value. Galatians 5:22 tells us, *"But the fruit of the Spirit is love, joy, peace, longsuffering, gentleness, goodness, faith, Meekness, temperance; against such there is no law."* James 1:5 tells us, *"If any lack wisdom, let him ask of God....and it shall be given him."* If we approach God with a pure heart to find the truth, God will direct our steps and bring us from the darkness of evil to the light of Christ through the example of Christ and His Apostles. Sadly however, there are those who cast blanket judgments on all things which are different from their personal interpretation. This can alienate many from recognizing someone whom God is using to extend an invitation.

Sadly, blanket judgments can also destroy the ability to nurture a relationship which could potentially win others to an important message because it undermines credibility and destroys the respect which, once lost, is difficult to regain. Christians want those who teach them to behave in a Christ-like fashion. The example Christ provided was of love, forgiveness, kindness and respect. While He rebuked sin, and unclean spirits, He did not judge and taught in parables so His message could be pondered without causing anyone to feel personally attacked. He prayed for those who would or did not understand His message rather than condemn them. He understood that if someone listened to His words, they might later also believe them. He did not alienate those He hoped would change their ways and follow Him.

Scripture also teaches us to beware the pride and arrogance evidenced by the Pharisees who condemned others and were then found lacking themselves. It teaches that God will be gracious to whom He will be gracious and that man cannot make this determination. Using the Holy Spirit and the fruits of the Spirit, we need to continually examine our hearts, our actions, and our inevitable private or public judgments and ask if God would approve the thoughts we entertain, and the example we have left with those with whom we have interacted. Most Christians seek the same path, but are perhaps at a different place along that path. They love God, are thankful for what Christ sacrificed on their behalf, and strive to be found worthy when Christ returns. Some know a great deal about scripture, some do not; some sin in ways that we wouldn't and we may sin in a way that they wouldn't; some give more of themselves to others than we do, some are more pure in heart than others, and *all have secret sins*. It is for God, not man to judge. God loves us because of what He sees in our heart and not because of a Biblical interpretation which we may or may not understand properly. He has provided us with the Holy Spirit with which to discern the true gospel of Christ. Further, He knows He can teach us as we mature because when we truly love Him and open our hardened heart, we are willing to ask for and accept His help.

Christian life is a learning process where we look for benchmarks which demonstrate a growth in faith, understanding, deed, and thought, and ask God to open our understanding. This is a far cry from the Christian who may misinterpret a word, an action or even scripture, yet decry and condemn this in others. As we review the march of Christianity, we can see that *God moved His people as was needed for their growth.* He began with the Jews, moved to the Apostles of Christ, to the birth of Catholicism, to the advent of Martin Luther and the Protestant movement, to the present day. This clearly teaches us that *our path needs to be adjusted on occasion* and that the mysteries of scripture are always unfolding and that what we may not believe or understand today may be opened to us tomorrow.

Scripture tells us that God wants all men to be saved, not just those with one idea or of one particular church, and also speaks about God's continued love for Israel. This lesson should be of great magnitude because it supports what scripture tells us about the pride and arrogance of those who condemn someone because they disagree on a particular point of doctrine as long as that doctrine still meets the test of the fruits of the spirit and what scripture tells us. Even if someone is correct in their interpretation they must teach in love, provide the right example and pray. God will do the rest.

An example however, of a current contention between Christians is praying for those who have died. This is practiced by approximately two thirds of all Christians worldwide yet approximately 8% of all Christians attribute demonic activity to this practice. Sadly these

8% do not know that there is a huge difference between *how* some pray for their dead. Thus to negate *all* who pray for the dead is a too strong and far reaching judgment and in part an erroneous assumption. Scripture tells us that different realms and prisons exist in eternity. Some who pray *for* the dead pray that God will provide mercy to the souls who occupy many of these realms. They do not pray *to* these souls but *for* them. They *pray only to God* and pray only to ask that He have mercy on these souls by allowing them to receive testimony in the realms in which they are held.

This represents a huge difference in practice and doctrine than those who pray *to* the dead and clearly shows that condemning *all* prayer for the dead may be in error. It may indicate that those who condemn prayer for the dead are not aware of the difference between these two practices. Scripture does *not* support talking to or praying to the dead or asking the dead to act as an intercessor. Scripture denounces the use of familiar spirits, necromancers, mediums, spiritists, and calling up the dead. The most notable passages are in Leviticus 19:31, Leviticus 20:6, 2 Kings 21:3-6, 1 Chronicles 10:13 and Deuteronomy 18:9. When King Saul prayed to the dead prophet Samuel for help, scripture clearly indicates that he incurred God's wrath and that God termed his action "abominable". Scripture also denounces praying to a graven image, or even erecting a graven image. Not only does God tell us in the Ten Commandments that He is a jealous God but also tells us to make no graven image. (See Exodus 20, Leviticus 26, Deuteronomy 4&5, Judges 17&18, Isaiah 40, 44, 45, 48, Jeremiah 51, Nahum 1:14, and Habakkuk 2:18).

Scripture does however support praying *for* the dead. An overview of just some of the scripture which references the support of praying for the dead is very revealing. I Peter 4:6 states: *" . . . for this cause was the gospel preached also, to them that are dead, that they might be judged according to men in the flesh, but live according to God in the spirit."* Note the word "also" meaning that both the living and dead received word about the Gospel of Christ, and note that the words "are dead" indicate the present tense. Further, the Apostles Creed tells us that Christ descended into hell after He died on the cross and remained there for three days. *"He descended into Hell and on the third day He rose again from the dead."* This supports the premise that while there He gave testimony to those who had died in their sins. It does not follow that Christ entered hell because of His sin....He was perfect and without sin.... but that He entered hell because His sacrifice could forgive the sin of others. Thus, if everyone in hell were beyond help, Christ would have had no reason to enter hell and bring them the hope of heaven which He had recently provided through His sacrifice.

I Corinthians 15:17-18 supports the words of the Apostles Creed where it says, *"And if Christ be not raised, your faith is vain; ye are yet in your sins. Then they also which are fallen asleep in Christ are perished."* Ephesians 4:8-10 says: *"Wherefore he saith, When he ascended up on high, he led captivity captive, and gave gifts unto men. (Now that he ascended, what is it but that he also descended first into the lower parts of the earth? He that descended is the same also that ascended up far above all heavens, that he might fill all things.)"* Scripture also describes Abraham's reaction when Christ entered hell. Abraham, faithful to God, but not living when Christ brought His sacrifice for our sins, evidently knew what Christ had achieved. John 8:56 tells us that Christ said, *"Your father Abraham rejoiced to see my day: and he saw it, and was glad."* John 5:25 explains, *"Verily, verily, I say unto you, The hour is coming, and now is, when the dead shall hear the voice of the Son of God: and they that shall hear shall live."* The key words in this verse are "and now is" indicating that the time is here (following the sacrifice of Christ) and that the dead can hear the words of Christ. Further, the words "shall hear", which mean "are willing to listen", indicates that not all will listen, believe, and repent so they can be saved. Scripture states that souls not worthy at the First Resurrection will not become the Bride, the Overcomers, or the Kings and Priests which scripture describes as the Firstlings who Christ will take upon His return.

The words of Peter also indicate that Christ preached His gospel after His death. 1 Peter 3:19 says, *"By which also he went and preached unto the spirits in prison."* And 11 Maccabees 12:43-45 teaches, *"For if he had not hoped that they that were slain should have risen again, it had been superfluous and vain to pray for the dead. And . . . Whereupon he made a reconciliation for the dead that they might be delivered from sin."* The words "made a reconciliation for the dead" clearly indicates that something occurred for those who had died which allowed them to be delivered from their past sins. There are many areas of scripture which provide insight into this question.

The parable of the rich man and the beggar who entered eternity on the same night provides clues about life after death. By depicting the beggar as resting in Abraham's bosom, it tells us that Abraham comforted the beggar after he died at the gates of the rich man's house. The rich man, who died at the same time, went to Hades (Hell) where he was tormented. This passage in the

Gospel of Luke is one of the Bible's most descriptive insights into death and clearly describes two places occupied by the dead, and the chasm between these two areas which could not, before the sacrifice of Christ, be bridged. This parable, found in Luke 16:19-31, spoken to the Pharisees, illustrates the chasm in eternity between those who in life pursued God and those who did not. Under the laws of Moses, the rich man was condemned for all eternity. When Christ brought the sacrifice which bridged the gulf between the Law of Moses and the Law of Love, those who had been condemned but who would accept Christ, believe and repent, would be allowed to cross from Hades to the bosom of Abraham.

The Biblical argument about eating pork is an example which relates well to this discussion. Roman 14:9-10 sums up this concern by saying, *"For to this end Christ both died, and rose, and revived that he might be Lord both of the dead and the living. But why dost thou judge thy brother? Or why dost thou set at nought thy brother? For we shall all stand before the judgment seat of Christ."* The verses that follow this one in scripture tell us not to judge what one believes "unclean" and another doesn't. Romans 14:18 says: *"For he that in these things served Christ is acceptable to God...."*

Because Christians differ in their interpretation of scripture, we must continually gauge our life of faith. Do we please Christ if we make harsh accusations against those who ask God to be merciful to those who have died especially if their words meet the criteria put forth as the fruits of the Spirit? Is there scriptural "proof" that demonic activity is at work in such an action? Do Christians have the right to judge this action and if so by what authority? And remember, praying *for* the dead is very different than praying *to* the dead or conjuring up the dead which may be the unjustified leap which those who make such harsh judgments have taken.

This raises the question about whether or not our personal salvation is in jeopardy when we demean and judge others when we do not have all the facts. Scripture teaches us to test that our actions are acceptable before God by discerning the spirits. Scripture tells us that we can accomplish this by comparing the *result* of our actions or beliefs or judgments to the fruits of the Holy Spirit listed in Galatians 5:22-23 which are *love, joy, peace, longsuffering, gentleness, goodness, faith, meekness and temperance.*

Additionally, scripture tells us that God knows our hearts and therefore, for our prayers to be heard, they require a sincere heart. When praying in the light of the fruits of the Spirit and aware that God knows our heart when we ask Him to help those who were less fortunate than we and died before knowing Christ, our actions certainly do include love, peace, longsuffering, gentleness, meekness….. and faith. Praying *for* the dead does fulfill this requirement while praying *to* the dead does not require a pure heart, nor this bevy of fruits. It is out of compassion and hope that people pray for those who appear to have had no connection to God while they lived, or children addicted to drugs who never gained the ability to understand God's offer before they died, or young people who died in an automobile accident who had never been brought to church by their parents and of course those who were aborted or miscarried. It is out of love…. not because demons inspire them…. that they pray for these souls and others in similar circumstances.

Bullet Points

Scripture tells us not to quibble over small differences.

Grace will cover disputes over legal issues wherever the true Gospel is taught.

False doctrines will be on the rise as the First Resurrection nears.

Doctrine should be tested against the fruits of the Holy Spirit.

False Prophets will be severely punished.

God promises to enlighten those who ask for His guidance.

Blanket judgments destroy credibility and respect.

Love should be a factor in all doctrine and deed.

Supporting Scripture

Galatians 5:26,	Romans 14:1,
Acts 15:1-2,	Acts 15:9-13,
Titus 2:7-8,	Mark 13:22,
Titus 2:15,	11 Corinthian 2:11,
Matthew 7:15-20,	Galatians 5:22,
Ezekiel 13:3,	Hebrews 13:9,
James 3:16,	Ephesians 5:11,
Ephesians 6:12-13,	James 1:5.

Chapter Thirty Seven

COLLECTIVE REDEMPTION

While Christians seek peace with all belief systems, and support the freedom of religion, scripture tells us to carefully preserve the accuracy of the Gospel. It is through the Gospel that we learn of Christ's sacrifice for us so each of us can seek the redemption required to become a child of God. One cannot bring about the redemption of another. It must be done individually. The gospel also teaches us that Christ was and is the personification of love and forgiveness, that He forgave even those who killed Him, and that He taught against envy and avarice, against hatred and vengeance and told us to love our neighbor.

Collective Redemption, sometimes referred to as Collective Salvation, is one of the most dangerous yet most successful satanic attacks on Christianity which has ever occurred. It is a doctrine which diametrically opposes the individual redemption offered through the sacrifice of Christ and has been directed toward a specific and highly religious population. It is a prime example of the warnings of false doctrine found throughout scripture and the cause of many good Christians being led astray. The doctrine of Collective Redemption began in the 1960's and advocates that unless reparation is made and the redistribution of wealth is attained *collectively, **no one*** can be redeemed. It teaches that mankind falls into one of two groups; the oppressor or the oppressed, and without working to reduce the oppressor and elevate the oppressed neither will be granted grace. This doctrine has become a major part of Black Liberation Theology. James Cone, one of its founders, and Reverend Jeremiah Wright, one of its best known current day advocates, teach their followers that they must collectively work toward the redistribution of wealth and reparation if they hope to find salvation. Their teaching is open to all, but directed primarily toward people of color, finding credence through the remembrance of the oppression which they and their ancestors experienced. This doctrine is based on the concept that Christ will seek restitution from the Jews because they were instrumental in His death. Further, that the believer must emulate Christ by obtaining restitution from those whose ancestors or themselves are, or have ever been instrumental in harming them or their ancestors. This has been one of the causes of a growing hatred inside our country toward Israel, a return of racism, and a growing movement to support the redistribution of wealth. Interestingly, this doctrine falls neatly into the political agenda of the Progressive Party within the Democratic Party and practiced by some currently high ranking political figures. Scripture however, clearly teaches that Christ was a victor and a conqueror, not that He was a victim, nor oppressed, nor that He hated those who harmed or even sought to harm him.

Christ is the personification of the perfect and unconditional love of God and gave His life for the *personal* redemption of anyone willing to follow Him and what He taught, to become a child of God. Christ warned His followers about the false prophets who would come after His death to bring them false doctrines. He also taught us to love our neighbor as ourselves and that we are not to seek revenge for any real or perceived wrong (Romans 12:19). Collective Redemption requires an act of vengeance which spawns hatred and has grown out of envy for one's neighbor. As mentioned in the previous chapter, one of the simplest tests to disprove doctrines taught by false prophets is to compare the fruit of the doctrine to the fruit of the Holy Spirit. Comparing the doctrine of Collective Redemption to the teachings of the Holy Spirit demonstrates their differences.

For example, Collective Redemption demands the redistribution of wealth and reparation, and thereby produces hatred/envy as opposed to love, unrest as opposed to peace, division as opposed to longsuffering, and vengeance as opposed to gentleness (Galatians 5:22-23). Matthew 7:16-17 tells us: *"Beware of false prophets which come to you in sheep's clothing.....Ye shall know them by their fruits...."* And Galatians 5:26 adds: *"Let us not be desirous of vain glory, provoking one another, envying one another"*. Sadly, many who were once true Christians have succumbed to this false doctrine of Collective Redemption and may lose their soul salvation because of it. It is especially sad to see these souls work with all their strength and heart to promote this ideology in the mistaken belief that they are doing God's work and thereby gaining their salvation. By perverting the true meaning of Christ's sacrifice for them individually, they and their ministers will suffer the wrath of God. Scripture describes the anger with which God views the perversion of His words and sacrifice, and provides warnings in almost every chapter of the Bible. 1 Corinthians 11:13 warns against false apostles, Acts 20:29 describes the wolves which will enter among Christians, Mark 13:13:23, 2 Peter 2:1 and Matthew 24:11, 24 and 25 bring similar warnings. Titus 1:10 addresses the many deceivers who will attack Christianity, and 1Timothy 4:16 warns to *"take heed"*. Acts 5:3 asks if Satan has filled our heart with lies, while 2 Corinthians 2:11 warns: *"Lest Satan get an advantage"*. Genesis 3:1 tells us how subtle Satan is, and John 8:44 tells us that Satan is a liar and a deceiver. Matthew 24:41 addresses the parable of the ten virgins who were all invited to attend a wedding, yet only half of them were allowed into the wedding because they had not made themselves ready and the door was locked to them.

This tells is that all Christians are invited to the First Resurrection but sadly only half will be ready by remaining faithful to the true doctrine and thus allowed to enter the wedding feast with Christ. Scripture clearly addresses the ministers who preach a false doctrine, warning them that they will be punished severely for leading others astray. Matthew 18:6, Mark 9:42 and Luke 17:2 are an example of these warnings and tell us that if someone causes a child of God to stumble, it would be better if they hung a millstone around their neck, entered the water and drowned rather than face the punishment of God. It is sad that many Christians have given themselves over to these false doctrines, but it is especially sad to see well meaning Christians perpetrate acts, entertain thoughts, and seek goals which they have been taught are godly when they are instead spawned by Satan. Those who have been misled will have a sad awakening one day and, just as described in the parable of the ten virgins, it will be too late for them to make the change which God requires. Scripture also tells us to speak sound doctrine (Titus 2:1) and to prove what we say and hear (Malachi 3:10, Romans 12:2, and 1 Thessalonians 5:21) by learning what God tells us in scripture. We must be especially careful as the end times unfold because scripture warns that the devil walks across the earth as a roaring lion seeking to devour us (1 Peter 5:8). Satan must destroy our faith to prolong his freedom and we must take his power very seriously. We must carefully guard the true doctrine of Christ and fight for our faith.

Many Biblical scholars and ministers have courageously spoken against the Collective Redemption tenet of Black Liberation Theology in an attempt to warn its followers against the satanic influence of this theology. We too must speak out and do our part to help those who are being misled and may, because of this doctrine, lose their soul salvation. We must listen carefully to everything we hear for even the smallest clues which will reveal Satan's subtle influence. Every one of us should prove the doctrines we hear by comparing them with what scripture tells us. Every one of us should warn our children, our relatives, our friends, and neighbors about succumbing to false doctrines which will cause God to say, *"I know ye not"* (Matthew 25:10-12). Every one of us must guard the precious gifts God has given us and help others find and follow the true doctrine which teaches that Christ gave His life for each of us individually, that God teaches and shows Himself through love, and that *we testify our Christianity by our loving actions toward one another.* Ezekiel 13:3 warns, *"...Woe unto the foolish prophets that follow their own spirit....."* Hebrews 13:9 warns, *"Be not carried about with divers and strange doctrines."* James 3:16 tells us, *"Where envying and strife is, there is confusion and every evil work."* Ephesians 5:11 warns us, *"And have no fellowship with the unfruitful works of darkness....."*

Scripture also teaches us that when engaging those whose doctrine is incompatible with scripture and fails the test of the fruits of the spirit, we face a dangerous religious spirit and must be very careful. Scripture clearly warns us that we must put on the armour of God in order to withstand these spirits if we face them in debate. Ephesians 6:12-13 explains, *"For we wrestle not against flesh and blood, but against principalities, against powers, against the rulers of the darkness of this world, against spiritual wickedness in high places. Wherefore take unto you the whole armour of God that ye may be able to withstand in the evil day, and having done all, to stand."* Hatred, destruction, vengeance, corruption, racism, and unrest are never from God and are actions which we must flee. Proverbs 14:7 warns, *"Go from the presence of a foolish man, when thou perceives not in him the lips of knowledge."* And the last words of the Bible found in Revelation 22:18-19 warn: *"..... if any man shall add.....and if any man shall take away from the words of this book of this prophecy, God shall take away his part out of the book of life....."* Further, those who follow the directives which have changed God's words may also lose their part in the book of life. However, we must have compassion for those who are misled and ask that God enlighten them and help them find the truth.

Bullet Points

Collective Redemption is a serious threat to Christians.

Collective Redemption, the doctrine of Black Liberation Theology, is a false doctrine.

Collective Redemption preaches that redemption cannot be attained individually.

Collective Redemption requires reparation and the redistribution of wealth for one to be provided their soul salvation.

Collective Redemption fits neatly into the political ideology of the Progressive Party.

Collective Redemption is inspired by Satan and can destroy the soul.

Supporting Scripture

Romans 12:19,	Acts 5:3,
Hosea 4:6,	Genesis 3:1,
John 8:44,	Matthew 24:41,
Matthew 25:10-12,	2 Corinthians 2:11,
Mark 13:23,	2 Corinthians 11: 13,
2 Peter 2:1,	Acts 20:29,
Malachi 3:10,	1 Thessalonians 5:21,
Matthew 7:15,	Matthew 24:11, 24, 25.

Chapter Thirty Eight

HATRED BY ANY OTHER NAME

Hatred is the opposite of love and opposes the tenets of Christianity. Hatred rears its ugly head in many forms using its tenets to create doubt, fear, suspicion, unrest and destruction. It is a satanic spirit which operates under many guises, some blatant and others hiding in ungodly and misleading ideologies. These spirits use their hatred toward those things they believe might threaten their existence. They work under a rhetoric which disallows disagreement with what it spawns because of its inability to prove its value through open and fair discussion. When discussion appears to disprove the ideology they propose, they resort to false accusation spawned by their hatred to distract from the godly truth of the issue at hand. It is a satanic attempt to force the personal ideology they have embraced or initiated, on all men, and in essence, is a threat and a method used by cowards because hatred rarely has the courage to be exposed for what it is.

Hatred wears many hats and does not have a place in the life of a Christian. However, today's Christian must understand what lies behind this force of ugliness and learn how to address it, unveil it, and respond to it. It is powered by evil and it is dangerous. Sadly, many actually believe that hatred is acceptable and believe that they are simply rectifying the wrongs of the past or avenging a current injustice. Some, driven by fear and inaccurate interpretation of the facts allow hatred to give them courage. The spirits which govern hatred have no remorse for bringing harm, for acting out their hatred. Some religions, and some ideologies, even some politics promote actions which produce hatred, and that spirit of hatred grows so strong in their heart that it dictates their way of life.

Hatred in and of itself is clearly satanic and in direct opposition to scripture. It opposes the example of Christ and the doctrine of His Gospel. It negates the work of the Holy Spirit which teaches love. It negates the scripture which encourages us to love one another and to overcome anger and forgive. Forgiveness is one of the key elements to our soul salvation. Scripture also tells us to leave revenge to God. Scripture teaches us how we are to behave toward one another and provides an excellent example in the story of the Good Samaritan. This story is found in Luke 10: 30-37, and speaks about a man who was attacked by thieves and left to die. Many people of different rank and different cultures passed him by without helping him. However, a Samaritan, someone from a culture not looked upon with favor, did stop and help the man, and Christ commended his mercy and his actions, and advised his disciples in verse 37, *"......Go, and do thou likewise."* This shows us that we are not to judge others by their rank or by their culture, but by their works.

Christ was asked by the Pharisees which was the greatest of the commandments and answered in Matthew 22:37, *"....Thou shalt love the Lord thy God with all thy heart, and with all thy soul, and with all thy mind. This is the first and great commandment. And the second is like unto it. Thou shalt love thy neighbor as thyself."* This clearly tells us that we are *all* brethren regardless of race or culture, fame or fortune, and must all care for one another in love. Armed with this information, the true Christian should consider another important thought put forth in a Native American proverb which says *"Don't judge a man until you have walked two moons in his moccasins."* What this teaches us is that we need to develop an understanding about what others may have experienced, what they may feel, or what they have been taught. Just as there were many circumstances which influenced and directed our Christian philosophy, non-Christians have been influenced by many circumstances as well, and some may have been those which espoused hatred and intolerance. Our effort to change minds may be admirable, but what assures our success is the love and example we provide which draws the heart of someone to us, and the *lack* of hate, envy, and class distinction they see in the tenets of true Christianity.

Actions have consequences, and if we cannot touch a heart or change a mind today, what we have said and done may change a mind somewhere down the road. We must remember that God desires to reach those who hate and may use our words and actions as a catalyst; He may be using us as a role model for a future turning point in someone's life. Timing is important and what might not work today may work another day, and bring the result we first hoped for, and thus initiated. We also need to remember that *the impression we leave rather than the intent we had* is of utmost importance. When someone is filled with hatred, certainly any negative word, look, or action can easily be taken personally and interpreted as a put down.

The spirit of hatred already has placed into the heart of those it holds captive, its perceived reason to hate, and it is important that we not add fuel to its fire. Christians must not hate. True Christianity and hatred cannot coexist. We may argue on policy, or ideology, we may differ in opinion, but we cannot hate because of it. Our world has long been one of a mixture of many cultures and colors, religions and traditions, yet every culture has at one time been mocked or abused by others. Even Christianity has been mocked and attacked. Further, it is an eye opener to realize that almost ***every*** culture has had their share of a form of slavery or bondage. The ancient Jews whom God loves so much were once enslaved by the Egyptians. England from which Americans fled had a class system which enslaved the poor through a form of bondage.

Thus, from Kings and Lords, Barons and Lairds to peons and serfs, slaves and servants, *a form of bondage has existed in almost every culture* in times past. Starvation threatened, taxes were burdensome, rank reigned, cruelties existed, and life was hard. These circumstances fostered hatred and envy because life was so difficult. Further, Christianity may not have been a part of the life of those in power who could have learned compassion from it. Those without power could have been strengthened through it. We also have to remember that scripture was not made available to the populace in earlier times and for some, neither was the ability to read. While many may have had a strong faith in God, they may have not understood that scripture advocates love and thereby, kindness. Further, it is difficult to love when living under hate without knowing God's words.

However, when emancipation was acquired, some who through the immigration which allowed them to flee the bondage of other countries and cultures, appreciated freedom and thus appreciated what their new country offered them and left their hate behind. They encouraged their children to speak the language of their adopted country, to excel in school, to respect the laws of the country, to appreciate the freedoms they had obtained and, through hard work and education, to reach the pinnacle of success.

They appreciated the liberties that their new life offered them and taught their children to appreciate them and never looked back. They were thankful for today and did not focus on their yesterdays. They harbored no hate for the bondage which earlier centuries or circumstances had created and looked toward a future which would not allow that to happen again. When given the opportunity to cast their vote in political matters they saw it as a God given freedom and both appreciated and utilized it by choosing the candidate who espoused the most virtue. As they developed their faith in God and began to know what scripture taught, they learned to lay aside the past and to love others as Christ loved them. Many, through prayer, developed the hope and strength they needed to change their life and their attitudes, and taught their children kindness, and to lay aside hate, thus God blessed His faithful children and blessed their honest labor and desire to overcome. Today, Christians must learn to be sensitive to the struggles of others and also to their history. That history may have left scars which can only heal with love and trust and time. Through love and patience and by being a role model against all hatred for any reason, Christians can win souls; they can deflect hate and thwart the efforts of evil and those spirits which whisper of past injustice to fuel present envy and hate.

God tells us in Colossians 4:6 *"Let your speech be always with grace, seasoned with salt, that ye may know how ye ought to answer every man."* And 11 Thessalonians 2: 3: warns, *"Let no man deceive you by any means: for that day shall not come, except there come a falling away first, and that man of sin be revealed, the son of perdition."*

Hate comes in many forms, some blatant and many hiding under the surface. Some hatred is the result of fear or envy, but it is most dangerous when it hides itself in an ideology which is not what it appears to be. (See Chapter 37) Hate is spawned by evil and aimed at breaking our faith and causing us to react, rather than act as God directs us. It is a part of the falling away of man from God and spurning the words of direction He has provided for us in scripture. We may have a past which gave us cause to hate, but if we love God and if we want God to love us, we must overcome our hatred in whatever form it shows itself and learn to love. We must leave all vengeance to God and hope that no vengeance will be necessary because those who brought us harm have themselves repented.

Bullet Points

Many attitudes and ideologies are an excuse to express hatred.

Hatred is satanic.

Accusations are used to distract from the issue in debate.

True Christians do not hate, seek vengeance, dwell on past injustices, or teach their children to hate.

Satan uses hate to separate and divide.

Rampant hatred, encouraged by evil is a sign of the end times.

Some political and religious ideologies are a disguise for hatred.

Supporting Scripture

Matthew 22:37,	Luke 10:30-37,
11 Thessalonians 2:3,	Revelation 2:10,
Colossians 4:6,	11 Thessalonians 2:7,
3 John 11,	1 Thessalonians 4:5-6.

Chapter Thirty Nine

THE SPRITUAL DANGER OF HALLOWEEN

Sometimes we base our decision to participate in an activity by the amount of risk involved. *"Is that ski slope too steep? Is there a rip tide today? Is it okay if I watch that movie? What would happen if I miss church this week?"* Our assessment of the risk directs our decision. But occasionally, despite a high risk, we choose to participate by convincing ourselves that if we are careful we will not be harmed. However, our best decisions are made when we have all the facts and ask if what we propose is pleasing…rather than displeasing….to God. We should always ask ourselves how we would feel if God were to join us in what we plan to do.

About 2,000 years ago in Ireland, England, and Northern France, the Celts, known as cruel and barbaric warriors who worshipped many gods, held a heathen festival filled with superstition and occult ceremony to honor the Celtic god, the lord of death, Samhain. The Druids, a more educated and priestly group within the Celtic people, taught that terrible curses and punishments would befall those who did not participate in the ceremonies honoring Samhain. The Druids believed that the realms of the dead and living became one on the night of Samhain, October 31st when this lord of death, allegedly gathered condemned and evil souls from eternity and allowed them to return to earth and associate with the living. The festival of Samhain was marked by the visitation of ghosts and mischievous spirits. While many writings say that human sacrifices were made, historical writings seem to indicate that they were animal sacrifices. Nevertheless, from the dying sacrifice, the Celtic priests predicted the future. Jeremiah 14:14 tells us *"They prophesy unto you a false vision and divination, and a thing of naught, and the deceit of their heart."* Deuteronomy 32:17 states *"They sacrificed unto demons, not to God; ...."* And Matthew 6:24: *"No one can serve two masters.....you cannot serve God and mammon."*

While the festival of Samhain was the origin of Halloween, (All Hallows Evening), the influence of these occult beliefs and practices persisted through the subsequent centuries. In AD 43 two Roman festivals joined this celebration. One was 'Feralia', which commemorated the passing of the dead, and the other honored the Roman goddess 'Pomona'." In 835 A.D, to convert this heathen custom into a spiritual celebration, Pope Gregory IV decreed November 1st as All Saints Day when departed souls would be prayed for. Thus, at this point these three festivals were joined together and were celebrated with bonfires, parades, and costumes.

Over the years some satanic groups considered Halloween the time when Satan could be called upon to exert his influence. An event called Irish Mischief Night, when fairies, elves, the traveling dead, and wicked supernatural spirits were thought to roam, was added to these events. These festivities, Samhaim, Feralia, Pomona, All Saints Day, Satanic groups and Irish Mischief Night combined into what we call Halloween and all but one are closely related to evil. Halloween celebrations champion a variety of costumes such as ghosts, witches, vampires, ghouls, skeletons, and bloody masks, fingers, and clothing.

Thus, Halloween trivializes and mocks souls who have died but whom God either deems His saints or those he still longs to save. God would never want us, His children, Christ's Bride, to join celebrations with their origins in evil and in overt opposition to God's love and His future plans for those who have died. Scripture tells us in 3 John 1:11 not to imitate evil: *"Beloved, do not imitate what is evil..."* and Ephesians 5:1, 11: *"Therefore be imitators of God as dear children...and have no fellowship with the unfruitful works of darkness, but rather expose them"*. Therefore, if our children wear costumes imitating witches and ghosts, zombies and vampires, magicians and shamans, and accessories with blood dripping from mouths and bloody fingernails, it could not be pleasing to God. We would not allow these to be worn to church or to the wedding feast with Christ, so why encourage our children to wear them at all? Would God think we honored the dead by wearing these costumes? Arguing that a more suitable costume would be acceptable is debatable for even mingling with the costumes we mentioned should give us cause for concern. We would know that these depict the Sanhaim ceremony and other satanic celebrations which promote the work of the underworld. Scripture warns that Satan is subtle; he can blind us, fool us, make us complacent, pervert God's words, and works unceasingly to prevent us from being a part of the Bride of Christ.

As Christians, we should carefully consider how Satan uses the celebration of Halloween to hurt the Holy Spirit within us and open our hearts to the spirits of evil. Further, that losing our soul salvation doesn't always happen overnight and invasion may not be noticed immediately....it can be slow and insidious...but it is always deadly. The opening an invading satanic spirit looks for can be unwittingly provided by us.....spontaneously or over time, and the threat to us is real. Scripture warns continuously that we are to watch for, beware, flee, and spurn all evil. Thus we should flee all activities which might open us, or our children, to these influences, and teach about the importance of doing so. Children are easily influenced by what they see around them and it isn't easy to dissuade them from what they may perceive as an evening of fun. Parents need to not only teach them why we spurn the trappings of Halloween, but also provide something Godly for them to do and consider a non-costume fall festival celebration which can be held in our churches, in our backyards, or the home of our minister or someone from our congregation. Campfires, hot dogs and marshmallows, games and fellowship with their peers, can make this day safe, fun and godly for our children. Sunday school and youth groups can also participate and neither they nor their parents will have to worry about their safety spiritually or physically, nor worry about razor blades in apples or poison in the candy. Further, through these thoughts and actions we can set an example for others and be sure not to displease God nor awaken the spirits so intent on harming our relationship with Our Heavenly Father.

Bullet Points

Halloween is a satanic celebration and most Halloween costumes dishonor the dead and thereby dishonor God.

Satanic spirits look for ways to enter mankind.

It is not appropriate for a Christian to celebrate Satan and his work, nor dress children in Halloween costumes to attend church.

We should create a Fall Festival Day which pleases God and is more fun than Halloween.

Supporting Scripture

Jeremiah 14:14,	Romans 14:9,
1 Corinthians 10:14,	1 Timothy 6:11,
Deuteronomy 32:17,	Romans 12:21,
Jeremiah 51:6,	Matthew 6:24,
Ephesians 5:1,	3 John 11,
Ephesians 5:11,	11 Timothy 2:22.

Chapter Forty

THE TRUTH ABOUT FENG SHUI

Feng Shui is the Oriental art of decorating one's home. It advocates practicality and a lack of clutter. Millions have flocked to Feng Shui and to Vastu, a decorating method used in India, because they promise good luck, harmony and tranquility, so fitting to our present lifestyle, our level of stress, and our desire to create a personal Bethany in our home.

However, through the promises these offer, and our desire to decorate our homes in a pleasing manner, by employing these decorating suggestions, our enemy has enticed us into jeopardizing our spiritual well-being. Innocent in premise, practical in application, touting commonsense in thought, and a lack of clutter in presentation, Feng Shui and Vastu appear a perfect choice for decorating in today's world and creating the refuge we seek to calm our fears. But, God warns of the power which lurks behind these practices and how they can become a power which can destroy our future.

The words of the First Commandment found in Exodus 20:2-3 tell us, *"I am the Lord thy God...Thou shalt have no other gods before Me"*. As the first commandment given to Moses, it is clear that God placed this commandment first; above all the others, and thus it should reign in importance. While we understand the first six words of this commandment, the last eight words leave us wishing for a list of what these "other gods" are.

We all agree that spending an inordinate amount of time and energy in any activity where we sacrifice time for God, or sacrifice our Christian integrity may constitute another god, and that whether it is a quest for financial security, power, fame, lust or beauty it could become a powerful motivator in some lives. But often these gods are easily identified, while the gods of Feng Shui are hidden, less easily defined. Satan rarely takes the obvious path.

As we research the many facets of Feng Shui, we find examples of the subtlety of the enemy's hook and realize how simple, innocent and practical another god can appear. Through this study, we are reminded that our enemy is a magnificent liar, making what he presents incredibly appealing and, on the surface, amazingly beneficial to our lives. He begins by providing us with a resource which promises to solve our most pressing problems, often love or money, and which initially appears safe, helpful, practical and logical.

Newspapers and magazines run ads for businesses which promise harmony, peace and well being through Feng Shui. Decorating books and magazine articles espousing its practical and psychologically sound aspects promise a foolproof method to attain a peaceful, harmonious environment. Even hair salons, gyms, housing developments, furniture stores, and hotels, tout their personal use of Feng Shui and its benefits.

Initially, we accept the premises put forth in these ads because they address simple common sense, practical, and psychologically sound ideas. But as the world of Feng Shui opens to explain its benefits, and offer its magic, we must look for its terrible danger, its hidden tenets, its subtle temptation… and the power behind it.

God gives us insight into His nature and provision, not only through scripture, but also through what we observe every day in our environment. As we experience what God has created throughout nature and our universe, we learn that He takes great interest in form and balance, color and harmony. From every flower, tree and unique snowflake, from the majesty of mountain and sea, we recognize a hand which desires and understands harmony, balance, design, beauty and peace.

God provides us with a glimpse into the perfection He can create by allowing us to witness the interaction between the various elements surrounding us. In nature, He shows us how miraculously the sand of the beach and the water of the ocean work together to allow a mutually beneficial interaction, how the weather and our crops work in mutual harmony to create their bounty, how our bodies respond to a balance of proper nutrients for good health, even the perfect harmony between an insect and the pollination of plants. We learn through these observations that a certain balance is required which only God can control. The book of Job asks question after question about who ultimately controls the earth, the atmosphere, and all things in the earth and the answer is always that only God controls them. What we also learn from this area of scripture is that despite fears of global warming, God controls all the elements of earth and our atmosphere. Other areas of scripture describe how God will destroy the old heaven and earth for the new...not man.

Feng Shui masters employ the use of the I Ching, an ancient Chinese book of revelation which advocates the use of "helpers" and provides a definition of who these helpers are. According to a book titled, "*I Ching, The Oracle of the Cosmic Way*", by Carol K. Anthony and Hanna Moog, I Ching Books, Anthony Publishing Company, Stow, Massachusetts, 2002, helpers are aspects of the Cosmic Consciousness, invisible, proficient in varied areas, are not angels, must be given a free hand in how to help, and *they* must be thanked afterward for their help.

Additionally, and in direct opposition to Biblical teachings, it is stated that to benefit from the wisdom of the I Ching and to draw the helpers into providing their assistance, man must *not* think of himself as a sinner or as born with original sin. They claim that this mistaken idea and belief will result in poison arrows being directed toward the person seeking help and will poison the true nature of that person. Thus, if man believes himself a sinner, neither the helpers nor the I Ching can be of use and a penalty is imposed upon that person. These beliefs are diametrically opposed to Scripture where God clearly tells us that we were born sinners and remain sinners. The sacrifice of Christ allows us to partake of Holy Communion for the forgiveness of sin. To deny that we are sinners denies the sacrifice of Christ, thus we deny Christ himself. This fact alone should warn Christians of its danger. Adding to its danger, Feng Shui masters use the Chinese calendar, Chinese astrology based on a 60-year cycle obtained by pairing the "Ten Heavenly Stems" and the "Twelve Earthly Branches", the psychological aspects of man represented by twelve animals, the four elements, numerology (KUA), compass direction, and yin/yang balance which they determine for each individual.

Used in conjunction with the magnetic compass, the Lo Pan and the Ba Qua, the astrological components become pivotal to directing the Feng Shui client toward a better life. Employing astrology, charts, chants and other tools for the purpose of divination are what scripture warns we carefully avoid and warns that they are controlled by Satan. .

In a book titled, "Many Infallible Proofs" by Dr. Henry M. Morris, Dr. Morris says, *"Astrology is unequivocally condemned in the Bible (see Deuteronomy 4:9; Isaiah 47:11-14; 11 Kings 23:5; Acts 7:42, 43; etc.), therefore we must by all means avoid any association with these particular teachings."* Dr. Morris states that astrology is *"synonymous with ancient polytheistic paganism and akin to the worship of fallen angels or demons"*. He further considers many so-called "ancient" myths and religions to be *"a corruption of the original revelation, rather than the raw inventions of men".* His book was written in 1974, and his examination of Scripture… applied then… still stands today. Once again, Christians are faced with a choice. Some have been led to believe that Feng Shui is simply a practical design application which reduces clutter and creates harmony. It does…that's the hook Satan uses to draw us. However, as we begin to trust the beneficial effects of employing the tenets of Feng Shui which promise to provide good luck and power if we bring certain elements into our life and remove others, we fall to worshipping another god and open the door to satanic influence. Even if we do not attempt to engage these promises but encourage others in the use of Feng Shui, we are held accountable for their fall. Malachi 2:8, 9 tells us: *"...ye have caused many to stumble....Therefore have I also made you contemptible....."*

Free will provides us with the right to make our own choices in life. Scripture shows us which choices please God and which do not and specifically what we must do to become God's children and ultimately the Bride of Christ. Thus choosing what will please God and protecting our spiritual life is always best…. but given our free will, it is up to us. Further, scripture clearly tells us that our lack of knowledge, our complacency in learning what He teaches through scripture will be no excuse. The Bride of Christ will be made up of those who have sought God's words and ways and placed them foremost in their life. God clearly tells us to flee the innocent appearing attractions which Satan uses to trap mankind. Scripture warns that we are to discern the spirits, watch, and make ourselves ready when Christ returns. Thus choosing even to "dabble a bit" is extremely dangerous and may rob us of our soul salvation.

Bullet Points

Feng Shui is an ancient Oriental approach to interior design.

Feng Shui employs the use of astrology, numerology, and chants which is displeasing to God.

Feng Shui masters use the I Ching to guide their recommendations and obtain spirit helpers.

I Ching helpers require that man not believe he is a sinner.

Scripture tells us that astrologers and prognosticators receive their power from Satan.

Employing other gods in our daily lives brings spiritual death.

Vastu is another decorating method which is used primarily in India and advocates that one arrange their interior rooms in a specific manner to prevent the anger of various gods.

Supporting Scripture

Exodus 20:2-3,　　　　　　Deuteronomy 4:9,

Isaiah 47:11-14,　　　　　　11 Kings 23:5,

Acts 7:42-43,　　　　　　　Deuteronomy 14:15,

11 Kings 21:3-6,　　　　　　Ephesians 5:11,

1 Timothy 6:11,　　　　　　Deuteronomy 14:19,

Revelation 3:21.

Chapter Forty One

ASTROLOGY, TAROT AND DIVINATIONS

It is sad that many Christians seek advice from tarot cards and astrology. Perhaps they are not aware of how strongly scripture advocates that the children of God *not* participate in such activity. Perhaps they do not understand that *the power inherent in these activities emanates from Satan* and opens the door to a spiritual invasion of one's soul. Perhaps they do not understand or acknowledge the subtly through which evil works nor the tools used to do so. Thus it becomes imperative for Christians to teach about this danger.

The actions suggested by an astrological chart or Tarot cards, may provide initial success, but they always bring destruction once someone is caught in its trap. These activities are not God's will, are clearly displeasing to God, and are described as incredibly dangerous to our soul salvation. Gathering scripture from many different areas in the Bible provides us with a myriad of warnings and clearly defined direction that we avoid such activity.

Deuteronomy 4:15,19 tells us *"Take ye therefore good heed……lest thou lift up thine eyes unto heaven and…… seest the sun, and the moon, and the stars, even all the host of heaven, shouldest be driven to worship them, and serve them…"*

And Isaiah 47:11-13 warns, *""Therefore shall evil come upon thee; thou shalt not know from whence it riseth……Stand now with thine enchantments, and with the multitude of thy sorceries……Let now the astrologers, the stargazers, the monthly prognosticators, stand up, and save thee…."*

When we ask ourselves why one would seek advice from these quarters, a myriad of reasons come to mind, none of which would stand before God. Our desire to know the future indicates a lack of trust in God and an impatience to obtain that which we seek. Further, when we make inquiries about the personal life of another, we seek an advantage which attests to pride and selfishness.

Even if we worry about someone and seek astrological advice because we wish to help them, we negate our faith, remove our concern from God's hands, and demonstrate a lack of trust that God will care for our concern. We are turning to another source of power to do this for us whereby the Holy Spirit must flee and a satanic spirit takes over. If we are asking these sources if danger awaits us, and what we should do to avoid that danger, again we have not asked for nor trusted in God's protection, but rather in satanic protection. We have not studied scripture to obtain God's words to guide us in what we should do or what we must avoid. But more importantly, when we turn to astrology, numerology, tarot cards, palmistry, Feng Shui or any other method which claim to offer information about or protection for the future, we, like Adam and Eve, open the door for Satan to work in our lives, not only in this current quest, but for all things which can then even harm future generations.. God gave Adam and Eve strict instructions which they disobeyed and which brought separation from God, and sin into their lives and the lives of others. God has given us strict instructions not to utilize the power through which the activities of divination operate and by disobeying we too bring sin into our lives, and potentially into the lives of future generations. In addition to disobeying God, we may lose God's help and open ourselves to a spiritual invasion and , as we said before, also create the potential for those spirits to bring those same sins, temptations and invasion into the lives of our children and future generations. Through these activities we disallow the Holy Spirit to live in our hearts and exchange this great and wondrous gift for a spirit of this world. That spirit may also invite other spirits and soon we could lose our ability to follow God and fall further into sin.

2 Kings 21:3-6 tells us, *"For he built up again the high places……and worshipped all the host of heaven, and served them. …And he built altars for all the host of heaven in the two courts of the house of the Lord. …and used enchantments, and observed times, and dealt with familiar spirits and wizards: He wrought much wickedness in the sight of the Lord, to provoke Him to anger."* Clearly these verses tell us that when we engage in divination we are dealing with "familiar" spirits and that we are worshipping other gods and serving them. There is no place in God's kingdom for these activities and no place among God's children for them. Neither would God allow the Bride He is

developing for His Son to engage these spirits. What might seem at first an innocent activity can cost us our soul salvation even if we simply "dabble" just a little bit.

Satan and his minions are stronger than we are, and in our arrogance we believe that we can choose to disengage any evil we encounter simply through the power of our own will and at any time. However, God warns that we cannot; that Satan can "trap" us when we least expect it, and that we must have no fellowship with evil because of its greater strength and power. Ephesians 5:11 tells us, *"And have no fellowship with the unfruitful works of darkness..."* Further, when the Apostle Paul wrote to Timothy he spoke of the many errors one can make which are displeasing to God and in 1Timothy 6:11 said, *"But thou O man of God flee these things; and follow after righteousness......"* Scripture tells us that *any* unrighteousness, *any* ungodly activity opens the door to the spirits of this world and thereby precludes the Holy Spirit from its activity in our life. Those spirits look for an opening into any heart and can bring other spirits with it. God warns us of this phenomenon and to open our hearts *only* to the Holy Spirit. He also warns that the Holy Spirit cannot dwell with these spirits and will leave us if we invite another spirit in.

There are many temptations in life, but we need to hold fast to what scripture tells us and remind ourselves of what God offers those who overcome those temptations. Revelation 3:21 promises, *"To him that overcometh will I grant to sit with me in my throne...."*

Bullet Points

Many believe that astrology and other divinations are harmless.

Satan has been given the power to produce signs and wonders.

Scripture clearly tells us that we must watch for the activities of Satan.

God's words throughout scripture warn against astrologers and all forms of divination.

Scripture tells us that these activities are controlled by Satan.

Those who engage in these activities will not be found worthy when Christ returns.

Supporting Scripture

Deuteronomy 4:15,   Isaiah 47:11-13,

2 Kings 21:3-6,   Ephesians 5:11,

Deuteronomy 4:19,   1 Timothy 6:11,

Revelation 3:21.

Chapter Forty Two

THE GIFT OF DIVINE PROPORTION

Exodus 31: 3-5 says: *"And I have filled him with the Spirit of God, in wisdom, in understanding, in knowledge, and in all manner of workmanship, to design artistic works, to work in gold, in silver, in bronze, in cutting jewels for setting in carving wood, and to work in all manner of workmanship."*

And Exodus 26:29 states: *"You shall overlay the boards with gold, make their rings of gold as holders for the bars, and overlay the bars with gold".* Through these and other directions for building Solomon's Temple, God tells us that He loves beauty and form. We too love a beautiful home.

When we read in Matthew 6:2: *"For where your treasure is, there will your heart be also."* we understand that when we treasure God above all things, and use our home to serve God, He will bless us. When we use our homes for prayer, Bible study, family discussions, fellowship, sharing experiences of faith, teaching our children, and accommodating the young and old, God will bless us for our heart will be with Him.

Amazingly, Nature, God's creation has provided us with a mathematical formula for creating perfect balance when decorating our homes. This formula is called Divine Proportion. Balance can be explained by examining a child's monkey swing which hangs from a tree limb by one rope. The monkey swing is made up of a rope which is has one end tied to one of the higher limbs of a tree and the other end tied underneath a platform used as a seat where the child sits, legs straddling the rope and both hands holding the single rope. The balance required on the monkey swing is an excellent tool for understanding how to balance a room in our home. Just as the swing requires balance not to tip, a room needs to be balanced by properly distributing the 'weight' of its architectural elements and its furnishings.

Without this balance, the room will seem to 'lean' to one side to our *subconscious* mind, and furnishings will *feel* as if they will 'fall off' the room's floor. Balance is the most important aspect of good design because it pleases the subconscious mind as well as the eye, and creates a sense of harmony. Architecture, accessories, style, size, colors, and textures affect balance, not only the furniture. Balance affects everything, everything affects balance.

However, balance doesn't require a pound for pound distribution, but rather the *illusion* of equal distribution throughout the space. Thus, a large item in one part of a room can be balanced by a corresponding size item, or the *illusion* of corresponding size, in an opposing part of the room. The balancing item could be furniture, but can also be architecture, color, drapery or plants. Disparities in size, delicateness, color, texture, and denseness must be considered, and when these balance from wall to wall and floor to ceiling, we internally sense its correctness.

One example of disparity is a fireplace of natural stone topped by a large mantle coupled with a white rattan décor of lace and ruffles. The 'weight' of the rattan does not offset the apparent 'weight' of the stone and mantle. However, through the use of the visual 'weight' of color, painting the furniture dark brown might work as would adding darker cushions. The determination of proper balance must not be about furniture alone, but begins with the existing 'weight' of architectural elements. Window treatments must also be considered.

The ancient Greeks learned that the oval is more pleasing to the eye than the circle, and the rectangle more pleasing than the square. From this, the Greeks determined that the most pleasing proportions of rectangles or ovals were those with ratios of: (2 to 3), (3 to 5), or (5 to 8). A ratio is a mathematical relationship between two numbers.

Fibonacci numbers are found in nature and connected to both the Greek ratio system and The Golden Ratio, though Fibonacci, a thirteenth century Italian mathematician, came later. The relationship between the Greek ratios (2 to 3), (3 to 5) and (5 to 8), The Golden Ratio (.618), and The Fibonacci Numbers is the mathematical series found by adding two consecutive numbers to obtain the next number in the series.

If we use the Greek ratios as an example and begin with one and two as the first two numbers and add these together, they give us the third number of the ratio. To move on we need only add the last two numbers together. Here, two and three gives five, and continuing we add three and five to get eight.

Thus, the first five Fibonacci numbers are 1, 2, 3, 5, and beginning with the 2, pairs of adjacent numbers correspond to the pleasing Greek ratios. Using the 2 and the 3 gives us the (2 to 3) ratio. Using the 3 and the 5 gives us the (3 to 5) ratio. Using the 5 and the 8 gives us the (5 to 8) ratio. We only need the first three for decorating.

Leonardo da Vinci used The Golden Rule to create the face of the Mona Lisa and the shape and dimension of her eyes before painting her. The mathematician Pythagoras and the builders of the pyramids used it as well. The spaces between columns in Greek architecture such as the Parthenon and even many graveyard crosses are some examples. Seashells, sunflowers, pinecones and pineapples are some mathematical examples found in nature and thus are referred to as Divine Proportion.

To obtain the ratio of a room, measure the width and length and convert these two measurements to feet, rounding off the inches. If a room measures 11' 8" x 18' 3" and the inches are rounded to the nearest foot, it would create the measurements of 12' x 18'.

Looking at the two numbers, find the highest common factor or divisor for both these figures. For example, 2 and 3 and 6 are all numbers that will divide into both the 12 and the 18. But, looking for the highest common factor or divisor, we would choose the 6 to work with.

We divide this common factor into the width figure, then into the length figure. If we have used the highest common factor, the ratio of the reduced width to the reduced length is the ratio reduced to its lowest form. For example, when we divide 6 into 12, the answer we obtain is 2. And when we divide 6 into 18, the answer we obtain is 3.

Our results then are 2 and 3. Our math result matches up to one of the three desirable ratios of (2 to 3), (3 to 5), or (5 to 8). Our ratio, (2 to 3) is one of the desirable ratios, indicating that the room is already in good proportion. Use the highest common factor or divisor, but if you haven't, then divide again.

However, if we assume that a room is 10 feet wide by 20 feet long, and when we find its ratio, it does not meet the pleasing Greek ratio criteria, we know that this needs attention. One solution would be to 'visually' elongate the 10-foot wall by two feet. If we could do this, it would create a 12 by 20 foot room which does meet the criteria. We cannot lengthen these 10-foot walls physically, but we can do it visually by creating the "illusion" of additional length. As an example, a piece of furniture that is both long in length and low in height can be placed on the 10' wall to create the desired illusion. A chair rail on only the two 10' walls, or wallpaper with horizontal stripes might also work.

Conversely, if the room was 13 x 20 feet, it would require that the two opposing 13' walls be visually "shortened". In this case, one might place a tall narrow piece of furniture, such as an armoire, on the 13' walls to achieve the illusion of shortening them.

Similarly, vertical wallpaper, or vertically placed moldings can be used. Thus, we see that there are many ways to solve the problem of disproportion once we have detected it. The mathematical formula for Divine Proportion detects it for you.

Once we understand the principles of balance and harmony through good proportion, we can decorate flawlessly. It is balance and proportion which is the all-encompassing rule for good design and provides the sense of harmony in our room. In most cases, it matters not the style, the age of our furnishings, or even the fact that nothing 'matches', *as long as the items and their placement provide the correct proportion and balance.*

What this teaches us is that God loves beauty and mathematics and that He has given us the means by which we can learn more about Him through nature and the creation He made just for us. We learn that He is sensitive to harmony and balance, and to perfecting the environment in which we live, and which He created with such loving care. Thus, we also know that if we ask our Heavenly Father to bless our home, and we use our home to serve Him, He will help us make our home our Bethany

Bullet Points

Our treasure should first and foremost be Our Heavenly Father.

God loves beauty, good design and artistic workmanship.

King Solomon was instructed to use certain colors, fabrics and designs to build the temple.

The Creation displays specific proportions used to create beauty and harmony.

We can use those same proportions to decorate our homes flawlessly.

Divine Proportion is a gift from God which we find in nature and which can be applied to our homes.

Supporting Scripture

1 Kings 3:9-13,	Exodus 31:3-5,
1 Kings 8:17,	Matthew 6:2,
1 Kings 7:17,	Exodus 25:10-14,
Deuteronomy 10:3,	1 Kings 7:49,
Exodus 26:29,	Genesis 6:14,
Exodus 40:20,	1 Kings 7:26.

Chapter Forty Three

THE QUESTION OF IMMERSION BAPTISM

Sometimes Christians do agree on substance, but not on degree. The question of immersion baptism is one such dispute. When we understand and accept scripture as God's word and through which we learn of God's plan of salvation, that Christ came to mankind to sacrifice His life for us and lead us to His Father and how we are to prepare for the First Resurrection, we trust scripture to provide all that we need. God provided is with the Old Testament so we could understand the events which led to the birth of Christ and His work of redemption. The New Testament brings us the life of Christ, the work of His Apostles, and the culmination of the marriage of the Lamb and the new home God will create. Together, the Old and New Testament act as a history of God's plan and the development of man's relationship with God, help us understand what role we play, and how we can be a part of the Bride of Christ at the First Resurrection.

Scripture teaches us that the harsh letter of the law which the Jews were required to follow in the Old Testament was *replaced* by the gentle and unconditional love taught by Christ. Through the sacrifice of Christ, sin could be forgiven through the new covenant of Holy Communion. This was one example of change and of the development of mankind. Another is that God gave the power of the Holy Spirit to Christ, and after Christ's sacrifice, gave the power of the Holy Spirit to the Apostles who offered it to all Christians to help them become the Bride of Christ. God gave Christ the Holy Spirit when He was baptized by John the Baptist.

When John the Baptist immersed Christ in the river of Jordan, the divinity of Christ was clearly demonstrated when the Holy Spirit entered him and bestowed its power upon Him. The study of all scripture pertaining to baptism, demonstrates that the baptism John provided Christ was not the same baptism we know today.

John's calling was to foretell the coming of Christ and to prepare the people for the act of repentance. Christ came to John the Baptist for three reasons. One was to fulfill a Biblical prophecy, another was to publicly establish Christ's divinity, and finally so that the power given to Christ by God would be clearly evidenced. During the baptism performed by John the Baptist, Christ was given the power of the Holy Ghost and through following Christ His apostles were later filled with the Holy Spirit on Pentecost. The Apostles were then able to use the power of the Holy Ghost to administer the sacraments, including the baptism we practice today.

While the word baptism means "to immerse, to submerge, to overwhelm, and is also used in the context of a "cleansing, a ritual washing, and a pouring out".

Most theologians assign the act of immersing or submerging not into water, but into Christ and His teachings. The Jewish baptism is considered an initiation or conversion.

Romans 6:4 tells us: *"Therefore we were buried with Him through baptism unto death...."* The word buried also indicates an immersion or submersion, and this piece of scripture indicates a submersion (death) of our sin by Christ's sacrifice. Thus, it can be concluded that it was not total immersion, nor any power from John the Baptist, but the power of the Holy Spirit which does the work of baptism. The water is a symbol of God's word and a conductor for the Holy Ghost, just as the power in the laying on of hands comes from the Holy Ghost and the hands acts as a conductor. One does not require total coverage for either to have an effect.

What *is* needed for the baptism taught by Christ is the power of the Holy Ghost, and John the Baptist did not have the Holy Ghost in him, nor did Christ later give this power to him. The Holy Ghost is *necessary* to make Baptism effective and the apostles of Christ were given that power on Pentecost. They in turn could seal others with the Holy Spirit.

If we look through scripture, we see in Acts 19:1-5 that Paul performed the sacrament of baptism on many in the city of Ephesus. He asked the people if they had received the Holy Ghost and they answered "no". Then they were asked why they were baptized by John, yet had not received the baptism of the repentance through Christ. This statement explains that John's baptism did *not* carry the power that baptism does today. John's baptism could *not* instill the Holy Spirit nor provide the forgiveness of sin. John's ministry was to speak of the coming of Christ and to call the people to repentance. When we read of John in scripture we read that he told the people to look for Christ, not him to provide these gifts.

Acts 10:36 speaks about the word which God sent to the people. It tells us that God's word explains that it is the preaching of peace with God through Christ which was and is important. To have peace with God one *must* have an indwelling spirit of God (the Holy Spirit) *and* have received the forgiveness of their sins. John the Baptist could not provide these since he himself did not have the indwelling of the Holy Ghost nor the power to forgive sins. Nor had Christ yet died in our place allowing that forgiveness. Another important consideration is that John the Baptist never taught the concept of inherited sin or the entering into a covenant with God as the reason for his actions which is the reason baptism is offered today.

Acts 10:37 explains that the ability to provide the baptism of Christ to mankind began in Galilee after the baptism which John the Baptist preached. Verse 38 explains that when God anointed Christ with the Holy Ghost and with power when he was with John the Baptist, *then* the work of the salvation for which Christ would give his life actually began. Again, *it is in the power which God gave Christ, and which Christ then gave His apostles, which gives baptism its power.*

Luke 12:49-50 also speak of the work which Christ was sent to do. These verses tell us how Christ explained that it is *His* work to kindle the fire in the hearts of the people and He says: *"What will **I** if it be **already** kindled?"*

Further, John the Baptist himself gave indication that it was not what he did which counted. In fact, in Matthew 3:6 John the Baptist states that what he was offering was to teach the people that they needed to repent of their sins and that Christ was coming to facilitate that repentance. It is interesting to note that what John did in his baptisms was, in essence, both the precursor to Holy Communion *and* to Holy Baptism, and *neither* could be effective except through the power of the Holy Spirit.

In Matthew 3:11, John admits that it would be Christ who would baptize in the future and that Christ would baptize with fire. Fire is another word used throughout scripture for the Holy Spirit. We can also note that John the Baptist never became one of Christ's apostles and in fact, scripture says of him in Matthew 11:11 that whoever shall be the *least* in the kingdom of heaven shall be greater than John which may imply the absence of the Holy Spirit in John.

We find in Luke 18:15: *"And they brought unto Him also infants that He would touch them"* and in Luke 18:16, Christ tells His apostles, *"Suffer little children to come unto me."* These verses teach us that we are to bring our children and infants to Christ and thus to all He offers, which includes baptism.

In Luke 8:10 and many other areas of scripture, God warns that we may not understand scripture correctly. While scripture is absolute and perfect because it is by and from God, our personal understanding is often limited. Christ understood this as well and therefore often taught in parables. But, God through scripture states that to a few will He grant the ability to unravel the mysteries of His Kingdom. Therefore we can pray that God will open our understanding of His word, and that He will not let our hearts be hardened to the truth. God wants us to understand and wants us to know everything He has planned for us, but He has also instituted a means by which those who might pervert His words would not have direct access through understanding them.

Finally, we are told in scripture that Satan is subtle and that he has the power to blind the minds of men. He does *not* attack in areas where we would easily recognize what he is doing. He will attack in subtle ways, in small ways which cause us to argue over a matter which could escalate into a contentious argument. He does this to prevent our coming into the fullness of the blessing which God through Christ offers us so freely. He does this to prevent that last soul God longs for from being found and brought into His flock.

God is a loving God and a circumstantial God in that only He knows the condition of a heart and what struggles that soul has faced. He may ask for more from one person and less from another because He sees everything and also sees an insincerity which the world may not see. Thus, Christians should simply agree to disagree on this matter and understand that it is the act of baptism and the heart's attitude toward it which God will consider and not how much water is used for that purpose.

Bullet Points

Christians often differ not on substance but on degree.

Immersion baptism is one such difference.

Christ is always to be our example of activity.

Scripture tells us that John the Baptist did not have the Holy Spirit.

John the Baptist called people to repentance but did not have the power to remand sin.

There is no scripture requiring full immersion for the sacrament of Holy Baptism to be performed and none refuting its effectiveness.

Supporting Scripture

Acts 19:1-5,   Acts 10:36,

Acts 10:37-38,   Acts 10:48,

Acts 11:16,   Luke 12:49-50,

Matthew 3:6,   Matthew 3:11,

Matthew 3:15,   Matthew 11:11,

Luke 8:10,   Luke 18:15,

Luke 18:16.

Chapter Forty Four

TESTIMONY AND TOUCHING HEARTS

There are three types of law under which we abide: The laws of nature, the laws of morality, and the laws of human society. One is the unchangeable physics of our world, another is the Ten Commandments in which we base our code of ethics, and another are those which are temporal or those which government may impose.

There is however another law which applies to Christians and is found throughout scripture. They are the laws of the heart and encompass all other laws. To understand and follow these laws requires an open willingness to embrace the Holy Spirit and ask Him to provide us with the fruits of the Spirit. Galatians 5: 22-23 tells us, *"But the fruit of the Spirit is love, joy, peace, longsuffering, gentleness, goodness, faith, meekness, temperance: against such matters there is no law."*

Each of these is a gift brought to us through the Holy Spirit which desires to reside in the heart of a child of God. These gifts require nurturing to grow to their fullest capacity and contain great power. We lose them when we lose the Holy Spirit. Some of us excel in one gift and need to nurture another, but all of them are important in helping us live our life as God asks and to help us draw other souls to God. Without the Holy Spirit, we will be ineffective in our testimony.

Galatians 5:17 tells us, *"For the flesh lustiest against the Spirit, and the Spirit against the flesh; and these are contrary the one to the other: so that ye cannot do the things that ye would."* If the balance we seek in our lives tips toward the flesh, the Holy Spirit can no longer indwell man to urge him toward perfection. Those actions which are considered of the flesh are listed in Galatians 5:19-21: *"Now the works of the flesh are manifest, which are these; Adultery, fornication, uncleanness, lasciviousness, Idolatry, witchcraft, hatred, variance, emulations, wrath, strife, seditions, heresies, Envyings, murders, drunkenness, revellings, and such like....they which do such things shall not inherit the kingdom of God."*

Ephesians 4: 25-32 tells us, *"Wherefore putting away lying, speak every man truth with his neighbor; for we are members one of another. Be ye not angry and sin not; let not the sun go down on your wrath; neither give place to the devil. Let him that stole steal no more; but rather let him labour, working with his hands the thing which is good, that he may have to give to him that needeth. Let no corrupt communication proceed out of your mouth, but that which is good to the use of edifying, that it may minister grace unto the hearers. Let all bitterness, and wrath, and anger, and clamour, and evil speaking, be out away from you with all malice. And ye be kind to one another, tenderhearted, forgiving one another, even as God for Christ's sake hath forgiven you."* These are the laws which the Holy Spirit of God places into the heart and what helps us make our life a godly one and our testimony successful. Satan however, wants to sabotage the Holy Spirit and its inspiration. Thus the Bible warns against false prophets and tells us that we will know them by *their* fruits which differ greatly from the fruits of the Holy Spirit of God. Matthew 7:16 tells us, *"Beware of false prophets, which come to you in sheep's clothing, but inwardly they are ravening wolves. Ye shall know them by their fruits."* In other words, what they produce does not match up with the fruits provided by the Holy Spirit.

Therefore, to have our testimony believed, to touch hearts, our own hearts must be touched and must contain the Holy Spirit to guide our every action. 11 Timothy 4:2 says, *"Preach the word; be instant in season, out of season; reprove, rebuke, exhort with all longsuffering and doctrine."* And Acts 20:28 says, *"Take heed therefore unto yourselves, and to all the flock, to which God made you overseers, to feed the church of God......"* While these scriptures were instructions from one apostle to another, today, we are all apostles of Christ and all asked to share the word of God. But we can only do this appropriately when we know God's words, and when we have the Holy Spirit to guide us in our words and deeds. Further, scripture warns us that what we see as a great fault in others should be compared to our own faults so we do not judge. Matthew 7:3-5 explains that there may be a speck in the eye of someone with whom we find fault and a beam in our own. But the beauty of our faith is that once we acknowledge our faults, God steps in with His incredible love to help us understand the merits of love and kindness, how to teach with love, how to overcome sin, and how to obtain forgiveness. Recognizing our faults and striving to overcome those faults helps us as we reach out with the hope to touch the heart of someone else.

Testimony can be likened to meeting a physicist and listening to him talk about quarks, photons, the uncertainty principle, and the theory of relativity. While the physicist fully understands his every word, we might not understand at all. Thus, we need to be aware that our conversations may create the same phenomena in a non-Christian. If we spoke only of things such as darkness and light, overcomers, the First Resurrection, the fiery pit, evil spirits and the Holy Spirit, someone who knew nothing of scripture could easily...and rightfully so within their scope of understanding....be unable to fathom what we mean and how our faith affects our life. Thus, the conversation of a believer must first contain the simple warmth of human kindness and an offer of loving friendship. Empathy for what our partner in conversation may be experiencing, and a respect for their feelings and ideas creates a bond of trust. God wants us to plant seeds and to do so in fertile ground. The seeds are our testimony. The fertile ground is the preparation we have done before the planting of those seeds. The respect and trust we have built and the continuity of our actions and the constancy of its love are like the fertilizer and the water which the ground requires to nurture the seeds. God will do the rest!

Bullet Points

Christians should want to share their knowledge of God with others.

Speaking with authority requires accurate information.

False prophets and false doctrines will be preached during the end times.

Christians must prove what they hear by knowing scripture.

Trust is obtained only when one acts the way they ask others to act.

God asks that we be overseers of our faith and an example to others.

Supporting Scripture

Galatians 5:22-23,	Galatians 5:17,
Galatians 5: 19-21,	Ephesians 4:25-32,
Matthew 7:16,	11 Timothy 4:2,
Acts 20:28,	11 Corinthians 2:11,
Romans 14:1.	

Chapter Forty Five

THE TOOLS OF THE TRADE

The early Apostles wrote many letters to the congregations to encourage them to live their faith according to that which Christ taught them. They understood and taught that a Christian's personal conduct was paramount to their success. The theme of these letters is well expressed in 1Timothy 4:16 which says, *"Take heed unto thyself, and unto the doctrine; continue in them: for in doing this thou shalt both save thyself, and them that hear thee."* Just as the work of a carpenter may require a hammer, and an electrician his pliers, the tools which are required for the work of a Christian come from his personal conduct which is learned from scripture and the Holy Spirit. This means that the Christian does have a specific task to fulfill. Colossians 1:10 explains, *"That ye might walk worthy of the Lord unto all pleasing, being fruitful in every good work, and increasing in the knowledge of God."* And in Colossians 4:6, *"Let your speech be always with grace, seasoned with salt, that ye may know how ye ought answer every man."* 1 Timothy 4:12-14 also teaches, *".....be thou an example of the believers, in word, in conversation, in charity, in spirit, in faith, in purity. Till I come, give attendance to reading, to exhortation, to doctrine."*

Knowing this, many Christians feel inadequate. Perhaps they are shy or reticent, feel that they have not learned scripture sufficiently to bring testimony, or that they must sing beautifully to join the choir, haven't the experience to head a committee, or being older have lost the strength for providing large fellowships. Yet they believe just as strongly as anyone else and may agonize over their concern that they have little to offer the church community. Nevertheless as 1 Timothy 4:14 clearly states, *"Neglect not the gift that is in thee...."* This tells us that there *is* a gift in us which we must contribute. Thus, the concerns of these Christians are legitimate concerns and should be addressed.

When a church community is healthy and both the ministers and the congregants strive to be good Christians, love should be the driving force of their actions and activities. Love is expressed through concern, empathy, consideration, understanding, and kindness toward everyone, and should *include* everyone and exhibit no favoritism. Thus, in this love, thought should be given to *every* age group from the smallest children, to the youth, to the young couples, to the middle aged, to the infirm and to those who are older. Each should be informed about what part *they* can play to provide cohesiveness to the congregation and how they can give of their best to the Lord…and one another. By succeeding in this, the ability for successful outreach and testimony will begin to flourish. When Christians meet the needs of church and family, and see these flourish, it follows that their outreach is successful.

To better understand the role of both the minister and the congregation in recognizing and promoting the need for oneness in all their members, we can read in 1 Corinthians 9: 5-7, *"Have we not power to lead about a sister, a wife, as well as other apostles, and as the brethren of the Lord....who planteth a vineyard, and eateth not of the fruit thereof? Or who feedeth a flock, and eateth not of the milk of the flock?"* And in 1 Corinthians 9:13, *"Do ye not know that they which minister about holy things live of the things of the temple? And they which wait at the altar are partakers with the altar? Even so hath the Lord ordained that they which preach the gospel should live of the gospel."* And in 1 Corinthians 9:19, *"For though I be free from all men, yet have I made myself servant unto all, that I might gain the more?"* 1 Corinthians 10:17 tells us, *"For we being many are one bread, and one body: for we are all partakers of that one bread."* Finally, 1 Corinthians 10:24 tells us, *"Let no man seek his own, but every man another's wealth."*

These verses teach us that the fate of one congregant affects every congregant and that we are to look after the health and well-being, and the participation of every member and not let jealousy or self-aggrandizement allow us to ignore the gifts and talents of some. Interestingly, scripture speaks of a congregational neglect which the apostles corrected. Acts 6:1-3 tells us, *"And in those days, when the number of the disciples was multiplied, there arose a murmuring of the Grecians against the Hebrews, because their widows were neglected in the daily ministration. Then the twelve called the multitude of the disciple unto them, and said, it is not reason that we should leave the word of God, and serve tables. Wherefore brethren, look ye out among you seven men of honest report, full of the Holy Ghost and wisdom, whom we may appoint over this business."* And Acts 6:5 tells us, *"...and they chose Stephen, a man full of faith and of the Holy Ghost, and Philip, and Prochorus, and Nicanor, and Timon, and Parmenas, and Nicholas...."* This demonstrates the responsibility of any who lead, to provide for all, and recognize and utilize the talents in all.

Similarly, Sunday school teachers and youth group leaders provide instruction for, and engage, the children. Other activities may utilize the ministers and choir to provide services to the congregants. The healthy congregation will also engage those who are older, or disabled, or ill, those who are shy, stumble with the language, and those with special skills, providing them with an opportunity to be an integral part of a working congregation. This can be as simple as offering the telephone numbers of those recovering from an illness, residing in a nursing home, or grieving. Youth groups can visit older members, or ask senior members to speak to them about their personal experiences of faith, or the skills they bring to their faith. A daytime Bible study for seniors can also be initiated. Sadly the spirits of jealousy, judgment and self-importance can hamper these goals and the Rector must watch for these spirits and banish them. Through the success of these efforts, we meet the admonition found in Acts 20:28 where we are told: *"Take heed therefore unto yourselves, and to all the flock, over which the Holy Ghost hath made you overseers, to feed the church of God, which he hath purchased with his own blood."*

Bullet Points

The wealth of each congregant is measured by the faith and joy in their heart.

Each of us is responsible for helping one another gather that wealth.

Everyone, from the youngest to the oldest in every congregation should be engaged.

This act of engagement comprises the tools of the trade of a Christian.

If we fail even one, we ourselves fail.

If we succeed we fulfill God's request to feed His church.

The spirits of jealousy and judgment can hamper these efforts.

Supporting Scripture

1 Timothy 4:16,

Colossians 1:10,

Colossians 4:6,

1 Timothy 4:12-14,

1 Corinthians 9:5-7,

1 Corinthians 9:13,

1 Corinthians 9:19,

1 Corinthians 10:17,

1 Corinthians 10:24,

Acts 6:1-3,

Acts 6:5,

Acts 20:28.

Chapter Forty Six

IS MEEKNESS WEAKNESS?

We often witness an encounter where whomever speaks the loudest and longest wins the argument. We see this behavior often, and also see that it is accompanied either by sarcasm, venom or threats, and more often than not, it lacks substance. This approach to a conversation or debate is based on feelings or emotion, rather than on sound principles, yet it is an action which appears to bring results. However, this behavior is clearly, simply and unequivocally satanic, not godly. It carries power from Satan and is used to intimidate, not to teach or discuss. The Christian is faced with the dilemma of seeing this approach work and feeling that any other approach appears weak. So what should the Christian do to gain confidence and approach such a situation where one will appear much stronger than the other?

The answer is two-fold. One is to pray and the other is to know what God tells us to do and to trust...to have faith... that following God's directives will bring results. What we must understand is that God enjoys demonstrating His love, His protection and His power to His children and He enjoys working through weakness to demonstrate His power to both the believer and the unbeliever. 1 Corinthians 1:27 tells us, *"But God hath chosen the foolish things of this world to confound the wise; and God hath chosen the weak things of the world to confound the things which are mighty."*

Even the Apostle Paul acknowledged that God worked through the weakness which the Apostle wished he could change. Paul said in 11 Corinthians 12:10: *"Therefore I take pleasure in infirmities, in reproaches, in necessities, in persecutions, in distresses for Christ's sake, for when I am weak, then I am strong."* And in the prior verse, 11 Corinthians 12:9 he said, *".....for my strength is made perfect in weakness."* Further, 1 Corinthians 2:3 says: *"And I was with you in weakness, and in fear, and in much trembling."*

Throughout scripture we find that God clearly tells us that He will always be with us when we need Him. Job 39:11-12 says, *"Wilt thou trust him, because his strength is great? Or wilt thou leave thy labor to him? Wilt thou believe him that he will bring home thy seed, and gather it into thy barn?"* In Malachi 3:10 God says, *"And prove me now herewith, saith the LORD of hosts, if I will not open you the windows of heaven, and pour you out for you a blessing that there shall not be room enough to receive it."*

In Psalm 91:15-16, God promises, *"He shall call upon me, and I will answer him; I will be with him in trouble;*

I will deliver him, and honour him". Psalm 27:1 tells us, *"The lord is my light and my salvation; whom shall I fear?....."* Psalm 34:7 says, *"The angel of the lord encampeth round about them that fear him and delivereth them"*. Jeremiah 33:3 promises, *"Call unto me, and I will answer thee....."* Isaiah 43:2 tells us, *"When thou passeth through the waters, I will be with you......"* And Hebrews 13:5 says, *"For he hath said, I will never leave you nor forsake thee."*

Further, Titus 2:1 says *"But speak thou the things which become sound doctrine."* 11 Corinthians 2:11 tells us, *"Lest Satan should get an advantage of is for we are not ignorant of his devices."* 11 Timothy 2:16 states, *"All scripture is given by inspiration of God, and is profitable for doctrine, for reproof, for correction, for instruction in righteousness"*. Titus 1:9 says, *"Holding fast the faithful word....that.... by sound doctrine both to exhort and to convince....."* And 11 Timothy 4:2 instructs, *"Preach the word; be instant in season, out of season; reprove, rebuke, exhort with all longsuffering...."*

These verses clearly tell us to learn God's words and then speak them boldly and with conviction to correct and to exhort. Scripture also tells to have faith that God will be at our side, loving us, and protecting us when we apply His words, and that we are to have no fear when doing so. We also learn that even if we see no immediate results from what we have said and done, God is working behind the scenes, using our words, our courage, and our faith to bring about a miracle. When there seems little hope because of our meekness, our longsuffering, and our forgiving hearts, yet we have spoken boldly of God's words and we have faith, God will always step in to give us the victory even if it is not immediately recognized.

Sadly, sometimes the too-zealous heart makes the mistake of not respecting the goodness in those who do not share their faith or traditions. They may become impatient and may judge, rebuke, condemn and debate too zealously and destroy the opportunity to bring fruitful testimony. This can occur in people of every faith and every background. We must understand that while many have no understanding of God's Plan of Salvation, or of Satan, or no knowledge of scripture, nor formal religion or education, or perhaps espouse opposing doctrines, nevertheless they may espouse the value system supported by the Judeo/Christian Bible. Further, they may be one of those whom God wants for His kingdom. Thus, overzealousness can harm the potential for opening a dialogue about the Gospel and the way one views their future with God. This harms our ability to bring a fruitful testimony.

Scripture tells us to be gentle in how we speak to one another, to not provoke one another to anger, and to love one another. It teaches that we are to draw others through our example and not by contentious debate. It shows us that when Christ and His Apostles went out to teach, they found many with honor and integrity and many who, without the benefit of being Christian, nevertheless provided their friends and families with love and respect. Many of these good people accepted what the Apostles brought them by accepting what Christ offered, but many did not. Some accepted in time, but not as a result of receiving their first testimony. Many lived their life with honor and integrity and were won to Christianity through love rather than a discussion about their faith.

The perfect example of a teacher is Christ. Christ was patient, loving, never threatened or condemned and taught with stories and by example.....and always gently. So it must be with any person of faith. Christians especially must never assume that they, and only they, "own" Biblical values. They do not. God clearly says in Exodus 33:19 that He will be gracious to whom He chooses, and show mercy to whom He wants to show mercy. Not to whom man deems worthy and not in the time frame man may deem appropriate.

The Bible also reminds us (in Mark 10:27) that what is impossible for man is possible for God, thus if we do not appear to make an impact, God still can. Prayer can also move God to perform the impossible both for the individual and those for whom they pray. Thus praying for others is something we should always do and something in which we can place our faith. Praying prior to testimony gives us greater power and keeps Satan at bay.

There are many admonitions throughout scripture about contentious debate. For example, Proverbs 13:10 says, *"....only by pride cometh contention."* And in Proverbs 17:4, *"Therefore leave off contention before it be meddled with."* And in Proverbs 18:6, *"...fools lips enter into contention."*

While scripture tells us to teach and rebuke, we are also reminded to withdraw when our words are not accepted. 1 Timothy 6:2-4 says, *"....these things teach and exhort....if any man....consent not to....the words of our Lord, Jesus Christ, and to the doctrine....he is proud"*. And in 1 Timothy 6:5 says *"....perverse disputing of men....destitute of the truth....from such withdraw thyself."*

What then is the answer to this dilemma? The answer is, was, and will always be....love! Knowing when to withdraw from an argument, coupled with our continued kindness, patience and prayer, and sometimes....quiet.... will allow love to be the victor. No one can come against such an attribute and there can be no lasting argument if one argues and the other simply...loves. And more importantly, this approach will leave another day for *fruitful* testimony...perhaps even by someone else. Our Heavenly Father works to open all hearts, wants all men to be saved, and only He truly knows what lives in someone's heart.

Being meek, or shy, quiet or even weak demonstrates a lack of pride and a lack of pretentiousness which allows God to become the driver of a conversation and a deed. The Holy Spirit can then speak rather than the man and gives strength and power to that mans words and actions. God loves to prove Himself and can do so easily in those who allow His power to govern their lives. Further, Satan is thwarted by love and by our lack of anger despite what he brings to any debate or conversation.

As mentioned above, in Malachi 3:10 God says, *"And prove me now herewith, saith the LORD of hosts, if I will not open you the windows of heaven, and pour you out for you a blessing that there shall not be room enough to receive it."* And in 1 Corinthians 2:3 *"And I was with you in weakness, and in fear, and in much trembling."*

Bullet Points

Even those who are meek and quiet should speak.

We will find confidence in reproving and exhorting with the power of God's words.

God works through our meekness, weakness, longsuffering and forgiveness.

Trusting that God will be with us brings strength and courage.

When it appears that we may fail, God is working behind the scenes for our victory.

Our faith can, in time, move mountains.

Supporting Scripture

1 Corinthian 1:27,	11 Corinthian 12:10,
1 Corinthian 2:3,	Job 39:11-12,
Malachi 3:10,	Psalm 91:15-16,
Psalm 27:1,	Jeremiah 33:3,
Hebrew 13:5,	Titus 2:1,
11 Timothy 2:16,	Titus 1:9,
11 Timothy 4:2,	Isaiah 43:2.

Chapter Forty Seven

A NEW YOU: TRANSFORMATION

God has promised us as written in Revelation 20:6: *"Blessed and Holy is he that hath part in the first resurrection...."* And in Revelation 21:7, *"He that overcometh shall inherit all things; and I will be his God, and he will be my son."* To understand who will be a part of the first resurrection and therefore an overcomer, we learn through scripture that they are those who accepted an invitation to a wedding feast and prepared for it. Revelation 19:7-9 explains, *"Let us be glad and rejoice, and give honour to him; for the marriage of the Lamb is come, and his wife hath made herself ready. And to her was granted that she should be arrayed in fine linen, clean and white; for the fine linen is the righteousness of saints. And he saith unto me, write, Blessed are they which are called unto the marriage supper of the Lamb....."* When we search scripture for information about a marriage supper, we find a number of parables which address this subject. Christ described a wedding feast as an analogy of those who would be gathered at the First Resurrection. He spoke about those who were originally bidden to attend a wedding and explained that when some would not accept the invitation, it was opened to others. Matthew 22:9 tells us, *"Go ye therefore into the highways and as many as ye shall find, bid to the marriage."* Then, in Matthew 2:10 we learn, *"So those servants went out into the highways, and gathered together all as many as they found, both bad and good: and the wedding was furnished with guests."* The parable ends with the words from Matthew 22:14, *"For many are called, but few are chosen."*

When we search further in scripture we find the parable of the five foolish and the five wise virgins. Matthew 25:10 tells us, *"And when they went to buy, the bridegroom came; and they that were ready went in with him to the marriage; and the door was shut."* This verse describes how the five foolish had not properly prepared and ran quickly to purchase what was required, but when they returned the door had been shut and they could not participate.

The Apostle John wrote in Revelation 3:5, *"He that overcometh, the same shall be clothed in white raiment."* And in Revelation 6:11 says, *"And white robes were given unto every one of them...."* Revelation 7:9 tells us, *"After this I beheld, and lo, a great multitude, which no man could number, of all nations, and kindreds, and people, and tongues, stood before the throne, and before the Lamb, clothed with white robes...."* Revelation 7:13 explains, *"And one of the elders answered, saying unto me, What are these which are arrayed in white robes?*

And whence came they?" Revelation 7:14 answers saying, *"......And he said to me, These are they which came out of great tribulation, and have washed their robes, and made them white in the blood of the Lamb."* And in Revelation 7:16-17 we learn, *"They shall hunger no more, neither thirst any more, neither shall the sun light on them, nor any heat. For the Lamb which is in the midst of the throne shall feed them, and shall lead them unto living fountains of waters; and God shall wipe away all tears from their eyes."*

These verses sum up what is required for the transformation required to be included in the wedding feast. The clue lies in two words: "overcomer" and "white robe". To be worthy we must be transformed in word and deed and become an overcomer by learning and doing God's words and by being faithful to God. If we do this work, we will be given a robe which is spotless, one washed clean of all our sin through grace. We will have asked forgiveness, have remorse for our sins, and have genuinely made an effort not to commit sin again. It is however not always easy to recognize the progress of a child of God as the changes they make might be slowly achieved. These may include the curbing of anger, moving tithes from pennies to the ten percent, a strong prayer life, and laying aside secret sins. Through these efforts, a transformation is taking place. Looking back over a period of time demonstrates those changes. 1 Peter 1:22 tells us, *"Seeing ye have purified your souls in obeying the truth through the Spirit unto unfeigned love....Being born again, not of corruptible seed, but of incorruptible, by the word of God....."* And in 1 Peter 2:9, *"But ye are a chosen generation, a royal priesthood, an holy nation, a peculiar people; that ye should shew forth the praises of him who hath called you out of darkness into his marvelous light."* And 1 Peter

2:25 sums it up by saying, *"For ye were as sheep going astray; but are now returned unto the Shepherd and Bishop of your souls."* And James 4:7, *"Submit yourselves therefore to God. Resist the devil, and he will flee from you."* Romans 12:1-2 clearly assures us, *"I beseech you therefore, brethren, by the mercies of God, that ye present your bodies a living sacrifice, holy, acceptable unto God, which is your reasonable service. And be not conformed to this world; but be ye transformed by the renewing of your mind; that ye may prove what is that good, and acceptable, and perfect, will of God."*

Sadly, our young people face a medium by which they are tempted to conform to this world. While we all make mistakes and all sin, our young people, despite their repentance, can have their sins exposed again and again sometime in the future. What they say and how they say it and what they admit is remembered by Satan and can be brought up again and again even if it was regretted and forgiven if it appears as *a written word or photo on Facebook* or another social media. This can bring them shame and cause them to lose their faith and thus their soul salvation. God forgives our sins and forgets them when we repent, but the world does not when social networking permanently records words and photos which, even regretted, can be opened by Satan to come back to haunt them. By keeping our youth captive, Satan prolongs his freedom. He knows what the Bible says and knows that God wants a certain number of souls to be ready when He sends His Son. Thus Satan works diligently to prevent the transformation from child of God to Bride of Christ and specifically attacks our youth.

Bullet Points

As we learn God's words and strive to act on them we are slowly transformed to grow into what scripture terms an "overcomer".

It is the overcomer to whom God will give a spotless white robe at the wedding feast.

Christ used parables to explain who will attend the wedding feast in heaven.

The wedding feast will occur right after the First Resurrection.

God will wipe away all sorrows and tears from that moment forward.

Social networking can be used by Satan to harm a child of God.

Supporting Scripture

Revelation 20:6,	Revelation 21:7,
Revelation 19:7-9,	Matthew 22:9,
Mathew 2:10,	Matthew 22:14,
Matthew 25:10,	Revelation 3:5,
Revelation 6:11,	Revelation 7:9, 13, 14,
Revelation 7:16-17,	1 Peter 1:22,
1 Peter 2:9,	1 Peter 2:25,
James 4:7,	Romans 12:1-2.

Chapter Forty Eight

THE CELESTIAL BODY AND THE SECOND DEATH

There is a reason why God provides us with information about our future. He understands that as the end times are fulfilled Christians will be persecuted and evil will prosper, thus He wants us to be assured that he will care for us in all things. By understanding His plan of salvation and what He offers, and knowing that our suffering is for a limited time, we can withstand the days of evil and the wiles of Satan. God also wants us to understand death; the torment that death and the second death brings to sinners and the hope and joy offered to those who strive to be God's children for whom natural death is not the end. Those who remain faithful to Him and have their sins forgiven will receive rewards which are so great that they are beyond description.

Yet throughout scripture God provides us with a glimpse of the new heaven and earth to strengthened us and show us what He wants to give us. For example, the Apostle

John, while on the island of Patmos, wrote about streets paved in gold. This was to help us comprehend the immense beauty of the City of God which those who remain faithful will enjoy. God calls the people who will be given these gifts His firstfruits and while others may enter heaven, this group will live and reign at God's side as the Bride of Christ, the overcomers, the kings and priests of His new world. The information God provides for His children through scripture includes a description of what happens to them after death. Scripture explains that when Christ returns we will have a celestial body which will never know sickness, sorrow, or death. 1 Corinthians 15:22 says, *"For as in Adam all die, even so in Christ shall all be made alive.* 1 Corinthians 15:35 says, *"But some man will say, How are the dead raised up? and with what body do they come? Behold, I shew you a mystery;* and 1 Corinthians 15:51 tells us, *"We shall not all sleep, but we shall all be changed."*

These verses tell us that all men must die, but that those who follow Christ will be made alive and will be changed. When we rise again after death we will be transformed from a terrestrial or natural body to a celestial or spiritual body. 1 Corinthians 15:40 tells us, *"There are also celestial bodies, and bodies terrestrial: but the glory of the celestial is one, and the glory of the terrestrial is another."* And 1 Corinthians 15:44 says, *"It is sown a natural body; it is raised a spiritual body. There is a natural body, and there is a spiritual body."* 1 Corinthians 15:47-49 tells us, *"The first man is of the earth, earthy; the second man is the Lord from heaven....And as we have borne the image of the earthy, we shall also bear the image of the heavenly."* This is an incredible promise and revelation, but there is also a warning which tells us that we must labor for this gift by being faithful, and by striving to learn and do as God asks. 1 Corinthians 15:58 tells us, *"Therefore, my beloved brethren, be ye steadfast, unmoveable, always abounding in the work of the Lord, forasmuch as ye know that your labour is not in vain of the Lord."* Psalm 1:1-3 tells us, *"Blessed is the man that walketh not in the counsel of the ungodly, nor standeth in the way of sinners, nor sitteth in the seat of the scornful. But his delight is in the law of the Lord; and in his law doth he meditate day and night. And he shall be like a tree planted by the rivers of water, that bringeth forth his fruit in his season; his leaf also shall not wither, and whatsoever he doeth shall prosper."* Here we learn who God will bless and thus what our behavior must be to be worthy of the celestial body which will rise at the First Resurrection. Although we all must die because of Adam, in Christ we will be made alive again. Psalms 1:1 tells us: *"walketh not in the counsel of the ungodly……but delight in the law of the Lord."*

The children of God await the return of Christ who will take from the earth those who are worthy to become His Bride. They understand that God wants a bride for His Son who is filled with the desire and ability to love. Thus, God's children strive to overcome the self-serving Adam-like nature and develop a Christ-like nature to achieve this goal. They understand that a loving father who seeks a bride for his son would want that bride to be kind, longsuffering, and forgiving. They also know that scripture warns that perhaps only half of those who are believers will meet the criteria required to become the Bride, causing us to wonder what will happen to those who, like the five foolish virgins, are left behind. These five foolish virgins were believers, but not prepared for the arrival of the bridegroom, thus not allowed to go with Christ when He came. (Matthew 1:1-13, and 24:40-41) The Bride will be those whom God deems the firstfruits or the overcomers and come from both the faithful still living on earth and the faithful from eternity. To be a part of the Bride of Christ is the hope of all the children of God and requires the development of the Christ-like and gentle nature of love and goodness, and the spurning of all things evil. This requires faith and the desire to be pleasing in the eyes of God.

Although not all who believe will be found worthy to become the Bride of Christ, our Heavenly Father longs for all men to be saved. He has made provision during the Thousand Years of Peace where those not taken at the First Resurrection will have the opportunity to come to Christ and following Satan's work once again for a short while, will be judged and become what scripture calls a lamb and enter heaven, or a goat and experience the second death. When Satan is again loosed to test these souls, he will have such great power that these new believers will be sorely tested. When judgment day arrives, each will be judged based upon their faith and past deeds. The lambs will be allowed to enter heaven, but not the City of God where the family of God will reside. When Satan is loosed many will lose their faith, and hatred and unbelief will gain in power and overcome many souls. Every deed will be seen, weighed and judged as opposed to the Bride of Christ taken at the First Resurrection whose sins were no more remembered. The goats who allowed sin and hatred to again govern their lives will be sent to the Lake of Fire for the second death where they will be in torment for all eternity. Thus, though not all are called to be the Bride, many will be a part of the kingdom of God and many will be cast into the Lake of Fire with Satan.

The second death is separation from God and from love for all eternity. There is no redemption from the second death, it is torment; it is life surrounded only with evil and it is for all eternity; it is forever. These words may seem harsh but are a reminder that not all believers will be a part of the First Resurrection and become a part of the Bride of Christ and thus the family of God. We need to clearly understand this so we strive harder to shed our old nature, become more like Christ, desire to leave all things evil and learn to love. Really love. Superficial love is not acceptable; it must be genuine, and from the heart which God reads accurately. (1 Corinthians 13:13 and 1 Corinthians 13:1-3)

What then is real love? How can we test our level of love? Perhaps we believe that we love because we hold fellowships in our home…..but who do we invite? Only those who have a similar level of education, status, manner of dress, financial assets? Or do we also include the lonely, the poor, the heavily burdened, the jobless, the sick? Do we believe that we love because we help with church activities…..but have formed a clique and push others away? Do we believe that we love because we tithe…..and never help someone who lost their job or cannot provide a Christmas or Birthday gift for their children? Do we include the widow and widower, the never married, those divorced and those who struggle to speak our language? Scripture tells us that faith without works is dead. But what are those works? Are they works of love? Are they self sacrificing as Christ's love was for us? Or are our works judgmental or given to gain personal accolades? Is our home open to everyone, and do we gladly bear one another's burdens and assist them through those burdens without judgment? Not all of us can do all things, but we must ask ourselves if what we *can* do is done with love and not to impress. God sees everything including the hidden recesses of our heart. He knows our motives and our faults and failings.

But God also knows our striving and hears our prayers to love more, and to grow in compassion. He knows that some are difficult to love, but His heart is moved when we forgive and overlook. Our Heavenly Father also understands that some of us are action-oriented and some are behind-the-scenes people. He sees both efforts and rewards them equally. If we are older and all we can do is send little notes of encouragement, or make a phone call to an invalid, God is overjoyed. We do not have to do large things, as long as we demonstrate our willingness to do our best and love. The Bride of Christ will be expected to be perfect in her love toward others by being, applying, developing, teaching, and giving love. When we truly love, we automatically desire to spurn what is not righteous in the eyes of God. We long to be with Him for all eternity where love will reign and evil will not exist.

The second death in the Lake of Fire is a state of existence in a place without God, without righteousness, and devoid of love. It is the final and forever separation of good and evil. It is a place of torment, a place filled with anger, hate, jealousy, envy, intrigue, back-biting, slander, lies, plots, terror and all things evil. It is a place to be avoided with every ounce of our being. But God wants us to be free of evil and to live with Him for all eternity in righteousness and love. He gives us every tool to do so. God's love for us is so great that He sent His

Son to give His life so we could be saved from the captivity of the sin which dooms us to the Lake of Fire. He has given us the gift of scripture to help us learn. He wants all men to be saved and He wants us to succeed.

Bullet Points

God provides the information we need to understand His Plan of Salvation.

Many do not understand how the dead will be raised when their bodies no longer exist.

Scripture tells us of the difference between a temporal body and a celestial body.

Only those who have been counted worthy will be given a celestial body.

When Christ returns, His bride will be given celestial bodies for their return to heaven.

Sadly, many will experience the eternal second death in the Lake of Fire.

Supporting Scripture

1 Corinthians 15:22,	1 Corinthians 15:35,
1 Corinthians 15:51,	Psalms 1:1-3,
1 Corinthians 15:40,	1 Corinthians 15:44,
1 Corinthians 15:47-49,	1 Corinthians 15:58.

Chapter Forty Nine

THE END TIMES

Most of us agree that the times in which we now live are the end times of which the Bible speaks. Despite this awareness few rush to assess their spiritual condition. Nor do they rush to assess the spiritual condition of those for whom they are responsible. Caught up in the harried pace of life and too busy to give God all that is possible, these believers may lose their soul salvation. Amazingly the Bible describes the conditions of the world when Christ returns and clearly predicts that we will be so engaged in our daily activities that we will be taken unaware and unprepared when the moment arrives. Matthew 25:40-42 tells us *"Then shall two be in the field; the one shall be taken, and the other left. Two women shall be grinding at the mill, the one shall be taken, and the other left. Watch therefore; for ye know not what hour your Lord doth come."* Sadly these verses and many others throughout scripture indicate that only half of those who want to be ready for that day will be ready. Matthew 25:10-13 tells us: *"....they that were ready went in with him.....and the door was shut. Afterward came also the other virgins, saying, Lord, Lord, open to us. But he answered and said, Verily I say unto you, I know ye not. Watch therefore for you know neither the day nor the hour wherein the Son of man cometh."*

There are many parables and much instruction throughout scripture where we read that God has asked *all* men to make themselves ready by learning of Him and striving to do as He asks and that God wants all men to be saved. But as we read these parables and the words of the Apostles, we learn that though many are called, few will be chosen. We also learn that no one knows when Christ will return and we therefore must always be ready. Matthew 24:36 tells us, *"But of that day and hour knoweth no man...but my Father only."* We also read that when men have spurned God's invitation and then realize that they were not a part of the First Resurrection, they will be in great agony. Matthew 22:12-13 says, *"....how camest thou in hither not having a wedding garment?.....Bind him hand and foot, and take him away, and cast him into outer darkness; there shall be weeping and gnashing of teeth."*

Scripture also tells us about the signs we will see as we approach the end times. Matthew 24:4-12,24 tells us, *"....wars, rumours of wars, famine, pestilences, earthquakes in diverse places, hatred toward Christians, betrayals hatred, false prophets with signs and wonders iniquity, no love"* Mark 13:12, 22 tells us, *"...brother shall betray the brother....father the son....children shall rise up against their parents....false Christ's and prophets...show signs and wonders".*

Luke 21: 25 explains, *"And there shall be signs in the sun, and in the moon, and in the stars....the sea and the waves roaring....Men's hearts failing them for fear...."* And 2 Timothy 3:1-7 tells us, *"...in the last days perilous times shall come. For men shall be lovers of their own selves, covetous, boasters, proud, blasphemers, disobedient to parents, unthankful, unholy. Without natural affection, trucebreakers, false accusers, incontinent, fierce, despisers of those that are good. Traitors, heady, high minded, lovers of pleasures more than lovers of God; Having a form of godliness but denying the power thereof....ever learning, and never able to come to the knowledge of the truth."* 2 Esdras 16:24 from the Apocrypha adds: *"At that time shall friends fight one against another..."* We are also told what Christ will find when He returns. 1 Thessalonians 4:16 tells us, *"For the Lord himself shall descend from heaven with a shout....then we....shall be caught up....to meet the Lord in the air....."* 1 Thessalonians 5:2 warns: *"For yourselves know perfectly that the day of the Lord so cometh as a thief in the night."*

Scripture likens the invitation which God extends to all of mankind to a wedding where everyone in the town is invited to come yet most of the people invited were either too busy, or too tired or too complacent to attend. Luke 14:16, 17, 24 explains, *"...a certain man made a great supper, and bade many......for all things are now ready........For I say unto you, That none of those men which were bidden shall taste of my supper."* When the First Resurrection occurs, Christ will return to heaven with the faithful. 2 Peter 3:10, 14 tells us, *"But the day of the Lord will come as a thief in the night.....Wherefore, beloved, seeing that ye look for such things, be diligent that ye may be found of him in peace, without spot, and blameless."* The wedding feast will take place for three and one half years while the horrors of evil work upon the earth. After this time elapses, Christ and those He took at the First Resurrection will return to earth to bring testimony to all who had spurned His teachings. Satan will be bound during this testimony and then loosed for a little while to test those who received Christ's testimony. After this Satan will be bound forever. Revelation 20:1-2 tells us, *"And I saw an angel come down from heaven, having a key to the bottomless pit and a great chain in his hand. And he laid hold on the dragon, that old serpent, which is the Devil, and Satan, and bound him a thousand years. And cast him into the bottomless pit, and shut him up, and set a seal on him, that he should deceive the nations no more....."* Those who choose evil over good will join Satan's final fate. Revelation 21:6 tells us, *"And he said unto me, It is done.....He that overcometh shall inherit.....But the....unbelieving, and the abominable...and all liars, shall have their part in the lake which burneth with fire....."*

We know that great difficulties will come, but as we see them begin and our anxiety levels rise, it should be a wake-up call for us. Acts 20:29 warns, *"For I know this, that after my departing shall grievous wolves enter in among you, not sparing the flock."* And Revelation 9:6 tells us, *"And in those days shall men seek death and shall not find it, and shall desire to die, and death shall flee from them."* Matthew 24:21, 22 warns, *"For then shall be great tribulation, such as was not since the beginning of the world to this time, no, nor ever shall be. And except those days should be shortened, there should no flesh be saved: but for the elect's sake those days shall be shortened."*

While there may be very little time before we are caught up in the terrors predicted by scripture, we need to look carefully at our lives, take note of our shortcomings, and make the necessary corrections. Christ has taught us the principles of Christianity which we must practice: love your enemies, do good to them that hate you, bless those who curse you, pray for those who despitefully use you, do to others as you would have them do to you, be merciful, judge not, condemn not, forgive, give, rejoice in the Lord, (Luke 6). He has also taught us to avoid adultery, fornication, theft, murder, deceit, covetousness, wickedness, lasciviousness, blasphemy, foolishness, and pride. Christ has taught us to be meek and kind, loving and faithful, to prepare ourselves as a Bride prepares for a wedding. If we fail to do this, if we are unprepared, have not developed as He has requested, when we want to go with Christ at the First Resurrection, we will be rejected.

But for those who are prepared, God tells us not to fear those days. He encourages us throughout scripture to be courageous. Psalm 27:14 tells us, *"Wait on the Lord: be of good courage...."* Psalm 31:24 says, *"Be of good courage, and he shall strengthen your heart...."* Isaiah 12:2 tells us, *"Behold, God is my salvation; I will trust and not be afraid...."* 11 Chronicles 19:11 states, *".....Deal courageously, and the Lord shall be with the good."*

There will be times when we are terribly frightened and times when our tears will flow and we will experience suffering. But Christians will know why, and will know that help is on its way. They have been comforted by

God's words. Revelation 2:10 has told them, *"Fear none of those things which thou shalt suffer...."* And Luke 12:32, *"Fear not, little flock; For it is your Father's good pleasure to give you the kingdom."* And John 14:27, *".......Let not your heart be troubled, neither let it be afraid."* However, we have also been warned that if we are not prepared we cannot expect to be part of the First Resurrection. The parable of the five wise and five foolish virgins clearly demonstrates that for half of those who proclaim themselves Christians, the door to salvation will not open to them. Matthew 25:1-13 tells this story and we read in Matthew 25:11, 12, *".......Lord, Lord, open up to us. But he answered and said, Verily I say unto you, 'I know you not."* God is giving us a wake-up call and providing us with every opportunity to prepare for what is to come. Every one of us should be praying for the wisdom to understand what we need to do to be absolutely sure that we are prepared.

In the end, we will experience God's wonderful promise revealed in Revelation 21: 4: *"And God shall wipe away all tears from their eyes; and there shall be no more death, neither sorrow, nor crying, neither shall there be any more pain....."* Therefore, we should say as Joshua 24:15 says: *"...As for me and my house, we will serve the Lord"*. And while we wait we must as John 16:33 and Acts 27:25 tell us: *"Be of good cheer"*.

Bullet Points

The Bible tells us what signs will occur before the First Resurrection.

These signs have already arrived.

When that day arrives we will be taken by surprise.

No one knows the day or hour when the First Resurrection will occur.

Scripture describes what we will witness when Christ return for the faithful.

Christ will take only one half of those who expect to be taken.

Those who are faithful will be protected.

Supporting Scripture

11Corinthians 5:1,	11Esdras 16:8-12,
Psalm 27:14,	John 14:23,
11Esdas 15:37,	Luke 12:32,
Acts 20:29,	John 2:17,
Revelation 9:6,	Isaiah 12:2,
Luke 6,	Matthew 24: 21-22,
Matthew 22:12-13,	Matthew 24:4-12, 24,
Matthew 24:36,	Matthew 25:10-13,
Matthew 25:40-42,	Mark 13:12, 22,
1 Timothy 3:1-7,	Luke 21:25,
Luke 14:16, 17, 24,	1 Thessalonians 4:16,
1 Thessalonians 5:2,	2 Peter 3:10, 14,
Revelation 20:1-2,	Revelation 21:6.

Chapter Fifty

PEACE AND THE ART OF BEING HAPPY

Those who see the silver lining in every circumstance and find their cup half full rather than half empty are those who seem to rise effortlessly above even the most difficult circumstances. If such an attitude were for sale, we would purchase as much as we could afford! Since all of us face problems which make our lives difficult it is natural to wonder how others seem to bear their circumstances with little fear. What makes ones person happy and another saddened by similar events? Why is it that some become discouraged, frightened, impatient and heartbroken when life throws us a curve and others take it in stride? Why do some fall into depression and others do not? And how can we become more like those who bear their burdens with nobility?

Once again the answer lies in understanding our Adam-like nature and why scripture tells us to shed that nature and develop a Christ-like nature. God provides us with everything we could possible want or need out of His incredible love for us, but we do not always understand how to use what is offered. The Adam-like nature came into being when Adam and Eve sinned, brought the knowledge of both good and evil into their lives and developed the need to defend and sustain themselves along with the emotions required to alert them to these needs. Sin by disobedience separated them from God and took from them His perfect care. Thus, the Adam-like nature, to survive without the all encompassing conversation, protection and provision they'd had from God, developed the automatic responses within their nervous system and stored memories in the temporal lobe of the brain which were for the first time, negative.

This phenomenon assured the continuation of the species through an automatic response. Mankind fell into what psychology terms "conditioning" as a protection and a drive which would assure their safety and sustenance. This occurred because of sin and produced the negativity with which we view our lives. Guilt, depression, hopelessness, and anger create the conclusion that God does not hear our pleas and we are unworthy of God's intervention. Because we all sin, Satan has a huge platform from which to accuse us of how little we deserve from God. Further, what Satan whispers to us is true! We don't deserve God's help. Nevertheless, God does help us because He and the Lord Jesus see our potential and hope to make of us a worthy bride! Thus God has provided us with an understanding of our human nature and the drives it commands. He shows us how to move into a Christ-like nature of trust so we can avoid the traps Satan lays for us through the Adam-like nature. Our Heavenly Father is omnipresent.... meaning that He is continuously and simultaneously present throughout the whole of creation. He is also omnipotent.... meaning that He possesses complete, unlimited, universal power and authority. Thus, we know that He can change our circumstances if He chooses to do so. From this we learn that it is not a matter of whether or not we CAN be helped but a matter of us believing that God WILL help. If we break this down into the impact this has on the process through which we deal with heartache, we must first understand the Adam-like nature and why we must overcome it.

God's love is unconditional and eternal because it is love in its purest form. But, we think of love in earthly terms where it can be fickle and may have diminished our ability to trust. Satan wants us to become conditioned to experiencing disappointment, fear, distrust and selfishness and thus unable to fully trust God. Let us imagine for a moment that we are young children attending pre-school. The teacher is God and the bully in the classroom is Satan. The teacher wisely allows the bully to act so the students can learn what comes of being a bully. She seeks to help her students choose goodness over cruelty, develop empathy for those who are bullied, and learn how to stand up to and ultimately overcome a bully's tactics. The students initially react with fear when the bully attacks, but over time learn that the teacher protects them before harm can befall them and they begin to trust her intervention. Thus those who develop confidence in the teacher believe they will be protected. They know the teacher, have noted her past actions, and trust that her deeds protect them. But those who do not know the teacher or the constancy of her deeds have not developed the confidence required to feel protected when accosted by the bully. *They haven't paid attention* and continue to react with fear while the students who were at first "conditioned" to fear the bully (The Adam-like nature) have now been "conditioned" to trust the teacher (The Christ-like nature).

Early in the twentieth century, a Russian scientist named Ivan Pavlov gained international recognition through an experiment he conducted with a dog. Food was offered to the dog immediately after the ringing of a bell, and in time the dog salivated whenever he heard a bell ring whether or not food was provided. This demonstrated the impact of memory on automatic reactions to current situations. A year earlier an American graduate student named E. B. Twitmeyer accidently conditioned the patella reflex (knee jerk) of a human subject to the ringing of a bell. Because people do not always meet our expectations, our Adam-like nature is conditioned to expect the worst when something unpleasant occurs. We become fearful and lose the self-esteem which provides us with our sense of self-empowerment. We fear what has occurred and become depressed and hopeless. Thus, examining what creates a happy person, despite a bevy of concerns, shows us that it is an attitude; a "conditioning" which prevents us from believing that help is on the way or a change will be beneficial. Unhappiness is actually a lack of trust in God's plan for us. It is a conditioning to expect the worst and not to expect a blessing. But God has always been, is, and always will be trustworthy. His love is pure and perfect and never fails. When we are faithful and ask for His help, He is at our side. Thus when we internalize this phenomenon we become "conditioned" in belief, faith and trust and overcome our fears. Fear is thwarted by faith. We can lose our faith when we allow Satan to make us feel unworthy by reminding us that we are sinners and thus unworthy of happiness or God's help. This negates the sacrifice of Christ and the gift of the forgiveness of sin....again, exactly how Satan wants us "conditioned" to believe. When fear appears, if we routinely list the times past when God protected us and actively tell ourselves that we have no need to worry, we can re-condition our memories. We must remind ourselves of God's love and that with the forgiveness of sin God no longer remembers our sin and places our striving above our failures. God understands what our Adam-like nature does to us and speaks to us through scripture telling us not to fear. Hebrews 13:5 says that He will never leave us or forsake us and in Isaiah 43:2 that He will be with us. Exodus 33:22 tells us that God will cover us with His hand, Jeremiah 33:3 promises that if we call, He will answer, and John 14:27 tells us not to let out heart be troubled. We must repeat these words to ourselves every day until we know them so well that they become a part of our internal belief system. As we practice these words and begin to trust in them...thus trust God... in time fear will leave and no matter what befalls us, *if we are striving*, God will see us through all our concerns and create a blessing from them. We will become conditioned to react with our Christ-like nature which finds peace through trust in the Father.

When Daniel walked into the lion's den, and Shadrach, Meshach and Abednego walked into the fiery furnace, they believed that God would look after them because they CHOSE to believe this. Free will is not just the choice to do good or evil, to bring harm or love, or to eat a second piece of cake or not, but it is also to choose how to think and what to believe. 1 Thessalonians 5:17

tells us to pray incessantly which is another way to condition our thinking and strengthen our faith!

Being happy is employing the art of trust. It is ours for the asking and then the taking. God wants us to be happy and offers us the means by which we can be happy. Trusting Him with everything in our life creates in us the child who comes to the Father knowing that the Father will care for them. We may not break our fear overnight, but in time by listening to our own words repeating God's words which tell us that we need not fear, we will overcome. A compelling alternative to unhappiness is to truly trust in God's plan for us and thank Him for His help. Scripture encourages us to trust God and through that trust find the peace He wants for us. 1 Corinthians 14:33 says, *"For God is not the author of confusion, but of peace....."* Galatians 5:22 tells us, *"But the fruits of the Spirit is love, joy, peace....."* And Colossians 3:15 says, *".....and let the peace of God rule in your hearts."* Further, scripture tells us not to lose our peace if we enter a home that is not worthy of our testimony. This verse further supports our need for fellowship with other believers to strengthen us. Matthew 10:13 warns, *"And if the house be worthy, let your peace come upon it: but if it not be worthy, let your peace return to you."* Luke 18:1 tells us, *"And he spake a parable unto them to this end, that men ought always to pray, and not to faint."*

As we move into the end times, God tells us to gather steadfastly in fellowship and the breaking of bread (Acts 2:42), and to bear one another's burdens (Galatians 6:2) and to pray without ceasing (1 Thessalonians 5:17). Through these activities we will be strengthened in faith and able to retain our peace. Scripture also tells us that to know and acknowledge God is *"health to thy navel, and marrow to thy bones."* (Proverbs 3:8) A lack of self-esteem, which grows out of a lack of understanding, can harm every aspect of our lives. It creates fear and anxiety and adversely affects our relationships, including our relationship with God. It also affects our health and well being. Without self esteem, without a sense of who we are and what we stand for, we cannot be spiritually successful spouses, parents, friends, neighbors or co-workers for we cannot be effective children of God. Further, Proverbs 3:3-6 tells us, *"Let not mercy and truth forsake thee; bind them about thy neck; write them upon the table of thine heart. So shalt thou find favor and good understanding in the sight of God and man. Trust in the Lord with all thine heart; and lean not to your own understanding. In all thy ways, acknowledge him and he shall direct thy paths."*

But God offers a final gift for these times, one that will add immensely to our peace. Christ speaks to us in John 14:27 and says, *"Peace I leave with you, my peace I give unto you: not as the world giveth, give I unto you. Let not your heart be troubled, neither let it be afraid."*

This tells us that as we pray we can ask that Christ give us the peace He promises us and ask that it may be added to whatever little peace we already have. Thus these five actions; learning what God wants us to know, having fellowship with believers through which we help one another with our troubles, praying unceasingly, conditioning our thinking to know that God will help us, and asking Christ for peace will carry us in peace to the First Resurrection. And we should always remember the words from Psalm 27:1, *"The Lord is my light and my salvation; whom shall I fear? The Lord is the strength of my life; of whom shall I be afraid?"*

Bullet Points

The harried and unsure times in which we live robs us of our peace.

Scripture tells us that we will have to endure great tribulation as the end times near.

God's words explain what is to come and how we can be protected.

Scripture also brings us words of great comfort for these times.

Fellowship with other believers adds to our wisdom and our courage.

Christ promises us His peace when we ask for it.

Supporting Scripture

Revelation 2:2-3,	Daniel 12:4,
Matthew 12:1,	Luke 18:1,
John 14:27,	Daniel 12:11-12,
Matthew 10:13,	Psalms 27:1,
Revelation 2:25,	1 Corinthians 14:33,
Galatians 5:22,	Colossians 3:15,
Acts 2:42,	Galatians 6:2,
1 Thessalonians 5:17.	

BIBLIOGRAPHY

The Holy Bible, King James Version, published by The New Apostolic Church, Canada, Thomas Nelson, Inc., Camden, NJ, 1972

James Strong, LLD, STD, *Strong's Exhaustive Concordance of the Bible*, Abington, Nashville, thirty fourth printing 1996, copyright 1890

Henry H. Halley, *Halley's Bible Handbook,* Zondervan Publishing House, Grand Rapids, Michigan, 24th edition, Copyright 1965

Henry M. Morris, *Many Infallible Proofs*, Moody Press, Chicago, 3rd printing 1977

Henry M. Morris, *The Bible and Modern Science*, Moody Press, Chicago, 1951, 1968

Donald Grey Barnhouse, *The Invisible War,* Zondervan Publishing House, Grand Rapids, Michigan, 12th printing 1976 copyright 1965

Robert Boyd, *Boyd's Bible Handbook*, Eugene, Oregon: Harvest House, 1983, pgs 122-124

Carol K. Anthony and Hanna Moog, *I Ching, the Oracle of the Cosmic Way*, 2002, Anthony Publishing Company. Stow, Mass.

Helen Gumienny Glowacki, *When Grandma Chased the Spirits,* 2008, *The Granddaughter and the Monkey Swing*, 2008 and *Abiding Faith, Hidden Treasure*, 2009, Helen Glowacki Publishing.

ABOUT THE AUTHOR

Helen Gumienny Glowacki is an interior designer, writer, teacher, and motivational speaker. She was the host, writer, and producer of the television series "The Contemporary Woman", broadcast by UA Columbia Cablevision. Her writing credentials include an extensive background as a freelance feature and staff writer for four newspapers and for various newsletters and magazines.

A graduate of William Paterson University, Helen received a Bachelor of Arts degree, magna cum laude, in Communications. She also received an Associate of Science degree with honors and is a registered nurse. She was listed in *Who's Who of American Women* and *Who's Who of Women Executives.*

Helen donates books to cancer centers, drug rehabilitation centers, prisons and also to mission schools of *The Henwood Foundation* to use her gift for writing to help others find the love and comforting presence of God. She also emails one of her books to those who wish to use it to bring testimony to others.

Those who have provided reviews of Helen's books tout her beautiful stories as spiritually uplifting and biblically correct. Her greatest joys are her husband, two children, four grandchildren, and time spent in her New Apostolic faith and in fellowship.

For more information:
Visit website: www.Helenglowacki.com
Email the author: helen@helenglowacki.com

List and Description of Novels

by Helen Glowacki (Book Size 6 x 9)

When God Broke Grandma's Heart: (208 pages) Rising from sorrow to become a beacon of faith Grandma struggles in an abusive marriage until God moves her from unequally yoked and broken to the healing of His love and forgiveness. Her granddaughter Sarah learns where to find answers to her problems and carries that legacy to those she loves. **Paperback: ISBN 978-0-9847-2110-8**

When God Took Grandma Home: (260 pages) About the heartache of drug addiction, of the enemy who destroys children through drugs, why God allows righteous anger, why we should pray for those in eternity and a description an incredible experience of faith for Matt and Sarah about why God allowed such heartache to occur. **Paperback: ISBN 978-0-49847-2111-5**

When Grandma Chased the Spirits: (208 Pages) The magnetism of idolatry, it's invisible power, and the heartache of bearing a child out of wedlock brings debilitating panic attacks to Mary and affects her husband Kevin. When Matt and Sarah tell them about their faith, God engineers a miracle to solve what that they thought impossible to resolve. **Paperback: ISBN 978-0-9847-2112-2**

The Granddaughter and the Monkey Swing: (284 pages) A wedding, a broken engagement, renovating and decorating a home through Divine Proportion, the truth about Halloween, and the gift of role models create a tender story of friendship. Helping through the planning and problems of a wedding culminates in the unveiling of a secret. **Paperback: ISBN 978-0- 9847-2113-9**

Grandma's Little Book of Poetry: The Story of God's Plan of Salvation: (277 pages) This beautiful whimsical story for all ages, begins when Sarah finds a manuscript in Grandma's desk and recognizes the story Grandma read to her and Josh and Caleb when they were children. Angels watch the inhabitants below them struggle to find God. **Paperback: ISBN 978-0-9847-2114-6**

Abiding Faith, Hidden Treasure: (262 pages) Serving in Iraq, Jim loses his faith to see a loving God allow so much heartache. Barbara invites him to dinner where Grandma shows him why creation and evolution co-exist and God's enemy creates the injustices Jim blames on God. Letters from the grave bring an incredible experience of faith. **Paperback: ISBN 978-0-9847-2115-3**

And Then They Asked God: (295 Pages) When Rebecca and Jayden arrive at their college campus they are overwhelmed by betrayal. Losing the values Rebecca once cherished fills her with guilt so monumental that she cannot forgive herself. Chaldeth the evil angel is defeated when God's grace frees Jayden and brings Rebecca's recovery. **Paperback: ISBN 978-0-9847-2116-7**

List of the "Why God Why" mini-series by Helen Glowacki

(Book Size 5 ½ x 8)

To What Purpose?: (126 pages) This first book in the *Why God Why* series answers questions about why we are here, what we need to learn, and what God plans for us. It is an excellent book for testimony and one you will share with others. **Paperback: ISBN 978-1-4507-7580-9**

Why God, Why?: (126 pages) This second book in the *Why God Why* Series describes why we experience heartache, its purpose, and how to face it. It answers questions about God's plan for us and what we need to do to be found worthy. **Paperback: ISBN 978-1-4507-7581-6**

Why Trust Scripture?: (126 pages) This third book in the *Why God, Why* Series addresses the challenges against scripture, who wrote the Bible, the importance of the sacraments, what role Satan plays, and how health and the Bible are related. **Paperback: ISBN 978-1-4507-7582-3**

What Should I Know about Life after Death and the Coming Tribulation?: (126 pages) What occurs following death, what will happen during the tribulation, and what the seven seals could mean to us are explained in this fourth book of the series. **Paperback: ISBN 978-1-4507-7583-0**

What Does God Want Me to do Right Now?: (126 pages) A concise explanation of what God asks of us, how we can live up to His expectations what is required to become a part of the Bride of Christ, and what God plans for the future with or without us. **Paperback: ISBN 978-1 4507-9076-5**

Coming Soon

Do The Little Sins Really Count? (126 pages) Most of us believe that the little sins don't really matter but scripture explains why they do.

List of Non-Fiction Books

By Helen Glowacki

(Book Size 5 ½ x 8 ½)

Politically Incorrect: The Get Some Gumption Handbook For When Enough is Enough: (406 pages) Fifty timely and controversial issues are examined under the politically correct approach and compared to what scripture tells us is the approach that God wants His children to take. **Paperback: ISBN 978-1-4507-9074-1**

Overcoming Depression: How To Be Happy: (258 pages) We all face heartache, and all feel sad from time to time. But depression lingers and can result from many different causes. It can rob us of hope and destroy our relationship with God. Thus our Heavenly Father tells us through scripture how we can tap into His blessing and His direction and brings joy out of tribulation. **Paperback: ISBN 978-1-4507-9077-2**

What No One Tells You About Addictions: (216 pages) Discussing the merits of tough love, the selfish co-dependency of the enabler, what scripture tells us about spiritual warfare and invasion, and generational sin, make this book a must read. **Paperback: ISBN 978-1-4507--9075-8**

Book Reviews

Reverend (District Apostle Ret.) Richard C. Freund, President of The New Apostolic Church, USA, Sea Cliff, New York: Magnificent writer, a story which makes the reader become emotionally involved, a joy to read, strong Christian values. *"When God Broke Grandma's Heart",* best seller quality.

Reverend (District Apostle Ret.) Richard C. Freund, President of The New Apostolic Church, USA. Helen's new novel, *"When God Took Grandma Home"* "Delights, brings comfort to those who grieve. Inspires, gives insight into the after-life, masterful portrayal.

Reverend Andrew Muliokela: New Apostolic Church in Alexandria, Virginia, formerly from Zambia Africa: *The Granddaughter and the Monkey Swing* and this series of books are awesome! A journey unlike another, I was reading a great novel, learning about confidence, love and support but also learning Bible verses at the same time! Helen Glowacki teaches through her books and I recommend them 100%. You'll enjoy the journey!

Reverend Frederick Rothe, (Ret. New Apostolic Church, New York) Palm Beach Gardens Congregation, Florida: Spent 48 years serving God and another 30 in the congregation. These books contain an accurate account of what God wants of us and why we suffer. The application of scripture and the people in the stories stand for the principles God wants in all of us.

Reverend Kevin Speranza, New Apostolic Church, Palm Beach Gardens, Florida: *And Then They Asked God* so happy I read this, weaves, documents biblical precepts, addresses political correctness, moral & political corruption, biased teaching, insidious growth of socialism renamed progressivism, self-importance, guilt and its debilitating power. WELL DONE! Identifies danger, artfully and Biblically addresses them.

Reverend Luke Jansen, Sr. V. P., Medical Connections, Boca Raton, Florida: "To Ms. Glowacki, author of **The Grandma Series**: grateful for your books, refreshing to find a Christian author who sees the *difference* between religion and spirituality AND that the two can and should be used in the same sentence.

Reverend Derryck Beukes, Montana-De Aar Congregation, Northern Cape, South Africa: Dear Helen, I personally often use your articles in my soul care visits, especially where youth are involved. I can assure you that your articles made a difference to my way of thinking, and I am busy encouraging fellow priests to read your works, as they are so factual and insightful! Thank you for your hard work. I thank God for you, and the wisdom He gave you! Please continue with the excellent work.

Deacon Shadreck Wilima, Overspill Congregation, Ndola, Zambia: Your articles prompt realistic examples which New Apostolic Christians need for their everyday living.

Youth Chairperson, Sunday School Teacher, Mulenga Ernest, Lusaka Central Congregation, Lusaka, Zambia: Through your writing I am constantly reminded of what to be aware of. I pray that God keeps you in the hollow of His hand, guards you and guides you to reach your brethren as you do me. Thanks for caring for the souls of many.

Reverend Aurelio Cerullo, Atripalda Congregation in Campania, Southern Italy: Dear Helen, your books and articles, and social networking bring brothers and sisters the words of our faith and touch the hearts of those who do not know our faith. Our goal isfound through the grace of the apostolate and in this sense, the word's from 1 Corinthians 15:58 assumes an important meaning: *"Therefore, my beloved brethren, be steadfast, immovable, always abounding in the work of the Lord, Knowing That your labor is not in vain in the Lord"*. Now that I am a minister of God for about a year I too am grateful to our beloved Father in Heaven for having opened the eyes of my soul, for having removed the plugs from my ears of my heart to hear and listen to His will in connection and communion with those who precede us, guided by the light of the Holy Spirit. God's work always evolves and adapts to the times and even via computers, cell phones and smart phones. I Thank God for having been able to know you, you're a very valuable pearl. God bless you richly.

Rev. Fred Krueger, (Ret.) Lutheran Minister 12 yrs and Clinical Social Worker 26 years, Dallas, Texas:

"Inspiring, grabs the heart, author headed to the bestseller list, a pleasure to read, masterful. *"When God Took Grandma Home"* filled with insight into God's plan!

NOTE: The articles which are referred to in these reviews are excerpts from Helen Glowacki's non-fiction books. Not shown are reviews by the ministers who oversee *The Henwood Foundation*'s New Apostolic Mission Schools in Zambia and review all reading materials prior to distribution.

Edith Stier, wife of a Ret. District Evangelist, Clifton, New Jersey: *The Grandma Series* helps those in need, inspirational, heartwarming, ends with a beautiful example of how God explains our pain, renews hope, shows us the way, creates miracles. I love this series.

Patricia Robinson, wife of a Ret. Rector, Indiana: 5 star rating: *When God Broke Grandma's Heart*: WONDERFUL INSPIRATIONAL NOVEL, enjoyed this book, well written, Bible references, how to achieve peace of mind and soul.

Rosemarie Schaal, wife of an Ret. Reverend, New York: *Abiding Faith, Hidden Treasure:* Reader develops empathy, feels emotion, hears a battle between scientific and spiritual knowledge. Skillful, detailed, brilliant, vivid, teaches that nothing happens that is not planned by Him.

Colette van Loggerenberg, wife of a Minister, Scottsville Congregation of Pietermaritzberg, South Africa: *Grandma's Little Book of Poetry: The Story of God's Plan of Salvation:* This has to be one of the BEST EVER books that I have read....If you ever get the chance to get one of Helen's novels...READ IT. It's like a fairytale but a TRUE fairytale.....Close your eyes and picture this: Grandma with her hair in a bun, glasses perched delicately on her nose, sitting in a rocking chair and her grandchildren sitting on the floor with BIG eyes hanging onto her every word.....but with a twist!!!!! If you have doubts about PRAYER...read this book. I LOVED IT...thank you!

Debbie Espeland, wife of a Rector, Palm Beach Gardens Congregation, Florida: 5 star rating: *When God Took Grandma Home:* HEARTWARMING! This book touched my heart. It is both heartwarming and very spiritual.

Aletta Venter, wife of a Deacon, Scottsville Congregation, Pietermaritzburg, South Africa: *"Grandma's Little Book of Poetry: The Story of God's Plan of Salvation".* What a learning process for me. Oooh I just **love** the way the angels are telling the story, **very original!** When is mankind ever going to learn? The inhabitant's lesson was to learn of good and evil. And they failed miserably each time. The devil has his agenda, and the inhabitants are the target. They call upon God for help, the angels rejoiced. Great….!!!

Aletta Venter, wife of a Deacon, Pietermaritzburg, South Africa: *"Abiding Faith, Hidden Treasure"* is the deepest and most rewarding novel I have ever read, touched my soul, made me cry, author's understanding of God's work is astounding, opens the mysteries

Lisa Mayo, wife of Minister, Palm Beach Gardens Congregation, Florida: Helen's *Why God Why* series of books gave me a new understanding of my faith. They are informative, so enlightening and in-depth, but in a way that is easily understood!!

Tammera Shelton, M.S. Psychology, Odenton, Maryland: I find *"When God Broke Grandma's Heart"* inspirational, beautifully portrays need to let go of negative events and that despite injustice, no pain is for naught.

Robert W. Rothe, USMC 1970-1976, Nevada: 5 star rating: *When God Broke Grandma's Heart:* Outstanding writer, kept me riveted, an angel sent to help through trying days. Thank you for helping me find peace.

Katharina Leipp, Schopfheim, Germany: This is the first time I have ever heard of a female New Apostolic author and I am very impressed by your articles. I have sent your link to my Shepherd and German friends and would like you to consider advertising in our German *Our Family Magazine*.

Claudine Visagie, South Africa: I'm trying to think of a way to introduce Helen's books and articles to others… especially to our youth. They are life changing!

Rabecca Mukuta Mukato, Lusaka, Zambia, Africa: Speaking on behalf of my Dad, District Elder Mukato, your articles are brilliant because they have changed me! Because of your articles my Dad has less headaches!

Robert Henry Parkes, Pietermaritzburg, South Africa: You are gifted with the verses and writings you do and are so inspiring to others. God is really using you as His special servant. You are really a wonderful person and we thank the Lord for you our sister in faith.

Frank Geores, from Port St. Lucie, Florida: *"When Grandma Chased The Spirits:* beautiful spiritual experience, can see caring nature and loving heart of author, eloquently reveals her love for God and search for truth. Worthy of the Star of Bethlehem rating. Thank you for sharing your magnificent gift.

Ben Lodwick, Avid Reader., from Brookfield, Wisconsin: Wow! An eye opener about God's plan of salvation, and why bad things happen to good people. Reminds me of Jim LaHaye and Jerry B. Jenkins "Left Behind Series". MUST READ!"

Dr. Walter Forman From North Palm Beach, Florida: *Grandma's Little Book of Poetry: The Story of God's Plan of Salvation:* a "wonderful book about success and failure in life. All Helen's novels are wonderful, a balm for the soul and an education to the seeker."

Susan Day, From Jupiter, Florida: *Abiding Faith, Hidden Treasure* : I hated to put it down, couldn't wait to pick it up, read all Helen's books, proves every point, shows what to do through God's words. I am 90 and Helen's books have helped me call on God.

Georgette Rothe, From Fort Piece, Florida: *Abiding Faith, Hidden Treasure* was more than I expected; a Biblical course making you re-evaluate your beliefs, enjoyed the journey very much.

Fred D'Alauro, from Palm Beach Shores, Florida: Internet 5 star rating: *When God Took_Grandma Home:* Remarkable! Inspirational, moving. Fascinating storyteller with a real message.

Debra Forman, Chester, New York. Internet 5 star rating: *When God Broke Grandma's Heart:* Written from the heart, shares the strong beliefs that shelters us in times of need, courage captivates the reader. Thank you.

Anonymous: Internet 5 star rating: *When God Broke Grandma's Heart:* WHEN LIFE GETS YOU DOWN, PICK THIS BOOK UP, it wrapped its arms around me. A wonderful read. Congratulations on an inspiring work.

A reviewer, a reader in Kentucky: Internet 5 star rating: *When God Broke Grandma's Heart:* Well written, heartwarming, overcoming heartbreak through God, touches your heart. A worthwhile read for all generations.

A reader: Internet 5 star rating: *When God Broke Grandma's Heart:* a must read for all generations. FANTASTIC!

A reviewer Internet 5 star rating: *When God Took Grandma Home:* Moves you, captivating.

A reviewer, a Kentucky reader: Internet 5 star rating: *When God Took Grandma Home:* MUST READ! Touching story of life's tragedies and how lessons learned from these heartbreaking events can turn into blessings.

Description of the Characters in the Novels By Helen Glowacki

Grandma: Grandma's life was filled with sibling betrayal and marital abuse. Her love of God, home remedies and famous boxing stance touches the heart.

Sarah: Sarah helps Grandma write her journal, learns about God's plan of salvation and the enemy who wants to harm her. She carries on Grandma's legacy of faith.

Matt: Matt, Sarah's husband, has a rock-like faith but when he loses a loved one, struggles with his anger with God, until he has a miraculous experience of faith.

Paul: Paul is Matt's older brother who earned a Captain's license for a seagoing tugboat. His faith sustains him despite enduring terrible circumstances.

Mary and Kevin: Mary and Kevin become Matt and Sarah's neighbors and friends. Mary's panic attacks end when God brings a miracle they never thought possible.

Elizabeth: Elizabeth adopts Rebecca, loses her husband twelve years later, is confronted with a potentially deadly illness and searches for Rebecca's birth mother.

Rebecca: Rebecca is Elizabeth daughter and Jayden's friend. Her father's death, the illness her mother faces, and a series of challenges at college almost destroy her.

John: John, a deacon, lost his wife to a debilitating disease, becomes Elizabeth's friend, and helps his daughter and grandson through a difficult divorce.

Jayden: Jayden is John's grandson and becomes Rebecca's friend. He has learned that prayer helps solve problems and he and Rebecca begin to share their faith.

Wade and Ruth: Wade is Jim's boss and friend who adopts two children from Iraq. Ruth is Jayden's mother and John's daughter who struggles to let go of the past.

Joshua and Debbie: Joshua, Sarah's younger brother, was demanding and judgmental until Caleb stepped in. Debbie looks to Joshua's family to be her role models.

Caleb and Ann: Caleb is Sarah and Josh's older brother and the family looks to him as they once looked to Grandma. Ann, Caleb's wife harbors a secret sadness.

Barbara and Jim: Barbara, Matt's sister is also Sarah's close friend. Her husband Jim plays devil's advocate in family debates, and matchmaker for his friend Wade.

Heza and Bara: Heza and Bara endured a suicide bomber attack when Bara was one and one half years old and Heza as she was born. They are adopted by Wade.

Chaldeth: Chaldeth is a fallen angel sent to destroy Grandma's family. He plots to bring great heartache to Rebecca and Jayden and their family to break their faith.

Durk: Durk, abused by a cruel father, is a sophomore at the college Rebecca and Jayden attend. He brings harm to Rebecca and Jayden but Jim gives him a second chance.

Professsor T. Nagorra, and Emils, and Dean Peerca:
These tenured professors befriend Durk and engage in activities that bring harm to the students and campus.

Professors Doog and Sendnik, and President Legna:
These three share a faith in God, a love for their country, and desire to be role models. They help save the campus.

"And the Spirit, and the bride say, Come. And let him that heareth say, Come, and let him that is athirst come. And whosoever will, let him take the water of life freely."
Revelation 22:17

www.ingramcontent.com/pod-product-compliance
Lightning Source LLC
Chambersburg PA
CBHW020729160426
43192CB00006B/161